ACCOLADES

"Pursuing our passions and feeling empowered to fully share ourselves with the world is a key aspect of well-being. In *Authentic Resilience*, Fatima Doman provides practical and proven strategies to do exactly that, and create a more vibrant and fulfilling life!"

—**Mark Hyman, MD**, 13X New York Times #1 bestselling author

"This ground-breaking book is a must read. In today's era of increasing stress, anxiety and depression, this book is a significant contribution to the rapidly exploding field of positive psychology and the development of resilience within each reader. Essential for all of us striving to live a meaningful, productive and vibrant life!"

—**Dr. Sandra Scheinbaum**, Founder & CEO, Functional Medicine Coaching Academy, Inc., author of *Functional Medicine Coaching*

"*Authentic Resilience* provides a brilliantly accessible toolbox for leading a happier, more successful, more resilient life. This is an important book for you — if you are interested in making the most of your gifts and talents, and to boost your well-being!"

—**Dr. Tal Ben-Shahar**, #1 bestselling author of *Happier and Choose the Life You Want*

"I highly recommend Fatima Doman's new book, *Authentic Resilience!* Everyone should learn to focus more energy in a positive way on their strengths. The tools in this book can shift one's mindset to look more for the good in themselves and others—increasing resilience and well-being. This book is a must-read in today's era of rising stress, depression and anxiety."

—**Daniel G. Amen, MD**, 12X New York Times #1 bestselling author

"Fatima Doman has written a wonderful book! Thorough and wise, it is simply a roadmap for growth. I found it comprehensive in its reach, yet easy to relate to, and spot on in advice quality."

—**Dr. Fredrick Luskin**, Director, Stanford Forgiveness Project, Stanford University

"It isn't often that a book can both educate and inspire. *Authentic Resilience* doesn't just succeed at these—it super-succeeds! Fatima Doman takes research and humanizes it, breathing life into it by telling personal stories. I was captivated by Fatima Doman's sharp mind, compassionate heart, and inspiring energy. You will be transformed by this book!

—**Dr. Everett L. Worthington**, Professor Emeritus,
Virginia Commonwealth University, Founder of REACH Forgiveness Program

"As a clinical psychologist and performance coach working with faculty members and physicians, I appreciate Fatima Doman's integration of practical skills and anecdotal examples with empirically-supported research. *Authentic Resilience* moves beyond the importance of good self-care, encouraging us to trust that we have unique strengths that help us keep moving forward with awareness, self-compassion, and the ability to set healthy boundaries and limits!"

—**Dr. Chad Buck**, Clinical Psychologist, Vanderbilt University Medical Center

"This book will help you build your resilience and well-being in a deceptively simple but transformative way - by learning to become an inner ally rather than being your own worst enemy!"

—**Dr. Kristin Neff**, bestselling author of *Self-Compassion*,
Associate Professor Human Development and Culture, University of Texas at Austin

"Fatima Doman's work is very important because people need a pathway to get to a positive destination. Her books are guides for how to get there—essential contributions to create a future that we can all thrive into!"

—**Dr. Bruce H. Lipton**,
renowned stem cell biologist and bestselling author of "*The Biology of Belief*"

"In the worst of times, we seek clarity, direction and knowledge that potentiates healing. In the best of times, we seek wisdom that will enable us to maintain our sense of thriving. Fatima Doman's insightful book provides a clear and inspiring pathway for either moment, reminding us that we are capable of grounding ourselves and moving toward our better selves on any day. It is a work that catalyzes our capacity to become larger, healthier and stronger within and in so doing, to cultivate goodness and richness both at home and at work."

—**Maria Sirois, Psy.D.**, author of A Short Course in Happiness
After Loss (and Other Dark, Difficult Times)

"Fatima Doman has had a profound and lasting impact on my former workplace, on me both professionally and personally, and on my daughter Aubrey in coaching her through a stressful career transition. This book is full of transformative wisdom—with helpful evidence-based resilience and well-being tools!"

—**Dr. Sue Hodges Moore**, Chief Strategy Officer, Ball State University (formerly Senior Vice President for Administration and Finance, Northern Kentucky University)

"Grounded in the science of positive psychology, *Authentic Resilience* provides insights into human performance, resilience and well-being—teaching practical ways to apply this exciting science in everyday life. In today's fast-paced and often stressful environments, this book is a must-read for anyone interested in fulfilling their own potential to flourish, or in coaching others to do so!"

—**David M. R. Covey**, CEO of SMCOV bestselling co-author of:
Trap Tales: Outsmarting the 7 Obstacles to Success

"*Authentic Resilience* is a masterpiece! Be guided by Fatima Doman's accessible tools based on evidence-based research and practical wisdom. The way you think of resilience will never be the same. Absolutely brilliant!

—**Stephan Mardyks**, CEO, Wisdom Destinations®

"Fatima Doman is onto something HUGE! Despite being able to carefully project on social media the most 'like-able' version of oneself, modern humans are encountering unprecedented levels of anxiety, depression, addiction, and suicide species-wide. It's sad, frustrating, and daunting. But Doman gives us the way forward in *Authentic Resilience*. Applying the latest science to everyday living, she provides concrete ways to make your life more authentic, more resilient, and more beloved. More people would feel whole if they read this book!"

—**Dr. Chelsea Shields**, Anthropologist, TEDx Speaker and former TED Fellow

"Fatima Doman has created resilience programs and books that have been a game changer in assisting countless youth and adults in building their resilience—using positive psychology tools to deal with stress. In an era of tremendous pressure and feelings of anxiousness, the *Authentic Strengths Resilience* evidence-based tools help anyone wanting to build their capacity for greater resilience, and to leverage their character strengths to flourish!"

—**Ember Conley EdD,** Superintendent, Mesa School District

"Fatima Doman's new book, *Authentic Resilience,* is much needed for the challenges we face now and into the future—as individuals, as families, in our schools, our workplaces and our communities. While there are many approaches to resilience, Fatima's focus on character strengths is what makes this book unique and powerful. Her model of exploring, empowering and engaging our strengths provides a framework for not only understanding strengths that perhaps we didn't know we had, but also an opportunity to learn about other strengths that we may need to develop when we face challenges and adversity. I highly recommend this book for anyone wanting to be their best self and live a flourishing life!"

—**Dr. Suzy Green, D Psych (Clin) MAPS**, Founder and CEO, the Positivity Institute

"This book is the most wondrous of creations! It is scientific and it is human. From the opening of the Introduction to the closing of the last chapter, I was won over by the combination of the genuine warmth of Doman's writing and the science behind the tools. This book does what many people believe is impossible, it uses positive psychology to help address negative experiences like anxiety, depression and stress. If you want to learn how to use trusted, evidence-based tools to build yourself up with your own strengths—and we all have strengths to build upon to create a more fulfilling life—this book is for you!"

—**Ruth Pearce, ACC, JD, PMP**, Coach, International Speaker and Author of Be a Project Motivator: Unlock the Secrets of Strengths-Based Project Management

"Coach and author Fatima Doman has created a fully functional, fantastic curriculum that is based on over 500 positive psychology studies and is world class! The practical, accessible content and tools she has created is nothing short of brilliant! She also now offers her content through cutting edge microlearning lessons, customized for various ages/grades with impressive analytics to improve the learner's experience. Students K-12, college/university, and corporations can access dozens of customized lessons for 5-8 minutes a day, meeting the learner when and where they are ready to learn. This transformative content can be easily added into any current instructional program. I truly believe that what Authentic Strengths Advantage® has to offer matches the core values of educational institutions around the globe."

—**Melissa Nikolai, M.Ed**, NBCT, Park City High School

"Fatima Doman's books and programs empower human development, achieving it through simplicity, science and human connection. Her latest book, *Authentic Resilience,* helps people to boost their resilience, happiness and well-being, and helps organizations to be more productive and supportive of their employees in these challenging times of change. Truly needed for today's world!"

—**Luciano Alves Meira and Anabella Meira**, Co-Founders, Caminhos Vida Integral, Brazil

"This is not simply a book—it is a powerful catalyst for positive and lasting change. Extraordinarily gifted coach and thought leader, Fatima Doman, translates Positive Psychology theory into practical steps that can be applied to everyday life. This book is a must read for every coach, leader, teacher, parent, student—anyone who wishes to truly maximize their resilience and well-being, and to tap into the power of their strengths!"

—**Jane Wundersitz**, CEO and Founder WunderTraining Australia, Positive Psychology Practitioner and Positive Culture Strategist

"Helping people recognize and understand their unique strengths will make a definite difference in developing an everlasting happiness throughout their life. Explaining and coaching authentic strengths and positive psychology is clearly one of Fatima Doman's many strengths. My own learnings from Fatima's books have changed my approach to life and there is no doubt that her new book will help shape and improve the lives of many to build their resilience and well-being!"

—**Marc Noël**, Father, Grandfather, Entrepreneur

"*Authentic Resilience* is must read book that helps people build their resilience and well-being! This book teaches the core principles of positive psychology that enable people to flourish. It brings a totally new perspective to coaching oneself and others, written by a truly great trainer and coach. This book is for everyone who wants to live a positive, productive and meaningful life!"

—**Edwin Boom**, CEO & Founder of MOOVS Training Company, Netherlands

"*Authentic Resilience* strikes at the core need to understand one's strengths, using them to navigate life's challenges and conquer forces that bring individuals down. Resiliency is essential for every person to overcome challenges and perform at their best. Not only will I use Fatima Doman's evidence-based tools to navigate my own life, I'm also thrilled to share it with the many guides of young children with whom I work!"

—**Joyce Sibbett, Ph.D.**, President/ Founder Dancing Moose Montessori School, Professor Emeritus Westminster College

"Resilience and well-being is not just a "feel good" imperative, it is a strategic asset contributing to an engaged and vital workforce. If we business leaders had used this book in the past, we would doubtless have reaped the benefits of a more energized workforce. I'm confident those benefits would have shown up on our bottom line. *Authentic Resilience* helps leaders recognize and unleash the collective strengths of those on their teams, boosting everyone's resilience —and in the process builds their credibility, career and their company!"

—**Kevin Cope**, CEO of Acumen Learning, and #1 bestselling author of *Seeing the Big Picture: Business Acumen to Build Your Credibility, Career, and Company*

"Fatima Doman's new book, *Authentic Resilience*, is the perfect partner to her programs we have used in our schools! It is both engaging, and practical. It builds upon the work our students are doing to build their resilience and brings that work to life with everyday examples. It encourages personal reflection through writing exercises which can serve as starting points for meaningful class or one-on-one discussions. Also, the new *Authentic Strengths Resilience* online modules provide great jumping off points to take deeper dives into many important topics. Character education teaches students how to be their best selves, and the tools and strategies to facilitate this work are easily accessible through the curriculum this important book supports!"

—**Brenda Yahraes, Ph.D.**, Interim Principal Harrisburg Elementary School, former Career and College Readiness Facilitator

"Authentic Resilience" will lead you to uncovering your strengths and to producing meaningful work. If you can't buy a large bottle of Fatima, this book is the next best thing to supporting your transition to "STRONG!"

—**Mark D. Cusick**, Co-founder of ZRG Partners, Global Executive Search Firm

"The Authentic Resilience book and training program is much needed for our children and families at risk. We want to influence children to become solution focused. The best way to begin is to help children know themselves and build on their own character strengths. Thank you, Fatima Doman, you have sparked life-changing positive changes in the lives of our families at risk!"

—**Diane Williams, MA**, Stanislaus County CA Office

of Education-Child/Family Services Division-Head Start

"We recognize the importance of each person—from the custodian to the CEO—in achieving equity, value and quality in the workplace. *Authentic Resilience* gives a unique perspective and a new set of tools that each person can use to discover and leverage their unique strengths. Fatima Doman's new book is a must read for anyone wanting to explore cutting-edge ways to increase their resilience and well-being. Improvement Sciences has partnered with Authentic Strengths Advantage® to infuse the principles of learning science and positive psychology, helping organizations improve outcomes. Together we deliver the right training, with the right technology, at the right time, to the right person - empowering each person with the awareness and application of their strengths to flourish in their personal and professional journeys!"

—**Michael Hunter, PhD**, Founder and CEO Healthcare Improvement Sciences, LLC

"This new book, *Authentic Resilience,* is a necessary read for practitioners, educators and parents—anyone wanting to help others explore their own strengths to build their resilience and truly capitalize on the value of individuals. We become better leaders and parents as we learn skills to empower ourselves with a greater understanding of our children, coworkers and students. Our influence will grow as we utilize the principles in this book to better relate to each other through the lens of strengths. Doman provides fresh insight and practical application that gives clarity to the science behind positive psychology. Each chapter is personally and professionally inspiring."

—**Dr. Jaynee Poulson**, Utah State PTA Health Commissioner, Professor at Weber State

University, Former CEO of The Life House Counseling Center

"A remarkable book that introduces people to the transformational world of character strengths, and their role in boosting our resilience and well-being. Fatima Doman's new book, Authentic Resilience, has made character strengths accessible to anyone and everyone. Research continues to show the profound, positive benefits that character strengths can have on our lives. I am grateful for Fatima's willingness to use her talents, experience, and knowledge to bring such a book to the world. Truly this book is a gift to us all!"

—**Tiffany Yoast, M.Ed**, Utah Valley University

"As a professor, one of the challenges I see in the rising generation of students is that many of them are focused on their weaknesses and allow their fears to influence their decisions. *Authentic Resilience* is an invitation to begin a transformational change to learn to recognize and develop our strengths to be more resilient and to flourish. This will empower the valuable contributions we can each make NOW!"

—**Dr. Darin R. Eckton,** Assoc. Professor, Student Leadership and Success Studies, Utah Valley University

"The world is changing fast, so stress and anxiety are inevitable—we need more strategic and proven tools to help increase our resilience. I believe *Authentic Resilience* will help anyone to bounce back from difficult situations and even to flourish in the midst of challenges! Thank you to Fatima Doman, the first trainer that opened the positive psychology door to me and who has never stopped empowering positive change in the lives of countless people. I am always grateful!"

— **Ruttanun Klewpatinond**, Learning Director and Founder of Plusitives Training Company, Thailand

"Written out of more than two decades of experience successfully coaching and training leaders around the world, Doman's new book, *Authentic Resilience*, lays out evidence-based, highly accessible, and personally transformative strategies for living a more resilient life. The all-important learning of becoming authentic includes first accepting responsibility for oneself, and then stepping onto the path of self-awareness and self-acceptance. I am thrilled about the possibilities for integrating Doman's approach into the First Year Experience university courses I teach, and for *Authentic Resilience* to become a game changer for students!"

—**Lisa Lambert, MBA**, Department of Student Leadership and Success Studies, Utah Valley University

"Authentic Resilience is an important book from an author I respect. Every great leader, whether at home and/or at work should read it. We live in a fast-paced environment that requires us to respond with agility in all aspects of our lives from communication, decision-making, conflict resolution, innovation to have room to deal with normal setbacks and continue to grow as a leader, no matter what stage. This is perhaps the best book I've seen that brings into one place all the best tools you will need to discover, apply and live your character strengths, and to realign with what matters to you that gives you energy. All this while learning to recognize and appreciate strengths in others too! You'll live with a deeper sense of vision, use your character strengths to shift into healthy habits, increase your resilience, and connect with a deeper sense of your authentic self—feeling happier and more fulfilled. A must-read!"

—**Angie Pincin**, CEO-Coach People Inc., Executive Coach-Facilitator

"Fatima Doman has done it AGAIN! With Authentic Resilience, Fatima has created an uncomplicated guide of instructive wisdom for anyone who has experienced a Dark Night of the Soul - whether that be a divorce, death of a loved one, or loss of a job or relationship. The tools offered in this this book will move readers from situational darkness into light, illuminating the path to greatness each of us deserves."

—**Shauna Wiest, MSLS**, Founder and CEO, Bespoke Grant Writing and Development

"In over 15 years of researching the blended family landscape for resources, nothing has resonated with our life experiences until now. We have found *Authentic Resilience* to be the perfect addition to our roadmap for living 1HappyLife™, making it an utterly essential resource in our co-parenting and blended family toolbox. From cover to cover, it is a life changer! This practical guide illustrates how to implement a strengths-based approach to personal well-being, facing and overcoming challenges, and developing healthy relationships. *Authentic Resilience* is an absolute must for co-parents and blended families looking for positive transformational and lasting change. No family should be without it!"

—**Chris and Karina Whetstine**, Co-CEOs and Co-Founders, 1HappyLife™

AUTHENTIC
RESILIENCE

Bringing Your Strengths to Life!

Foreword by Daniel G. Amen, MD

Fatima Doman

Published in the United States by Authentic Strengths Advantage, LLC
www.AuthenticStrengths.com

Copyright © Fatima Doman 2020
All rights reserved.
This title is also available in an e-book via Authentic Strengths Advantage, LLC
ISBN: 978-1-7348688-0-7
Library of Congress Control Number: 2020906761
Printed in the United States of America

Note to the Reader: Throughout these pages some names and identifying features within stories have been changed to preserve confidentiality.

In loving memory of my dear friend Allyson Lyle.
Your example of authentic resilience will live on for generations.

CONTENTS

FOREWORD

By Daniel G. Amen, MD

Twelve-time *New York Times* #1 Bestselling Author

"It is during our darkest moments that we must focus to see the light."
—Aristotle

Virtually all of us have felt anxious, depressed, traumatized, grief-stricken, or hopeless at some point in life. It's perfectly normal to go through hard times or experience periods when you feel panicked or out-of-sorts. How you respond to these challenges makes all the difference in how you feel—not just immediately, but in the long run.

All of us want to quickly stop the pain and to become more resilient. Unfortunately, many people self-medicate with energy drinks, overeating, alcohol, drugs, risky behavior, or wasting time on mindless TV, video games, shopping, to name a few. Although these substances and behaviors may give you temporary relief from feeling bad, they usually only prolong and exacerbate the problems, or cause other more serious ones, such as energy crashes, obesity, addictions, sexually transmitted diseases, unhappiness, relationship problems, or financial ruin.

I am Daniel Amen, MD, a psychiatrist, brain-imaging researcher, and founder of Amen Clinics, which has one of the highest, published success rates in treating people with complex and treatment resistant mental health issues, such as anxiety and mood disorders, post-traumatic stress disorder, ADHD, and more. Thanks to all of this experience, I understand how critical it is for you to know *what will help you feel better right now and later.* There are plenty of things that may help in the short term but will make you feel worse—or cause more problems—in the long term. What you need are evidence-based tools and strategies to help you build your resilience now, and to maintain your resilience in the future.

One of the most important secrets to our success at Amen Clinics is that we focus on understanding, healing, and optimizing the physical functioning of the brain (hardware), then focus on properly programming it (software), in that order. Both always work together, and if you ignore one while only working on the other, you will have a harder time increasing your resilience to consistently feel positive emotions.

This is where Fatima Doman's book, *Authentic Resilience*, comes in. I believe that Fatima's decades of meaningful work with positive psychology coaching is part of the important "software" that I mention above. The science of positive psychology, upon which Fatima bases her coaching books and tools, is a perfect companion to my brain health techniques in building resilience. This book you are reading utilizes the latest research to help you build your resilience by tapping into your strengths of character, that innermost part of yourself that can lead you to good decisions and positive outcomes in all aspects of your life.

The science-based tools you will learn in this book can help you discover your authentic strengths for sustainable motivation, calm your inner critic, and give voice to your inner coach by connecting the intelligence of your brain with the wisdom of your heart. This book will also help you overcome "comparanoia" and perfectionism, reframe negative experiences in ways that better serve you, leverage the skills of practicing gratitude, mindfulness and optimism, increase your emotional intelligence to strengthen your relationships, and much more.

Change is easy, if you know how to do it. But it is hard if you keep doing things that continue to reinforce negative behavior circuits in the brain. If you were an anxious child, for example, odds are you still feel anxious as an adult unless you did something to rewire the anxiety circuits in your brain. Anxiety built specific connecting highways (neural networks) in your brain. If you deal with pressure by drinking alcohol or lashing out at those around you, you are likely to continue that behavior whenever you feel stressed—unless you develop a new model of doing things.

Once the brain learns how to do something, it becomes wired to do it automatically and reflexively through a process called neuroplasticity. New learning and change require strategy, effort, and resources, which is why we often get stuck. I find this to be true in my own life and I bet you do too. Depending on what you've taught your brain to do, this neuroplasticity can help you develop and maintain good habits "superhighways of positivity and success" or it can cause you to get stuck in "ruts of negativity" that steal portions of your life.

Marcus: Too Many Negative Thoughts

The parents of fourteen-year-old Marcus brought him to see me because he was struggling with schoolwork and with his temper. He was depressed, had trouble focusing, was easily distracted, procrastinated, and took longer to complete assignments than ever before.

When I met Marcus, it was clear he struggled with many negative thoughts. He repeatedly referred to himself as stupid, and during our first session he told me:

"I hate school."

"I can never be as good as other kids."

"I'm a terrible person."

"I am an idiot."

"I am a failure."

"My teachers hate me."

"It's my parents' fault for not letting me quit."

His thinking was in a rut. The highways in his brain were headed straight toward negativity, failure, and depression. When I showed Marcus his brain and compared it to a Ferrari whose engine was revved too high, he smiled, saying he liked that analogy. To help Marcus get control over his mind, over the next two months I taught him principles of disciplined thinking that we all should have learned in school.

Every Time You Have a Thought, Your Brain Releases Chemicals

That's how your brain works. You have a thought, your brain releases chemicals, electrical transmissions travel throughout your brain, and you become aware of what you're thinking. Thoughts are real and they have a powerful impact on how you feel and behave. Just as a muscle that's exercised becomes stronger, repeatedly thinking the same thoughts makes them stronger too.

Every time you have an angry, unkind, hopeless, helpless, worthless, sad, or irritating thought, such as "I'm stupid," your brain releases chemicals that make you feel bad. In this way, your body reacts to every negative thought you have. Marcus was exercising his brain to feel depression, sadness, and failure. I asked him to think about the last time he was mad. How did his body feel? When most people are angry their muscles become tense, their hearts beat faster, their hands start to sweat, and they may even begin to feel a little dizzy. Marcus told me he got dizzy and sweaty, and felt confused and stupid.

Similarly, every time you have a joyful, hopeful, kind, optimistic, or positive thought, your brain releases chemicals that make you feel good. I asked Marcus to think about the last time he had a happy thought. How did he feel inside his body? When most people are happy their muscles relax, their hearts beat more slowly, their hands become dry, and they breathe more evenly. Marcus told me about an outing with his father, where they went fishing and had a great time. When he thought about it, he said he had felt peaceful and happy. He didn't feel stupid.

At Amen Clinics we have biofeedback equipment that measures physiological responses. I taught Marcus to think of his body as an "eco-system" that contains everything in the environment, such as air, water, land, cars, people, animals, vegetation, houses, landfills, and more. A negative thought is like pollution to his whole system. Just as pollution in Los Angeles or Beijing affects everyone who goes outdoors, so too do negative thoughts pollute your mind and your body.

Your Thoughts are Hardwired to be Negative

Given our ancestry, negative thoughts protected us from early death or becoming supper for more powerful animals. From our earliest times on earth, being aware of and avoiding danger was crucial to survival. Unfortunately, even when the world became safer, negativity bias remained in our brains. Researchers have demonstrated that negative experiences have a greater impact on the brain than positive ones.[1] People pay more attention to negative than to positive news, which is why news outlets typically lead broadcasts with floods, murders, political disasters, and all forms of mayhem. According to research from the content marketing website Outbrain.com, in two periods of 2012 the average click-through rate on headlines with negative adjectives was an astounding 63 percent higher than positive ones.[2] A negative perspective is more contagious than a positive one, which may be why political campaigns typically go negative at the end. Even our language is not exempt: Sixty-two percent of the words in the English dictionary connote negative emotions, while 32 percent express positive ones.[3]

Psychologist and author Rick Hanson has written that the brain is wired for negativity bias.[4] Once we start looking for bad news, it is quickly stored in the brain to keep us safe; but positive experiences have to be held in consciousness for more than 12 seconds before they stay with us. "The brain is like Velcro for negative experiences, but Teflon for positive ones," Hanson writes. Psychologist Mihaly Csikszentimihalyi, author of *Flow: The Psychology of Optimal Experience,* writes that, "Unless we are occupied with other thoughts, worrying is the brain's default position … we must constantly strive to escape such 'psychic entropy' by learning to control our consciousness and direct our attention to activities which provide 'flow,' activities which give positive feedback and strengthen our sense of purpose and achievement."[5] Discovering and leveraging our character strengths is one such activity.

Negative emotions supersede positive emotions, which is why it is critical to discipline our natural tendency toward the negative and amplify more helpful thoughts and emotions. This is why positive psychology coaching is so helpful.

Thoughts are Automatic and Often Lie

Thoughts are based on complex chemical reactions in the brain, memories from the past, the quality of our sleep, hormones, blood sugar, and many other factors. They are automatic, reflexive, random, and overwhelmingly negative. Plus, they are often erroneous. Unless disciplined and bridled, they will lie to you and wreak havoc in your life. Marcus thought he was stupid. He told himself that multiple times a day because he had trouble staying focused and didn't perform well on tests. Yet, when we tested him, his IQ was 135, in the top one percent of all people. I told him it was critical to question and not believe every thought that went through his head.

It's important to examine your thoughts to see if they are true, and if they are helping you or hurting you. Unfortunately, if you never challenge your thoughts, you will simply believe them, and then act out of that erroneous belief. If, for example, I thought, *"My wife never listens to me,"* I'd feel lonely, mad, and sad. I would give myself permission to be rude to her or ignore her. My reaction to the lie I was telling myself could cause a negative spiral in my marriage.

By repeatedly allowing his undisciplined thoughts to invade his mind; telling himself he was stupid, a failure, and a terrible person; that he hated school and was hated by his teachers, Marcus was more likely to behave in ways to make those terrible things happen. I told him that his brain makes happen what it sees, which is why it is critical to get control over your thoughts.

Is it Really Possible to Feel Better Fast?

Many people, mental health professionals included, think therapy needs to be long, hard, and painful. Or if you start medication for anxiety or depression, it is a lifelong commitment. Certainly, some people will need help longer than others, but, in my experience, many people can feel better fast if they engage in the right behaviors and strategies, which include knowing about and optimizing your brain, and learning positive strategies such as utilizing your character strengths consistently.

Think about it: You know you can make yourself feel worse almost immediately—by dwelling on the worst possible outcome of a situation, spending time with highly toxic people, or sabotaging each of your senses with dreadful sounds, smells, tastes, touches, or sights. You can just as easily make yourself feel better, for which Fatima will share positive psychology tools in the following pages to help you do so.

Helping people change their feelings and behaviors and optimize their lives has been my passion as a psychiatrist for the past four decades. I see a similar passion for helping people in the work of Fatima Doman. Everyone should learn to focus more energy in a positive way on their strengths. This book can help shift one's mindset to look more for the good in themselves and others. I encourage you to utilize the transformative positive psychology principles in this book to feel better fast, and to help those you love to do the same.

AWAKENING RESILIENCE

By Fatima Doman

"There's something in everybody that longs for that awakening to be more true to yourself."[6]

—Eckhart Tolle

My Journey

What makes people resilient? I became interested in this question of what makes people resilient because I grew up in circumstances where resilience was stretched to its limits. I was born in Angola to Portuguese parents, and my family immigrated to the United States fleeing a war when I was three years old. Before we fled the country, our family survived a night where 40 families in the country were massacred under the cover of darkness. Terrorists had gone from farmhouse to farmhouse killing entire families.

Although it happened far from our home, when morning came and news spread, our little farm community congregated at the local church. Families brought mattresses and provisions, and everyone stayed together for protection. Men with guns drawn watched for the next attack. Women tried to keep children quiet and calm for three days until the immediate threat had passed. My mother describes the scene that I was too young to remember clearly. The image, however, is not hard to conjure in my mind, having heard my parents tell the story many times and having felt their strong emotions as they told it. I feel transported back to that place and time. I can literally feel their fear, desperation and stress.

My parents lost everything they had worked for: their home and business virtually overnight. Soon they found themselves in a new country, unable to speak the language, and working long and exhausting hours at manual labor jobs. They were good, decent, hard-working people burdened by uncommon challenges. My father, an adventurous man in his youth, felt "cheated" by "bad luck" and often ruminated about what he had lost. High blood pressure and a heart condition took his life too early.

My mother, a deeply religious woman, although affected by the stress, did her best to focus on the positive. Eventually, however, she began to suffer from depression and other serious health problems. Despite her challenges, my mother was often a beacon of light for me, a woman of great faith and courage. She was the fragile thread that held our family together during those tumultuous times. Although her strength wavered in the midst of such intense stress, I remember hearing my mother say, "Aren't we lucky to have come to the U.S.?" "We're so blessed to have survived, our entire family intact." My mother, a mild and shy 4'11" woman, had been a school teacher in Angola. However, because of the language barrier in America, she found herself working in a turkey plant on a cold, wet assembly line, cutting the breast off the bone of turkey after turkey.

My mother would come home, visibly tired, wearing her rubber boots and hard hat, feathers sticking to her clothes. She was scarcely through the door before she would ask about our schoolwork. She encouraged us to do our best in school, knowing that was likely our only hope for a better life. She would pick me up from school in her old, dented, green Ford Maverick, get out of the car in her hairnet and rubber boots and yell, "Fatinha! Estou aqui!" (Little Fatima! I'm over here!). As an awkward adolescent I sometimes felt embarrassed, wishing she would wait in the car, but today I remember those times with deep emotion and pride — my hard-working mother doing her best to raise five kids and put food on the table.

I noticed the fingerprint of euphemisms that my parents would use on a regular basis. Sayings like "aye que miseria" ("oh what misery") were common to my ears. I often longed to hear more optimistic language from my parents, and it was painful to watch them struggle. At a relatively young age, I found myself wondering why some people were able to have a positive outlook on life despite hardships, and others — in the same situations — seemed crushed by circumstances beyond their control. It seemed as if the people who bounced back from adversity were thinking more good thoughts and expressing more appreciation for the little things in life, developing confidence in themselves and others. I became determined to live as if it were possible for me to have not just a good life, but to flourish.

My desire to explore how people can awaken their resilience and thrive no matter their circumstance led me to positive psychology. While coaching and speaking around the world, I have discovered that regardless of the culture, socio-economic status, or belief system, the positive principles of good human character resonate with virtually everyone. If I was teaching in Asia, people would comment on how it seemed to come right out of Buddhist or Taoist beliefs; when I was in Africa, the Middle East or Southeast Asia I was asked if the material had been inspired from the Quran; when working with Hindus, I was told it reminded them of the Bhagavad Gita, while in western countries people said it was reminiscent of Christian teachings.

I have come to see through many years of working with thousands of people that those looking for help through life's challenges are searching for practical ways to apply their culture's deeply valued strengths and wisdom.

I, like you, continue to face the inevitable challenges of life. I'm writing this book not as a "perfect" person who doesn't struggle, but rather as an imperfect human being, sharing what has worked for me and for others I've witnessed. In my life, I've had my share of disappointments and failures. I know what it's like to face health and relationship challenges, fall short, be disregarded, feel overwhelmed and discouraged, and even to be betrayed and bullied. I recognize that very few people have been spared these and other difficulties in their lives. Everyone encounters occasional hard times—some of us keep those experiences to ourselves for various reasons.

Significant and unusual challenges have surfaced while writing this book—it has been one of the most stressful periods I and many have gone through. Given the pandemic crisis the world is facing as I write these words this book feels more relevant than ever. Like so many, as a wife, mother, friend, community member I'm concerned not just for myself, but also for the most vulnerable harmed by this crisis. I can say with all honesty, however, that when I apply the principles in this book, my life and my relationships flow more smoothly, I'm more productive, and I feel greater inner peace.

I feel humbled and grateful to share these evidence-based principles with you that I believe can help you stay optimistic and strong in the face of adversity. May this book awaken the amazing strengths within you that are a source of your own resilience.

Your Journey

"Through your awakening, you awaken others."

—Solara An Ra

I welcome you on your own journey toward greater resilience, empowered by your authentic strengths. If you have picked up this book, you are wanting to help yourself and others to build resilience to deal with the challenges that life inevitably presents to us. It's part of the human experience.

The principles you will learn have been shown to enhance the quality of life for countless people by increasing their happiness, life satisfaction, achievement, fulfillment, and resilience. These principles are grounded in scientific research and people who apply them report a greater ability to create sustainable, positive change in their lives.

So, what is resilience? The Oxford Dictionary defines it as "the capacity to recover quickly from difficulties."[8] Researchers María Luisa Martinez-Marti and Willibald Ruch explain, *"during our lives we face a variety of challenges, from daily hassles to major life events. Although some people become overwhelmed by these events, many people manage to endure them extremely well, with no apparent disruption in their functioning. The study of psychological resilience seeks to understand why some individuals are able to withstand stress better than others."*[9]

Other definitions include:

"the ability to cope with whatever life throws at you"

"being resilient is positively associated with happiness"

"some people can be knocked down by life and return as a stronger person than ever before"

"a resilient person works through challenges by using personal resources, strengths and other positive psychological resources"[10]

Based on my own experience, I would add to these definitions that resilience is not something that is a one-time pursuit "once and done," but rather it's something that we have to work on every day. Resilience is a lifelong process of learning and growth.

It's important to remember that each of us can learn how to navigate the occasional rough waters of our difficult experiences. Maria Sirois, PsyD offers words of encouragement as we embark on this journey of building our resilience:

> *"One of the common myths about resilience is that some people are simply born with it, while the rest of us aren't. The good news is that anyone can build the skills necessary to cope and even thrive in difficult times."[11]*

Because you have picked up this book, you are proactively creating your own thriving life. I've noticed a shift in people like you, who are increasingly interested in building their resilience and in living from their strengths. In the midst of the stress, disappointments, failures, and the chaotic noise of modern life, countless people are choosing resilience over fear. J.K. Rowling shares her own resilient journey, reconnecting with her wholeness, in her 2008 Harvard Commencement Address:

> *"Failure meant a stripping away of the inessential. I stopped pretending to myself that I was anything other than what I was...I was set free, because my greatest fear had been realized, and I was still alive, and I still had a daughter whom I adored, and I had an old typewriter, and a big idea. And so rock bottom became a solid foundation on which I rebuilt my life."[12]*

A Growing Need in Communities

There is a growing need for tools that help people build their resilience. Resilience-building resources are resonating broadly, from schools, to the corporate world, to communities and essential services personnel.

Let me share one such example of a community on a quest for resilience-building tools. The mountain town I live in was forever changed the week two thirteen-year old boys fatally overdosed on a new opioid drug. The boys had purchased the drug—twice as potent as heroin—on the Internet in two short keyboard clicks. Feeling immense sadness and somber resolve to warn others, school superintendent Ember Conley wrote in a School Administrator article[13]:

> *"At times, it is hard to separate the lines between my role as a school leader and my role as a parent...Not only was the school district and community suffering from the loss of two students, we had teachers, staff, siblings [and friends] of the deceased students feeling tremendous pain...a cloud of grief settled into the school. Parents arrived to pick up their children. Staff kept working, putting plans into place for their most acutely affected... We were now part of a national crisis, the scourge of opioids."*

Conley asked me to be a resilience presenter and panelist in town hall meetings, and to work with the district teaching my strengths-based positive psychology program, along with experts in other fields. She realized her staff needed to use all resources at their disposal to share knowledge that would help keep students safe and help them build their resilience:

> *"First, we learned about trauma-informed, resiliency-focused measures that could be applied in our district. We began with community conversations and circles of support to allow healing and education, and we co-sponsored a film series to raise awareness.*

Second, we reviewed...resilience, perseverance and grit...and we provided [Doman's Authentic Strengths Resilience] training to all of our counselors, health teachers and nurses who have most access to students in the life skills curriculum...This training uses the motto "Moving from what's wrong, to what's strong." The elementary schools have begun using mindfulness in all classes to teach students the benefits of breathing, working through situations and not becoming emotionally charged. We are seeing some effects of these tools. A principal walked out to the playground during recess when she noticed two boys sitting...eyes closed, breathing deeply. When she asked what they were doing, they admitted they had gotten angry playing soccer and instead of fighting decided to do their breathing!...The Authentic Strengths [Resilience Program] has been a game changer in assisting our youth in building resilience—using positive psychology tools to deal with stress...In an era of tremendous pressure and feelings of anxiousness, the tools and training have built capacity...and truly increased the confidence of both staff and students grades K-12 to leverage their character strengths to flourish."

Finally, we came together as a community...we organized Lunch and Learn information sessions...to give parents practical strategies for talking with their children...with the support of the county health department, county council, city council, [governmental] and non-governmental partners, we [addressed] youth risk factors and youth protection."

Although building our resilience is only one part of the solution to the growing epidemic of stress, anxiety and depression, it is a vital part, nonetheless. When we are facing challenges, it's helpful to have a toolbox and fill that toolbox with as many supportive tools as possible. These resilience tools are *not* intended to replace medical and mental health professionals that offer important tools. The tools you will learn in this book are intended to *add* to your toolbox, rather than to replace any other tools you are already using or may use in the future to help you weather life's storms.

A Universal Need

On another occasion, I saw evidence of this universal need to tap into one's inner strength when I presented to one of the largest law enforcement departments in the United States. I had been warned not to expect much interaction or buy-in from the captains and lieutenants in attendance. The training leader said, "Don't let them intimidate you, Fatima. You will probably be looking at a lot of blank, stoic faces and they may even be openly hostile to positive psychology. Don't expect them to talk much."

What I encountered was the opposite. When we discussed that the law enforcement profession carries with it some of the highest suicide and divorce rates of any profession, they were eager for solutions to their problems. The challenge, they told me, is that to survive on the streets they have to be extremely fast and adept at following highly skilled training in the moment. What if they could also train for resiliency and develop the ability to come down faster off the adrenaline rush to a place of emotional and mental clarity? What if they could develop the very strengths that are shown to counteract post-traumatic stress and to nurture conditions for post-traumatic growth? They were so energized by the skills and tools of the strengths training that I often could not get them to stop talking in their groups and to move on to the next topic!

One of the captains came up to me after the training and said he would like to see character strengths training taken to the prison system.

He said, "Could you imagine the impact if we provided this information to each new inmate? Most of them have probably never had anyone help them identify their strengths."

That captain's comment reinforced my commitment to share this empowering information with as many people as possible. As you learn the motivating concepts within these pages, you will tap into your authentic strengths, that core part of yourself that energizes you and fills your life with meaning, purpose and sustainable inner strength.

Our Roadmap

Many people, after reading my first book, *Authentic Strengths*, told me that they would like to see that information made accessible to everyone—not just geared to professional coaches. Especially now, during times of increased stress, people have requested a new book written for the masses, with a focus on how to apply the principles, practices and tools in everyday life as well as while in crisis. Therefore, I've added recently updated tools, new practices, research and practical application that I believe will help anyone build their resilience in the midst of life's inevitable stressors. This new book is a revised and expanded version of my first book, written in a way that is simplified and applicable to everyday life. Most importantly, this new book contains important fresh content essential to building resilience. Many of the concepts and examples will be familiar to the readers of my first book, but I offer more common language, additional relatable stories and anecdotes to bring it to life, and day-to-day uses for what you will learn in the book you now hold in your hands.

Each time I've shared the principles in this book, people pull me aside and confide their own struggles—and more importantly their hopes for a better future. I'm humbled by their honesty and inspired by their vulnerability. From the husband and father reeling from his sudden job loss and fearful of his family's future, to the TV producer who whispered that his daughter had survived her second suicide attempt, to the teacher who confided she'd been gang-raped and was rebuilding her life, to the educator whose son is a recovering opioid addict reconnecting with his strengths, to the woman who held a gun in her mouth, then set it down when she heard an inner voice say she was "worthy and beautiful" the way she was created—they all inspire me to continue sharing the tools that have helped them and those they love.

I've spent decades studying resilience and human flourishing so that I could condense what I've uncovered into a simple, practical, three-step process within the pages of this book. My hope is to help you awaken your authentic resilience, which I believe can be found in your strengths of character. As you learn how to cultivate more resilience in your life, even in the midst of your darkest hours, you will be empowered to live abundantly and to bring forth your potential—your personal contribution to the world.

First, you will learn tools designed to **explore** your strengths, understanding how your strengths have helped you in the past, and how to leverage their power in building your resilience in the future. Next you will learn how to **empower** your resilience with your strengths, understanding your own intrinsic source of sustainable motivation that can propel you forward in life. And, finally, you will learn to **engage** your strengths, moving beyond just thinking about using your strengths to actually *living* your strengths daily —all while honoring and appreciating the strengths in others. These three, easy to remember steps can take your life and the lives of those you influence in fulfilling new directions.

ENGAGE
Strengths in Action
Reflect, Reveal, Recalibrate/CSQ

EMPOWER
Strengths Motivation
Feedback/Feed Forward
Motivation Grid/STRONG Goals

EXPLORE
Strengths Awareness
Life Sketch/Whole Life Scale
Best Self/STRONG Filter/STRONG Thoughts

CHARACTER STRENGTHS

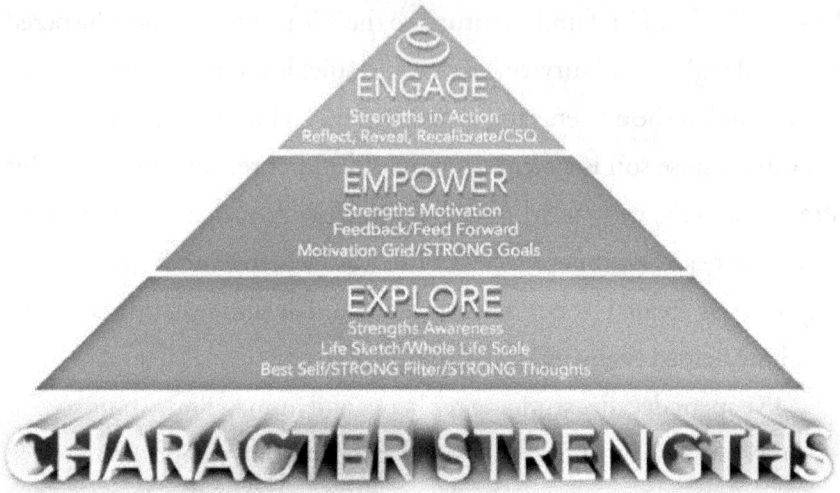

The concepts and tools in this book are based on scientific research and are designed to help you increase your resilience in the midst of life's challenges. Many highly regarded universities and institutes conduct positive psychology research that is referenced in these pages, and I have drawn from this extensive research to create a self-coaching process that I believe can serve you well.

What is Positive Psychology?

Can resilience, optimal functioning and happiness be learned? Positive psychologists say "yes!" The science of positive psychology provides an evidence-based approach to creating your own thriving life. While traditional psychology focuses on the disease model, "what's wrong" with people (one's weaknesses), positive psychology balances this by focusing on "what's strong" in people (one's strengths); by studying optimal functioning and strengths of character to help people improve their lives.[14]

Throughout the twentieth century, traditional psychology measured and addressed human pathology, a valuable and needed contribution. Now, in the twenty-first century, a movement toward developing equally robust assessment tools and interventions exists to study human flourishing—people's strengths and virtues. Positive psychologists have developed reliable and valid measures of strengths, well-being, and approaches to happiness and life satisfaction.[15] As a result, scientists can now assess strengths like hope, perseverance, leadership and love, in as precise and reliable ways as we measure anxiety or depression. Enriching and broadening the past, positive psychologists have put together a list of *Character Strengths and Virtues* or the CSV[16], as a counterpoint to the famous *Diagnostic and Statistical Manual of Mental Disorders*, or the DSM, which classifies mental disorders.

A Tipping Point

We are at a critical tipping point in history. The world is steeped in negativity bias[17] and scarcity mentality. We are inundated daily with disturbing news of mass shootings, climate change, volatile politics, unrealistic social media pressures, etc. Stress, anxiety, and depression are rising at alarming rates.[18] Many people carry a deficit perspective of themselves and of others. As a result, many people aren't aware of how it affects their own well-being, and their relationships in their personal lives, at school, at work, in their communities, etc.

But the good news is that we can learn to become our own resilience coach, and also to engage with others from a positive perspective—giving our attention to what's strong instead of what's wrong. As Carol Kauffman of Harvard Medical School has said, *"In essence, the clinician is trained to follow the trail of tears. Positive psychology coaches shift attention from what causes and drives pain to what energizes and pulls people forward. They follow the trail of dreams."*[19]

Positive psychology doesn't pretend that mental and emotional issues don't exist. However, this fundamental, expansive, and exciting science focuses tremendous time and energy on the wholeness and strengths within people. This is a new, and much needed empowering focus on living a thriving life. I have noticed that what is observed, comes to the forefront. So why don't we learn to treat ourselves in this way—discovering our own wholeness concealed within—becoming our own best coach? One of my dear friends, Cheryl, shares below how she did just that...

> *I had a lot of negative self-talk beginning in my late teens that resulted in a severe eating disorder. I was constantly telling myself how I wasn't as good as others. I would say to myself that I was fat, that I wasn't smart or disciplined. My inner critic was so loud that I wasn't even aware of my inner coach. This self-condemnation made me want to escape from myself and all these self-hating thoughts. I pretended to others that I was happy, but when left to myself, all I had were my self-deprecating thoughts finding so many things wrong with me. I struggled with this for 17 years and the pattern had become deeply ingrained in my brain. Drawing on my strength of bravery, I finally sought help and was admitted to a treatment facility.*

> *I began to recognize how some of my character strengths could help me hear and reactivate my inner coach, and to recognize my many negative thoughts. I realized I had the option to not believe these destructive thoughts. I could choose to see my strengths—I could choose something different!*

> *I committed that for one week I would recognize every time I bullied myself, and then replace that criticism with something loving to myself. In these moments, I chose to repeat "I love myself, I accept myself." I have a very developed strength of loving others and wondered*

if I could use this strength to love myself. At first, I felt like I was repeating my new mantra right after finishing saying it, because my thoughts were on such an automatic critical mode! By the end of the week, however, I found my critical voice diminished dramatically. I even began to add to my mantra things like "I am learning and growing every day and I am worth it," using my strength of spirituality by remembering my infinite worth. This was the beginning of my recovery.

Learning to have self-compassion and accept that I'm human, imperfect, and yet have great value, helped me be brave enough to take the scary steps towards a full and happy life. This allowed me to really SEE ME and see the GOOD in me, which led to hope and productive actions.

No one overcomes adversity or reaches their personal best without being inspired or guided part of the way. Whether you use the tools in this book to coach yourself, or pay it forward and coach others (like Cheryl is now doing), these timeless principles can bring out the best in you and in those you seek to positively influence. You will learn to build resilience, foster self-compassion and self-acceptance, achieve optimal functioning, increase your well-being, and contribute positively in your relationships and in society by reconnecting with your highest and best self—your strengths of character. Let's tip the scales toward positivity bias and abundance mentality—authentically empowering you for sustainable positive change to love the life you live!

EXPLORING YOUR POTENTIAL

"You have to find what sparks a light in you
so that you in your own way can illuminate the world."[20]

—Oprah Winfrey

CHAPTER ONE

MOVING FROM WRONG TO STRONG: YOUR SPIRITUAL DNA

"Greatness is on the inside. It's about character."[21]

—*Stephen Covey*

Imagine you found a flower bud in your garden — you see the bud but are unsure what flower will unfold from it. If you have a predetermined wish or requirement for it to be one vs. another, such as wanting an orchid to be a geranium or a tulip to be a rose, you will be disappointed when the "wrong" one unfolds. You will focus on what's "wrong" with it and try to change it, and in so doing you may harm it and prevent it from reaching its potential. If so, it will wither.

Unfortunately, the world is full of withered and withering people because they, or others around them, have not respected and nurtured their innate strengths, nor valued their uniqueness. Often the loud inner critic joins in the game by suppressing a person's authenticity and trying to coerce them into some preconceived ideal.

All living things — people included — have innate tendencies that define our uniqueness. Though we certainly share many characteristics, our uniqueness defines us as individuals. It represents our character and what we treasure about ourselves. Regrettably, too often people are viewed as lumps of clay to be molded to certain specifications, behaviors, beliefs, or job descriptions that suit the desires of others, ignoring their unique needs in the process. While inanimate objects can be molded how we want, we cannot do the same to living organisms without risking doing harm.

What if we could learn how to see and appreciate our and others' authentic character strengths rather than trying to mold self or others into some preconceived ideal? How would that positively impact resilience, learning, achievement, overall life satisfaction and fulfillment? Truly wise people—individuals, parents, teachers, coaches, leaders—create the conditions for themselves and others to flourish and soar.

Using the science of positive psychology, we now can identify the strengths that define who we are at our **best** —the qualities that, when nurtured, can improve all areas of our lives. Developing an awareness of these strengths helps us to focus on "what's strong," instead of "what's wrong." As decades of research and hundreds of studies have now shown, people who express their strengths tend to be more resilient, happier, more engaged, energized, less stressed, and higher achievers.[22]

In my twenty years of coaching, I have yet to encounter a more powerful tool for increasing resilience. I have witnessed significant positive change when people come to understand and use their character strengths, while appreciating the character strengths in others.

Understanding Character Strengths

"Character strengths serve as those crucial influencers that help us embrace the positive, endure the mundane, and navigate and manage the struggles."[23]

—*Dr. Ryan M. Niemiec*

Character strengths are those aspects of your personality that define what is best in you. Collectively, they are responsible for your greatest achievements and fulfillment. Scientists have identified 24 strengths that are the basic building blocks defining our individuality as people, psychologically speaking. We each possess all 24 of these strengths in different degrees and combinations.

These strengths are universally valued — in the East and in the West—across the world's diverse cultures. An international team of over 50 scientists investigated, classified and confirmed the character strengths you will learn about in this book. Positive psychologists define them as positive traits that are beneficial to self and others. They lead us to positive feelings, relationships, achievements, vitality, and into engaging and meaningful life activities. We flourish when we identify and flex our strengths.[24] [25]

If we want to build up any of these strengths, we can learn to do so. People aren't born missing key character strengths — we just may not have focused on exercising a particular strength, perhaps causing it to atrophy. The key is developing an awareness of our strengths and how to optimally use them, in order to build our resilience.

Dr. Martin Seligman is considered by many to be the father of the positive psychology movement. He explained in his groundbreaking books, *Authentic Happiness* and *Flourish,* that once we know what our best qualities are, they open up a vital pathway to engagement—at work, at school, in relationships and in life. Due to the science of positive psychology (which focuses on what's strong about a person) vs. the old psychology that has used a problem-focused approach, we now can help people design their own future powered by their strong suits.[26]

I use the VIA Character Strengths Survey[27] because it is a scientifically valid, peer-reviewed tool that helps you to focus on what's strong instead of what's wrong. For example, the survey might show that a person's top strengths are leadership, kindness, curiosity and creativity. All 24 of the VIA character strengths matter equally. No one strength is more important than another. The 24 VIA character strengths depicted below are done so with permission from the VIA Institute on Character, with the images modified:

Wisdom	**CREATIVITY** • Originality • Ingenuity	**CURIOSITY** • Interest • Openness	**JUDGMENT** • Open-Mindedness • Rational Thinking	**LOVE OF LEARNING** • Interest In Gaining Knowledge	**PERSPECTIVE** • Wisdom • Big Picture View
Courage	**BRAVERY** • Courage • Valor	**PERSEVERANCE** • Persistence • Industriousness	**HONESTY** • Authenticity • Integrity	**ZEST** • Vitality/Enthusiasm • Energy/Vigor	
Humanity	**LOVE** • Loving/Being Loved • Close Relationships	**KINDNESS** • Generosity/Nurturance • Care/Compassion			**SOCIAL INTELLIGENCE** • Emotional Awareness • Relationship Intelligence
Justice	**TEAMWORK** • Citizenship/Loyalty • Social Responsibility			**FAIRNESS** • Just • Not Biased	**LEADERSHIP** • Organizer • Encourager of a Group
Temperance		**FORGIVENESS** • Mercy • Letting Go	**HUMILITY** • Modesty • Humbleness	**PRUDENCE** • Careful/Cautious • Practical Reason	**SELF-REGULATION** • Self-Control • Disciplined
Transcendence	**APPRECIATION OF BEAUTY & EXCELLENCE** • Awe/Wonder • Elevation	**GRATITUDE** • Appreciation • Feeling Blessed	**HOPE** • Optimism • Future-Mindedness	**HUMOR** • Playfulness • Lighthearted	**SPIRITUALITY** • Faith • Purpose

This chart of the 24-character strengths above is categorized into six virtue categories as follows:

- Wisdom: Cognitive strengths for the acquisition and use of knowledge
- Courage: Emotional strengths that exercise will to accomplish goals in opposition

- Humanity: Interpersonal strengths that involve tending and be-friending others
- Justice: Civic strengths that underlie healthy community life
- Temperance: Strengths that protect against excess
- Transcendence: Strengths connected to a larger universe and that provide meaning

Positive psychology research is continually shedding light on our understanding of character strengths and the following are four key characteristics of strengths:

- First, strengths are positive traits all humans possess.
- Second, they are universally valued, meaning that they are valued in all cultures around the world.
- Third, strengths are expressed in varying degrees, or at different levels. For example, one person may be very high in expressing courage, whereas another person may be more moderate in expressing courage.
- And fourth, they are learnable! The exciting news is that anyone can learn how to express any of the 24-character strengths more fully at any time.

Discover Your Unique Strengths Profile

You can discover your own unique VIA strengths profile. Simply visit AuthenticStrengths.com and click on the button, "TAKE THE FREE STRENGTHS SURVEY." It's fast and easy. After you take the VIA survey, you can download the free report immediately. In your report, you will find a ranking of your 24-character strengths with your most-used strengths at the top and your less-used strengths at the bottom. You will be referring to this report on some of the exercises that follow.

As you review your report, it is important for you to know that lower ranked strengths do not indicate a "weakness." We call these "less-used strengths," which means that you do not express these strengths as often as your top, more dominant strengths. For example, scoring low on honesty does not mean that a person lies a lot. In fact, the VIA strengths scale does not assess lying or dishonesty at all, nor does it assess any other weaknesses. The VIA report only assesses strengths, and how much they are used.

Your Top Strengths

Let's take a look at the different categories of character strengths. Some strengths are more strongly represented in us (and therefore rise to the top of the report) and are core to our identity, to who we are. These are called our "signature strengths" or "top strengths." Top strengths are like a fingerprint—they define our uniqueness and represent our authentic selves. Our top strengths are those that feel almost as important to us as breathing. They come naturally, and we feel energized and satisfied when we are expressing them. And when others see them in us, we feel understood in an important way. If we are unable to express these parts of ourselves for some reason, we might feel like we are suffocating or dying inside. That's why focusing on our top strengths and how to put them into play—at work and in life in general—is so important.

As you look at your strengths survey results, in particular your top strengths, ask yourself these questions to determine whether a character strength is truly a top strength for you. It's helpful to write down and reflect on your answers:

- Is it authentic?
- Does it show up often?
- Do others notice it?
- Does using it energize me?
- If unable to express it, would I feel empty?

Because we care so much about our top strengths, we tend to expect others to care as much as we do and can become upset when they do not. Take, for example, a person high in "fairness" who will tend to become upset whenever he sees instances of others (or himself) being treated unfairly. In other words, our top strengths are also our hot buttons — that emotional trigger that fires when others act in contradiction.

Your Situational Strengths

The next category of strengths is called "situational strengths." These are strengths we call forth when we need to. For example, a man shared with me that although he does not like public speaking and was terrified to speak at a school board meeting, he was able to do so because the education of his children was very important to him. So, he called forth some of his less used strengths—bravery and leadership—which were best suited to the situation to help get him through the public speaking. However, because these were lesser strengths for him, it was exhausting to do it. So, people can "step up" and invoke any strength when needed.

Situational strengths, unlike top strengths, are not as important in defining who we are. For example, while some people may have perseverance as a top strength—meaning that in general they like to work at things diligently and rarely give up—others who do not have this as a top strength may still be able to use their willpower to persevere when the situation requires it. For the first group of people who have it as a top strength, persevering marks what they love to do and is a strength that is energizing to them. However, for the second group who have it as a situational strength, perseverance is something they call forth only when they need to perform in a given situation. Interestingly, in the second group, it can be draining to use their situational strength of perseverance. The difference between situational strengths and top strengths is that people *need to express* top strengths to feel whole and energized, but they are comfortable expressing situational strengths *only when they are needed*. Therefore, you may feel more energy after expressing a top strength and less energy after expressing a strength lower on your report.

The more you use *any character strength*, your comfort level with that strength will increase and you may experience more energy with it over time. This is why we will do some strengths-building activities later in this book, to flex all of your character muscles over time.

Strengths You Tend to Combine

Character strengths rarely exist alone—they mostly occur in combinations. Like a well-tuned orchestra, the right combinations can amplify the strengths of all the various instruments and make them each sound even better, complementing one another.

Take, for example, the following story of how the strengths of humor and social intelligence (the ability to understand others) can be a powerful combination: Mary was grieving the death of her husband Fred, when Tom, who worked with Fred for years, came up to her. He mumbled through his tears a funny story about Fred that lifted Mary's spirits. Through her tears, Mary laughed. In his grief, Tom had called forth his strengths of humor and social intelligence to console Mary. But humor applied with too little social intelligence can be offensive (*i.e.,* if Tom had told Mary a disparaging joke about her husband, it would have had a reverse effect on the situation). Yet, when humor and social intelligence exist together, that combination becomes endearing and one of the most powerful strengths in social situations, helping to strengthen relationships (*i.e.,* bringing levity to a challenging situation or project by seeing the humor in it). Other examples of powerful strength combinations are prudence and creativity, or judgment and zest, or leadership and teamwork, or honesty and kindness, etc., because they moderate and balance each other.

Think of a creative person who combines their strength of creativity with their strength of prudence to ensure that their creative project is complete and on time. Or consider a person using their strength of zest to infuse their work with energy and passion, yet who balances it with their strength of judgment in considering all aspects of a project before diving in. Or recall a time someone has been honest with you on a sensitive subject but balanced their strength of honesty with their strength of kindness toward you. Our middle strengths can play a role in moderating our top strengths to make them work better. Also, our top strengths can combine in unexpected and extremely powerful ways.

You Can Build Your Strengths

There may be times in your life where you encounter the need to build strengths that you previously have not focused much energy or attention on. Most likely this will emerge after a life event that changes your motivation to use a strength that had been somewhat dormant in the past. Perhaps you have new school or work demands, or something in your personal life has changed to call for a fuller expression of a particular strength, such as a new relationship or personal interest. Or, you may simply be at a point where you are interested in growth and this includes growing your repertoire of "go-to" strengths. The strengths you choose to build are most likely those strengths that you feel would help you most in some aspect of your life. It can be very motivating to target such strengths that you want to build. Let me share a letter with you from an inspiring woman named Ally, who during a time of personal growth, was able to build strengths with great success:

"Strengths coaching was a real eye opener for me. It revealed several underutilized strengths that were preventing me from fully implementing some of my signature strengths. Of my top strengths, two

of them are curiosity and love of learning, while one of my lowest ranked strengths is perseverance. All of a sudden, I realized why I am constantly starting fascinating writing projects and never completing them. I abandon the old idea or project because I'm so excited about learning about a new one; and with little perseverance, it's a perfect storm for never finishing anything I start. In fact, I had become so discouraged over the years that I was to the point of not even starting anything — assuming I wouldn't finish!

Another top strength is kindness driving me to be genuinely interested in helping people and wishing I could make an impact on their lives. But with social intelligence ranked almost last in my strengths ranking, I often don't connect with people the way I would love to.

I always assumed these were character flaws that were an unchangeable part of my personality. Then I read Authentic Strengths and realized that my strengths ranking wasn't set in stone. I have all 24 strengths and I can build upon my lesser strengths! I may have been neglecting some of them, but they're all at my disposal! This idea really motivated me, and I decided to test it one morning. Instead of my usual minimal "medium starch" and no eye-contact interaction with the attendant at my neighborhood cleaners, I consciously decided to test using two of my signature strengths, curiosity and kindness to raise my social intelligence. Well, after twenty years "Carla" and I now greet each other by name, and I will be interested next time I drop off cleaning to hear whether her daughter got into the journalism program. And my errands will go from automated to energizing because of the genuine human connection.

Buoyed by this simple success, I'm also working on that never-finishing-anything issue. Perseverance has taken on tremendous importance for me — I now truly care about finishing what I start. I even keep a list by my desk of everything I finish. Projects big and small that never made it past the good idea stage are now making the list of accomplishments — everything from planting a rose in honor of my mother to web-publishing past speeches - and each thing I complete returns the energy of accomplishment rather than the dejection of unfinished failure."

The Shadow Side of Strengths

Another important aspect of strengths is overuse and underuse—learning to use our top strengths well—and to modulate them according to any given situation. I like to call this the "blissful middle," because avoiding extremes of overuse and underuse leads to optimal expression of strengths where we experience our best selves.

However, when you overuse or underuse a strength, you are in what is known as the "shadow side" of strengths. This means that you are missing out on the great power that can come from using that strength optimally. Underusing or overusing a strength can create problems and that's why it's important to know how to use them optimally. An example of overusing is this quote by Abraham Kaplan, "Give a small boy a hammer, and he will find that everything he encounters needs pounding." This example of the boy overusing a skill is much like someone who is good at "prudence" may sometimes overuse it and become seen as a naysayer and overly cautious and fearful person. Take a moment to review the "shadow side of strengths" chart below:

UNDERUSE	OPTIMAL	OVERUSE
CONFORMITY	CREATIVITY	ECCENTRICITY
DISINTEREST	CURIOSITY	NOSINESS
NON-REFLECTION	JUDGMENT/OPEN-MINDEDNESS	NARROW-MINDEDNESS
UNINFORMED	LOVE OF LEARNING	KNOW-IT-ALL
SHALLOWNESS	PERSPECTIVE	OVERBEARING
COWARDICE	BRAVERY	FOOLHARDINESS
GIVING UP	PERSEVERANCE	OBSESSIVENESS
PHONINESS	HONESTY	RIGHTEOUSNESS
SEDENTARY	ZEST	HYPERACTIVE
EMOTIONAL ISOLATION	LOVE	EMOTIONAL PROMISCUITY
INDIFFERENCE	KINDNESS	INTRUSIVENESS
SOCIALLY AWKWARD	SOCIAL INTELLIGENCE	OVER-ANALYZING
SELFISHNESS	TEAMWORK	DEPENDENT
DISMISSIVE	FAIRNESS	DEMANDING
COMPLIANT	LEADERSHIP	AUTHORITARIAN
MERCILESS	FORGIVENESS	PERMISSIVE
SELF-ABSORBED	MODESTY/HUMILITY	SELF-DEPRECIATION
RASH	PRUDENCE	OVERLY CAUTIOUS
SELF-INDULGENCE	SELF-REGULATION	OVERLY RESTRICTIVE
LOW EXPECTATION	APP OF BEAUTY/EXCELLENCE	PERFECTIONISM
RUGGED INDIVIDUALISM	GRATITUDE	INGRATIATION/OVERPRAISE
NEGATIVE / APATHETIC	HOPE	UNREALISTIC
OVERLY SERIOUS	HUMOR	GIDDINESS
UNCERTAINTY	SPIRITUALITY	FANATICISM

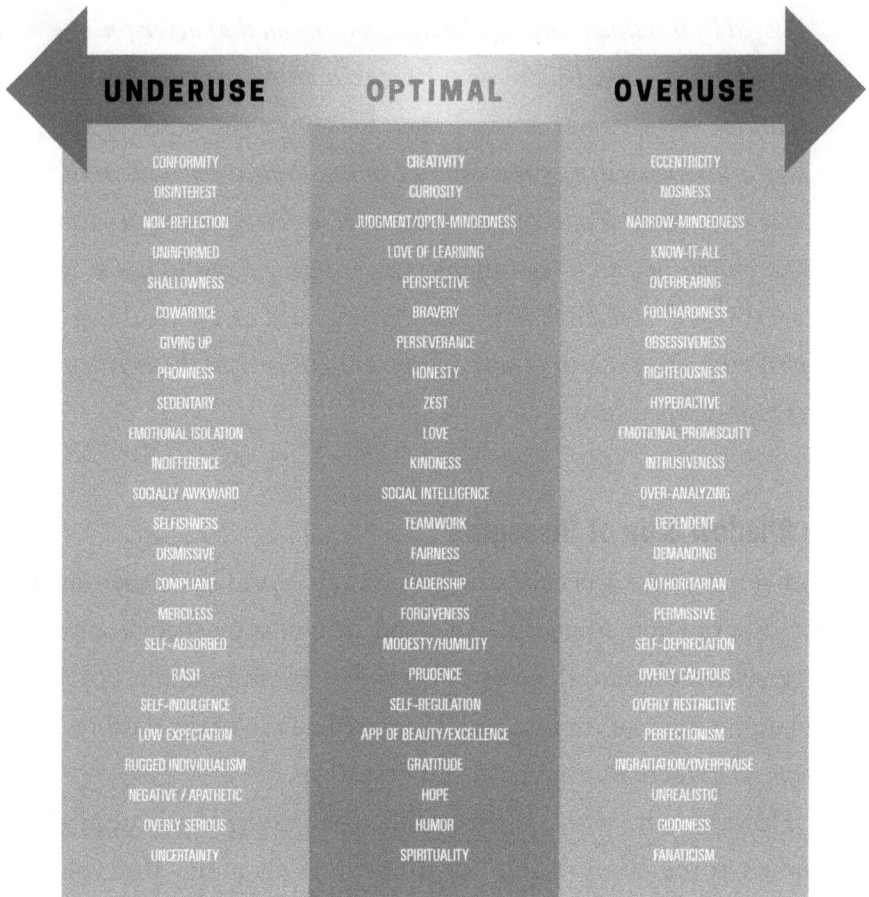

(Adapted from VIA Institute on Character Optimal Use Chart.)

Introducing Your Positivity Journal

Throughout the following chapters you will have an opportunity to capture your aha moments and insights. I encourage you to dedicate a separate journal as your "Positivity Journal." Take the time to look inward, and to invest energy into building your own resilience, as you learn to shift your focus to your authentic strengths.

STRONG Questions in Your Positivity Journal

As you encounter Positivity Journal exercises throughout this book, you will notice powerful, self-coaching questions for you to answer. Because these questions are rooted in positive psychology research and are designed to build resilience—mental and emotional strength, I call them "STRONG Questions." Watch for examples of STRONG Questions throughout this book and take the time to really ponder these questions and to answer them. So, are you ready to write your first entry in your Positivity Journal? You can begin with these questions below:

Positivity Journal STRONG Questions

- What are some examples of challenges you have experienced when overusing or underusing a strength?
- How can you consistently be more aware, and shift to optimally using your strengths? (Developing this personal awareness will help you to be more effective, and to enjoy the benefits of optimal use.)

Your Strengths Snapshot

Learning all of this great information will not make much difference in your life unless you *use it*! It's helpful to create a "snapshot" of your strengths in order to have them front and center as a reminder. A strengths snapshot allows you to reflect on your top strengths, which are most often the top listed 5 strengths from your strengths report. List the ones that truly feel authentic to you as your top strengths and write them down.

Next, write down your most common strengths combinations, which are the strengths you tend to combine for best effect. For example, I often combine my strengths of social intelligence and teamwork for greater expression of each of these strengths. Some of the common strengths combinations that people tend to use, although not an exhaustive list, can be seen below. Every individual is different, but you may see powerful strengths combinations below that you recognize using in your own life:

- Fairness & Leadership
- Gratitude & Hope
- Leadership & Teamwork
- Fairness & Teamwork
- Gratitude & Zest
- Judgment & Perspective
- Gratitude & Spirituality
- Leadership & Social Intelligence
- Honesty & Perseverance
- Creativity & Perspective
- Fairness & Forgiveness
- Curiosity & Zest
- Humility & Leadership
- Self-Regulation & Zest

- Honesty & Leadership
- Hope & Zest
- Humility & Fairness
- Love of learning & Perspective
- Humor & Social intelligence
- Kindness & Leadership
- Humor & Kindness
- Curiosity & Hope
- Humor & Zest
- Kindness & Teamwork
- Love & Honesty
- Prudence & Judgment
- Self-Regulation & Perseverance

And lastly, think of a strength(s) you would like to build going forward and write this in your strengths snapshot as well.

Positivity Journal

Take a few minutes to create your own strengths snapshot, considering these three important areas of self-reflection:

- Top Strengths
- Strengths Combinations
- Strengths to Build

Positivity Journal STRONG Questions

I encourage you to choose 2-3 of the following questions, and journal about them:

- Do your top strengths reflect the real you? Do others notice?
- What are some ways you can consistently bring your top strengths forward for greater energy and engagement in life?
- What strengths have you used optimally in past successes?
- What strengths can you call forth when visualizing a positive outcome to a challenge?
- What strengths combinations have worked well for you in the past that you want to utilize more intentionally and effectively in the future?
- How will the strengths you identified that you want to build in the previously mentioned "strengths to build" section of your "strengths snapshot" serve you best?
- Do you want to share your strengths snapshot with someone you trust to get constructive input? (Many people like to share their strengths snapshot with a confidant in order to get another's perspective and support with their growth plan.)
- How did it go sharing your strengths snapshot? What did you learn about yourself? How was your experience identifying ways to build a strength that you want to leverage more in your life?

Unwrapping Potential Within

"Our self-esteem, our self-worth, our sense of confidence, our well-being... stem directly from the way we think of ourselves in the world."[28]
—*Gregg Braden, The Science of Self-Empowerment*

One of the deepest human needs is to be understood and seen for our potential—our hopes and good intentions deep within. But what if that vision of our highest, best self has been obstructed by layers of non-constructive criticism, damaging life events and environments, or the wrong focus? It is more important than ever for people to shift the way they see themselves by using the empowering lens of their strengths of character. Our very well-being depends upon it. This is precisely why the groundbreaking science of positive psychology is so exciting, because it connects us in a tangible way with our strengths and virtues—the infinite potential within each of us.

I once watched a lecture by Mohammad Yunus, Nobel Prize winner and founder of the "micro lending" movement. He's CEO of Grameen Bank that gives low interest loans to the poor and has lifted over 500 million people out of poverty. Yunus said, *"All human beings are born entrepreneurs. Some get a chance to unleash that capacity. Some never got the chance, never knew that he or she has that capacity."*[29]

Yunus was willing to invest in the potential of the very poor people he encountered on the streets of Bangladesh. Interestingly, the repayment rate for these micro-loans made to these "poorest of the poor" is much higher than that of traditional lending. Could the empowering intention with which these loans are made—to help people find their potential and flourish—influence the perception and overall success of those receiving the loans?

In the midst of life's hardships we each possess an inner compass that can guide us and light the path to our potential. And when given the opportunity to discover our potential, we tend to rise beautifully to the occasion. So how do we connect to, and better understand this potential within ourselves?

Our Spiritual DNA

I was in awe when I heard a five-year old boy named Koby, wise beyond his years, describe in his own words how he understands character strengths. Koby simply said, "Character strengths are the keys to your heart that make your spirit rise and allow you to do things better." Our character strengths are in essence our potential—the highest expression of our humanness. They are that part of us where human virtue and goodness reside. We could consider our character strengths as our "spiritual DNA" because collectively our character strengths give meaning and purpose to our lives, enabling our spirits to soar.

Specifically, the strength of spirituality has been defined as the ability to see one's place in the scheme of the universe (or the outer world) and thus to find meaning and purpose in everyday life. [30] Spirituality has also been defined by scientists as *"the search for, or connection with 'the sacred.'"* They continue:

> *"The sacred might be that which is blessed, holy, revered or particularly special. This can be secular or non-secular: sacredness might be pursued as the search for a purpose in life or as a close relationship with something greater; the sacred might be experienced in the forgiveness offered by a child, an awe-inspiring sunset, a profound experience during meditation or a religious service, or the self-sacrificing kindness of a stranger. As a character strength, spirituality involves the belief that there is a dimension to life that is beyond human understanding."* [31]

I use the words "spiritual DNA" here not in a religious sense, although it can certainly be that for many people, but to describe the inner worth and potential that each of us carries within. This inherent worth and potential characterizes the resilient, unconquerable human spirit. Additionally, research findings on the benefits of the strength of spirituality found that spirituality had these benefits:

"[Spirituality] provides a sense of being grounded, increases optimism, and helps provide a sense of purpose for life. These in turn contribute to an overall sense of well-being. Youth who describe themselves as spiritual show better self-regulation and academic performance and tend to see the world as a more coherent place. Spirituality has also been linked to many character strengths, including humility, forgiveness, gratitude, kindness, hope, love and zest."[32]

Embracing Your Uniqueness

Traditionally, character has been thought of in moralistic terms as opposed to practical terms, resulting in a black or white judgment as to whether a person is "good" or "bad." This traditional approach can lead to narrow belief systems that prescribe a handful of character strengths for the way we all "should" be. Positive psychology recognizes that human goodness can be expressed in many ways and allows each person greater latitude to find his or her own way of living a "good life." Like facial characteristics, our character strengths come together in ways that define our uniqueness. So, while traditional approaches have led to efforts to make us all the same, the science of character strengths leads us to embrace our uniqueness, while respecting the uniqueness in others. Sizing up a person's character is no less complex a task than sizing up all of a person's physical attributes. A fair description of both ends up being a description of a variety of features. All 24 character strengths add value to our own lives, and to the lives of others.

CHAPTER TWO

EMBODIED RESILIENCE: CALM THE INNER CRITIC GIVE VOICE TO THE INNER COACH

"The greatest glory in living lies not in never falling,
but in rising every time we fall."[33]

—*Nelson Mandela*

Consider a high-performing musician who in her quest for perfectionism is painfully self-critical each time she makes a mistake. Is that internal, criticizing voice the key to her success? What if there was a better, more sustainable way to bring out the same, or an even higher level of excellence? What if the key to unleashing greatness is to calm the inner critic and to give voice to the inner coach?

I was deeply moved as I witnessed a coaching demonstration by Benjamin Zander at a Harvard Coaching Conference. Ben, conductor of the Boston Philharmonic, had brought an amazing string quartet to the event. Although the following experience was likely "staged" it still made an unforgettable impact on those of us watching. When a member of the string quartet made a mistake, Ben stopped the musicians in the middle of the piece they were playing. The errant violinist's expression was excruciating as she hit herself on the top of her head in frustration. Ben good-naturedly prompted her "I need you to stand and throw your arms up in the air and say, 'How fascinating!'" She tentatively did as she was asked. "Good," he said. "Now try it again." Eventually she was smiling broadly and once again relaxed enough to carry on with the performance.

Rather than making a mistake an occasion for fear and humiliation, Ben welcomed it with exuberance, neutralizing the shame. He was making an unforgettable point for those of us in attendance. I witnessed how a mistake could be viewed as a "fascinating" opportunity for learning, and I was filled with emotion. Removing negative thinking from a traditionally embarrassing experience was transformative for both the orchestra and those of us in the audience.

As I sat in my chair watching a mistake turn into a growth experience, I was transported to past occasions when I had been paralyzed by perfectionism, and my own self-criticism. But now, my heart felt lighter and more expansive, as I tuned into my own inner coach. My inner critic was calmed — and in that space, I could hear what I needed to hear: "Celebrate the victory of not putting yourself down. That is a big win." my inner coach told me. I invite you to learn how to make beautiful music in your own life as you discover your inner coach.

Reigning in Self-Talk

"Changing the destructive things you say to yourself when you experience the setbacks that life deals all of us is the central skill of optimism."[34]

—*Dr. Martin Seligman*

Let's do an exercise that shows how self-talk affects us. It's helpful to really pay attention to how your body feels as you read the following two distinct lists of words, rather than just passively reading the lists. This enables you to tune into your body and to observe what your body is trying to tell you. The list on the left characterizes the inner critic and the one on the right characterizes the inner coach.

The world's wisdom literature points to the body's innate knowing or wisdom if we would only stop long enough to listen. Also, observe the thoughts that pop into your head as you read each distinct list of words, and pay attention to the emotions you experience.

Now, mindfully read the inner critic list first, followed by the inner coach list below:

Coach vs. Critic Model

INNER CRITIC	VS	INNER COACH
Weakness-focus		Strengths-focus
Problem-oriented		Solution-oriented
Fixed mindset		Growth mindset
Blame/Judge		Learn
Disregard		Respect
Know it already		Curious
Afraid of change		Open to change
Either/or thinking		Creative thinking
Use "but"		Use "and"
Looks for offense		Looks for intent

Coach vs. Critic Model, © 2014-2020, Authentic Strengths Advantage, LLC.
(Inspired by the following: Columbia University Coaching Certification Program Learner/Judger Model; Marilee C. Goldberg's, The Art of the Question 1998 p. 161-178).

Positivity Journal STRONG Questions

- Did you notice any changes in how your body felt as you read each list?
- What did you observe about the thoughts you experienced as you read each list?
- What emotions did each list evoke for you?
- Which list had a more positive impact on you? Why?
- Take a moment to make a mark on each of the arrow continuums in the Coach vs. Critic model above, indicating where your mindset is currently. Notice if you are leaning more toward a coach or a critic mindset. I call this a "mindset check."
- Consider what you want to work on going forward. After you have marked the arrows, write down some strategies for moving to the inner coach side.
- What positive changes will you make to turn down the volume on your inner critic and to raise the volume on your inner coach?

Embodied Resilience

This simple exercise evokes many insights for people. Without fail, people report discernable physical, mental and emotional manifestations depending on the words they are reading. It is not surprising that positive psychology research is showing similar mind-body correlations to self-talk, thought patterns, and the resulting emotional states. You may have heard the saying, "the issues live in our tissues"[35] inferring that our bodies store information. I've had workshop participants tell me after doing this exercise that they felt old back or knee pain resurface while reading the critic list of words, and during their reading of the coach list that pain melted away. Perhaps you can relate to this because you've felt similar tensions in your body when exposed to very negative news, messages or imagery, for example. The opposite may be true for you as well.

For instance, you may have felt your body relax or feel energized after experiencing an uplifting movie or song.

I've also had people report that they noticed their shoulders droop, their heads lower, their hearts harden, their posture slump, and report a general sense of "heaviness" while reading the critic list. Interestingly, while reading the coach list people have reported feeling lighter, able to breathe better, lighter and open hearts, better posture, and an overall sense of empowerment and well-being. I call this "embodied resilience."

So, what is embodied resilience? It's developing your awareness of what is happening in your body related to your life experiences and your resulting reactions to them, in order to improve your resilience and overall well-being. As Megan McDonough, CEO of the Whole Being Institute states: *"Embodied positive psychology engages the body in the kinesthetic experience of living the science of flourishing. ... As the definition explains, embodiment gives visible form to an idea."*

McDonough goes on to explain:

"Cognitive understanding and knowing is not the same as realizing, living, and experiencing. Embodiment physicalizes an idea, making it concrete in the here and now. As the definition explains, embodiment gives visible form to an idea. By embodying Positive Psychology, you become a walking expression of the idea. Embodied Positive Psychology is the experience of:

- *Cultivating mindfulness through the body, by focusing on the breath and anchoring our attention in the present*
- *Engaging the body as part of the learning process—physically moving in order to understand an intellectual concept*
- *Exploring and inquiring as much about our inner world as our outer world*

- *Sharing, connecting, and networking, because the "we" helps provide context for the "me"*
- *Leveraging the body's capacity to change the mind (instead of enforcing the mind's will upon the body)."*[36]

Embodied Resilience: Inner Coach vs. Inner Critic

The brief mindset check activity you did earlier is significant because each of us engages in self-talk every day. When our self-talk is negative, such as what Daniel Amen, MD calls "automatic negative thoughts" or "ANTS"[37] for short, it can take a toll on our resilience and well-being. So, it's very helpful to learn to turn down the volume on our inner critic, who focuses on the negative, and to turn up the volume on our inner coach who elicits our wholeness. Let's explore the two mindsets further...

The self-criticism of the inner critic is a double-edged sword because, when we engage in this type of self-talk, as Dr Kristin Neff has said, "we are both the attacker and the attacked." For example, musicians are notorious for being self-critical. And, according to a survey reported in The Music Quarterly, musicians in 78 worldwide orchestras rated their job satisfaction lower than that of prison guards! Self-inflicted criticism, it seems, sucked out the joy from their career for many of the musicians who were studied. So, why do you think people are often self-critical?

Many people believe that self-criticism is necessary to motivate themselves. In fact, research is showing it's not a great motivator at all. Dr. Neff states, "Self-critics are much more likely to be anxious and depressed — not exactly get-up-and-go mindsets. They also have lower self-efficacy beliefs (i.e., less self-confidence in their abilities), which undermines their potential for success."[38]

The habit of self-criticism engenders fear of failure, meaning that self-critics often don't even try achieving their goals because the possibility of failure is unacceptable. Even more problematic, self-critics have a hard time seeing themselves clearly and identifying needed areas of improvement because they know the self-punishment that will ensue if they admit the truth."[39]

Thoughts that bring about despair or discouragement can become obnoxiously loud, drowning out our inner coach and preventing our character strengths from expressing themselves. Negative thoughts are lies that sabotage, drain and upset.[40] If you suffer from this, it's a signal that your inner critic is directing the action.

Aaron Beck, the father of cognitive therapy, began helping his patients identify and evaluate negative thoughts. He found that by doing so, patients were able to think more realistically. This in turn led them to feel better emotionally and behave more functionally. He discovered that distorted thinking has a negative effect on our emotional state and behavior.[41]

Our inner critic thrives on distorted and inaccurate thinking such as catastrophizing "My dreams are doomed to failure," all-or-nothing thinking, "she never supports me," or discounting positive experiences "he only helped me because he wanted the credit." Beck helped people become aware of and observe their distorted thinking, teaching them how to challenge its effects, in essence awakening the inner coach.

Back to the two columns of words—the columns represent the self-talk we are tuning into at any given time. We will periodically stop throughout this book and do what I call a "mindset check" to determine which voice you are focusing on currently—the inner critic or the inner coach. This mindset check is a powerful part of the learning process in becoming a coach to yourself and eventually sharing what you learn with others. The goal is to turn down the volume on the debilitating voice of the inner critic, and to develop the habit of listening more consistently to the constructive, empowering, positive, resilient, growth-inducing messages that come from your inner coach.[42] Even when we've made a mistake, we can correct ourselves and better motivate change with constructive self-talk, spoken as an inner coach rather than as an inner critic.

Fortunately, the inner coach is the opposite of the inner critic. Learning to tune into the language of our heart, the source of our inner coach, reconnects us with our highest and best self. As we develop the skill of listening to our inner coach, we may discover a sincere desire to make positive changes. This is a life-altering shift for many people as they break free of despair and discouragement that has paralyzed them in the past.

The Wisdom of the Heart

"Within each of us there exists an organizing and central intelligence that can lift us beyond our problems into a new experience of fulfillment even in the midst of chaos. It's a high-speed, intuitive source of wisdom and clear perception, an intelligence that embraces and fosters both mental and emotional intelligence. We call it "heart intelligence."[43]

—*Doc Childre and Howard Martin, HeartMath Institute*

Your inner coach offers encouragement —which comes from the Latin word *cor* meaning "heart" — or — "to hearten and inspire." Consider that for a moment. It is a fundamental shift to recognize that perhaps the most important job you can take on is encouraging yourself and those around you.

Think of your inner coach as the wisdom of your heart—the encouraging self-talk that you can tune into. The world's revered teachings use the heart as a metaphor for the seat of compassion, connection, human spirit and empathy—a place of inner-knowing that can guide us through life's challenges. Your heart, when coherent and tranquil, is like your inner coach—intelligent, calm, and seeing more clearly than the inner critic that can plague your mind with endless discordant and non-productive thoughts.

The key to invoking your inner coach and silencing your inner critic is to first take the time to quiet the mind. As you fully embrace the present moment as the "observer" of your inner world, you can connect to the wisdom that resides in your heart. It is from this place of stillness that one hears what many refer to as the profound "whisperings of the heart."

Although the benefits and effects have been reported for many years, science continues to take a serious look at how this quieting of the mind and calming of the heart through mindfulness, and other practices benefits us. Centering practices such as mindfulness, yoga, deep breathing, mantras, loving kindness meditation, prayer, or other contemplative practices affect not only our psychology, but also our physiology. These calming practices have been demonstrated to affect the body's biochemistry, metabolism, heart rate, blood pressure and brain chemistry. [44] [45] [46]

As Megan McDonough, CEO and Co-Founder of the Wholebeing Institute shared during a conversation with me: *"The brain, body, and breath are inextricably linked. We are physiologically constructed in a way that a change in one affects a change in another. So, when you slow and deepen your breathing, especially elongating the exhale, the body relaxes. When your body relaxes, your brain releases different chemicals. Your nervous system moves from the fight or flight response to rest and digest. We are not prisoners of habits of body, breath, or brain. We can break the cycle in any of the three points."* [47] [48]

When we learn to synchronize our hearts and our brains in a coherent way that empowers our potential, we can create our best life. Living in such alignment can enable us to rise above the distraction and chaos of life's challenges, and to remain centered in our authenticity to find the best solutions to our challenges. This is a significant part of building resiliency.

An excellent example of such alignment is found in the book, *American Scandal* by Pat Williams, which describes Mahatma Gandhi's famous speech before England's Parliament. The British government had vehemently and violently opposed Gandhi's efforts for Indian independence, having jailed Gandhi multiple times. However, Gandhi spoke eloquently before Parliament for nearly two hours, and at the end of his talk he received a standing ovation from the very statesmen who had sought to destroy his revolutionary ideas!

Afterward, a reporter asked Mahadev Desai, Gandhi's assistant, how Gandhi had been able to deliver such a passionate and compelling speech without any notes. "You don't understand Gandhi," Desai responded. "You see, what he thinks is what he feels. What he feels is what he says. What he says is what he does...He does not need notes."[49]

Gandhi was being guided by an inner wisdom and intelligence that enabled his brilliance. His strengths of character illuminated a path out of the violence for all in attendance. Gandhi's example of being centered and fully aligned in his purpose inspires us to develop this alignment of heart and mind, and to live an authentic life empowered by our character strengths.

The Heart–Brain Connection

The HeartMath Institute[50] is a pioneering organization, whose research has revealed that the heart and brain communicate with one-another and share intelligence. Their tools and techniques are based on over thirty years of scientific research on the psychophysiology of stress, emotions, and the interactions between the heart and brain. There are hundreds of studies utilizing their techniques or technologies to achieve beneficial outcomes, and the findings offer an innovative approach to improving well-being. [51]

Most of us have been taught in school that the heart is constantly responding to "orders" sent by the brain in the form of neural signals. However, it is not as commonly known that the heart may actually send more signals to the brain than the brain sends to the heart! Moreover, these heart signals can have a significant effect on brain function — influencing emotional processing as well as higher cognitive faculties such as attention, perception, memory, and problem-solving. In other words, not only does the heart respond to the brain, but the brain also responds to the heart.[52]

The HeartMath Institute has demonstrated that different patterns of heart activity (which accompany different emotional states) have effects on cognitive and emotional function. During stress and negative emotions, when the heart rhythm pattern is erratic and disordered, our ability to think clearly, remember, learn, reason, and make effective decisions is limited (this helps explain why we may often act impulsively and unwisely when we're under stress). The heart's input to the brain during stressful or negative emotions can have a profound effect on the brain's emotional processes—reinforcing the emotional experience of stress.

In contrast, the more ordered and stable pattern of the heart's input to the brain during positive emotional states has the opposite effect—it facilitates higher cognitive function and reinforces positive feelings and emotional stability. This means that learning to generate heart-brain coherence, by sustaining positive emotions, not only benefits the entire body, but also affects how we perceive, think, feel, and perform. Similar connections of positive emotions enabling better performance and beneficial mental states have been shown repeatedly in positive psychology research, most notably by Dr. Barbara Fredrickson.[53][54]

According to the HeartMath Institute, when we experience uplifting emotions such as appreciation, joy, care, and love (think character strengths here), our heart rhythm pattern becomes highly ordered. This is called a coherent heart rhythm pattern. When we are generating a coherent heart rhythm, the body's systems operate with increased efficiency and harmony. It's no wonder that positive emotions feel so good — they actually help our body's systems synchronize and work better.

The science is still developing, and the complex interaction of the mind and the body continues to be unraveled. Traditional techniques of stillness and deep breathing have been shown to have demonstrable benefits.

Below is a technique from the HeartMath Institute that I've used to benefit myself and my coaching clients in de-stressing and building resilience. Find a comfortable place to practice this technique where you will not be interrupted. This technique is a great way to calm the inner critic and to give voice to the inner coach.

Quick Coherence® Technique

1. Focus your attention in the area of the heart. Imagine your breath is flowing in and out of your heart or chest area, breathing a little slower and deeper than usual. Find an easy rhythm that's comfortable.
2. As you continue heart-focused breathing, make a sincere attempt to experience a positive, regenerative feeling such as appreciation or care for someone or something in your life.

In summary, these are the "Quick Steps":
1. Heart-Focused Breathing
2. Activate a positive or renewing feeling

Regularly taking time to shift into a state of heart coherence has been shown to increase resilience in those who practice this technique. I use it when I'm stressed or feeling overwhelmed, and the calming, centering results are fast, beneficial, and lasting for me.

According to the HeartMath Institute, "It's our theory that heart intelligence actually transfers intelligence to the emotions and instills the power of emotional management. From our research at the HeartMath Institute, we've concluded that intelligence and intuition are heightened when we learn to listen more deeply to our own heart."[55]

Discovering your potential and awakening your resilience is a matter of getting in touch with and giving voice to your inner coach, that authentic part of yourself. Tapping into the wisdom of your heart can amplify your inner coach and be a powerful guide for leading you to your personal best.

Resilience Gets Real

Sometimes life unexpectedly sends us experiences that demand we build our resilience like never before. An example of someone who was thrust into a situation that challenged his very sense of self is Mike. It had been a month since Mike had been fired from his job—he was still reeling from the blow of having the ground pulled out from under him, when he came to me for coaching. A husband, father, and self-proclaimed over-achiever, Mike was stuck in ruminating self-doubt and his inner critic was in high gear. During our coaching sessions, Mike peeled back the layers of what he described as a "devastating and highly unanticipated job loss." Mike's keen intelligence and sincere desire to learn and grow from the painful experience propelled him to pour his energy into the tools throughout this book as he worked to rebuild his resilience. In Mike's own words:

> *"The shame I felt after having been 'let go' was overwhelming. Even though I hadn't violated any rules and had given my best efforts, to my dismay, my boss unexpectedly announced that I wasn't a 'good fit' and terminated my employment—without severance pay. I was*

experiencing the emotional equivalent of a flat tire—utterly de-flated. Even the best military vehicles cannot run forever on a flat tire and I felt incapacitated. Thirty days after being fired, I knew I needed to seek out new tools to pump up my 'flat tire.' What I was doing simply wasn't working and I was sinking into further despair. A friend suggested I try strengths coaching. In the sessions that followed I quickly came to realize that I could leverage my strengths to reframe what had been an excruciating experience into a hard-won growth opportunity.

I chose to focus on my top three strengths to rebuild my career. First and foremost, I've used my strength of 'kindness' toward myself (self-compassion) to regularly engage in self-care rituals like turning down the volume on my inner critic, amplifying my inner coach, exercising regularly, eating healthy food, and reading empowering books to restore my sorely depleted confidence. I've enjoyed doing acts of kindness for my wife and daughter as well, lifting the mood in our home.

Second, I've called forth my 'leadership' strength to create a deliberate action plan to guide my research and application for new jobs. This has been a tremendous boost in lifting me out of the dejection I was feeling, giving me hope, purpose, and clarity so that I could positively move forward into the next chapter in my life.

Third, I've re-awakened my top strength of 'social intelligence' to rekindle relationships with my support network—people whom I've supported in the past and are more than happy to return the favor. This strength has always attracted good people and good situations into my life, and I am working to recreate more of those past high points going forward.

I've learned how absolutely critical it is to be authentic—releasing me from the burden of trying to be all things to others—knowing confidently that I am now always calling upon my best self. And I no longer obsess over what others think. Even when new challenges come as they inevitably will, I now recognize that adversity is part of being human—I'm not being singled out—and through it all I can learn, grow, and remain grounded in my strengths!

Focusing on my strengths has produced an 'undoing effect' on the negative emotions I felt—genuinely creating a positive new perspective. For example, when I would start to feel the heavy sadness in my heart and the deep shame in my gut from having been fired, I became very deliberate in my thoughts and self-talk. I listed all of the objective reasons I am a capable, hardworking employee, and a benefit to any employer. I intentionally called upon my self-kindness, self-leadership and social intelligence, among other strengths, to move me past those moments. I've made the shift from 'what's wrong to what's strong.' When I look in the mirror as well as deep into my heart, I now recognize the affirming voice of my inner coach!"

When you become the observer of your thoughts you may begin to recognize debilitating negative thoughts trying to sabotage your connection to your inner coach. This is the moment to practice going deeper into your heart's calming wisdom by connecting to your authenticity—your strengths of character such as gratitude, hope, self-kindness, courage, perseverance, etc. Counter critical thoughts by thinking of all the objective reasons you should reject them, and by reminding yourself of your strengths best suited to the challenge you face.

As I coached Mike to reframe his situation in a way that better serves him, I asked him to consider what he would do differently the next time he faces a challenge—how would he re-write the story. He explained:

"I now recognize that perfectionism (my inner critic) has not served me. Highly driven people like me can be overly focused on achievement and I've discovered it can be an 'Achilles' heel' for me. In the past, I had been hyper vigilant around my own errors, as well as the errors of others. Moving forward, I am learning to use my strength of 'prudence' balanced with my strengths of 'kindness' (toward myself and others) and 'social intelligence' to soften my perfectionist tendencies.

Also, after I was let go, I reacted too quickly with fear, anger and distress—I couldn't find my footing and desperately needed an anchor. Through coaching with Fatima, I realized that I was being hijacked by my own emotions.

I've learned that quieting my mind by seeking stillness allows me to tap into my inner coach, which helps me move forward in a positive direction. So now, when I have a tough moment, I breathe deeply and just sit with the feeling, working through it first, without immediately reacting like in the past. It is in this stillness that I can better understand situations objectively. The tools in this book helped me learn to do this. For example, using the STRONG Filter and STRONG Thoughts Tools to shine a light on counterfeit, debilitating, negative thoughts and emotions, and using the Connect-Care-Create Tool to center myself. I have extinguished the shame that wasn't serving anyone—myself, my family, my future employer, etc. I now see that my toxic emotions were not rooted in objective reality, and it feels liberating to remove shame from my self-concept."

In light of the fact that people are engaging in multiple careers throughout their lifetimes, it's inevitable that most people will experience some sort of "failure" at work, whether it's being passed up for a promotion, mishandling a project, being demoted, job loss, etc. People must learn these resilience tools, Mike told me, so that they can *"learn how to rise out of the ashes and become even stronger and more employable than ever before."* Mike has now started his own business and is actively engaged in creating a new and better future. You will learn more about the tools that Mike used later in this book.

True Liberation

When we listen to our inner critic who devalues our beliefs, attacks our self-worth, and blocks our initiative, we give away our stabilizing, self-motivating, inner power. To clear a path through life's most difficult experiences, we must turn down the noise of the inner critic that rings so loudly in our ears. When we practice mindfulness, and make the important journey from our head to our heart—connecting the two—we can begin to hear the still small voice of our heart—our inner coach.

An example of this is Jewish psychiatrist and Holocaust survivor Viktor Frankl, who under the most difficult circumstances imaginable, used the ability only humans possess—to choose his own thoughts to create a meaningful personal vision in the midst of hellish chaos. He liberated himself to live fully—long before allied forces marched in.

While in four Nazi death camps, including Auschwitz, Viktor chose to base his behavior and values on his own self-awareness rather than to react to how he was defined by his captors. He saw himself lecturing to his future students about the insights he was learning daily, using his innate power to exercise his character strengths, inspiring others to do so as well.

In his own words: "We who lived in the concentration camps can remember the men who walked through the huts comforting others, giving away their last piece of bread. They may have been few in number, but they offer sufficient proof that everything can be taken from a man but one thing: the last of the human freedoms—to choose one's attitude in any given set of circumstances, to choose one's own way."[56] He and others were in effect calling forth their inner coach—their highest and best selves, even in the most extreme conditions.

Fortunately, we can retrain our focus to our inner coach, and to notice our character strengths so we can appreciate the best in ourselves, in others, and in each moment. When we choose to listen to our inner coach, who expresses our personal vision and values, we inspire both ourselves and others to be more resourceful, creative, whole, and in the process build our resilience.

Transforming Problems into Solutions

Too many people relinquish their resilient inner power because they form an identity out of their problems. They go through life obsessively focused on having been victimized or treated unfairly. But who among us needs more problems? Why would we want to spend more time identifying with problems? The most important thing we can do is to cultivate and invest energy into solutions that create what we want, not draining our energy on problems.

Life's toughest problems are not solved by having all the answers, but rather by asking the right questions. People who ask solution-focused questions that are rooted in strengths gain clarity, purpose and insight to solve their problems. Solution-focused questions and self-reflection are part of the vital process of learning and growth.

Research reveals the impact of solution-focused vs problem-focused coaching questions. Although both types of questions enhance goal attainment, solution-focused questions generate better results in helping us achieve our goals. Why? Because people are more energized and motivated by the positivity of solution-focused questions. Rumination (obsessively repeating negative thoughts) decreases when we ask ourselves solution-focused questions, while insight increases. Better self-regulation, better mental health, better quality of life and increased life satisfaction result.[57] Solution-focused coaching has also been shown to enhance goal striving, well-being and hope, and the gains people made toward their goals were maintained for extensive periods of time.[58] So why not be our own best coach and use solution-focused questions with ourselves?

Here are some examples of problem-focused questions:
- How long has this been a problem? How did it start?
- What do I think about this problem?
- What impact is thinking about this problem having on me?

Now pay attention to the difference in these solution-focused questions:
- Imagine the solution—what does the solution look like?
- What are some ways I could use my strengths in creating the solution?
- What impact is thinking about the solution having on me?

Positivity Journal STRONG Questions
- What did you notice about the two different types of questions?
- Which would you prefer to ask yourself, or have others ask you? Why?

Solution-focused questions are one of the most powerful tools in strengths coaching. For maximum benefit, I suggest you make a habit of asking yourself questions that combine a solution focus with the use of your strengths. You probably noticed that the STRONG Questions you have answered thus far also orient you toward solutions. As I mentioned earlier, I use the descriptor "STRONG" because these types of questions are rooted in positive psychology research and are designed to build resilience—mental and emotional strength.

The right question can unlock a wealth of understanding and unleash a world of potential. Simply ask yourself open-ended, solution-oriented questions about how, what, when, and where your strengths can be used. Then, listen! Slowing down and quieting your mind enough to listen to the promptings of your heart—your inner coach—will guide you in discovering your own inner wisdom. Your inner coach is your true nature, fully in the present moment.

Encourage yourself to not just state or think about hopeful solutions, but also to *feel* the effects of the solutions—as if the situation is already resolved. Take time to linger in the positive emotions that this evokes for you. This act of faith is central to creating what your heart visions for you. See yourself using your strengths, thereby empowering any solutions with added motivation.

Illuminating Your Strengths

"Nothing can dim the light which shines from within."[59]

—*Maya Angelou*

So, now that you have identified the difference between the inner critic and the inner coach, let's explore ways in which you can shine a light on your strengths and become your own best coach.

Think of one of your favorite teachers, mentors or inspiring coaches that you have known. What did this person do that brought out the best in you? How did you feel when you were in this person's presence? What did you learn from this coach?

When I ask people in my workshops to answer the previous questions, they usually describe feeling "seen" for their strengths by their favorite coach—seen for their "best self." They recall how this coach or mentor treated them with respect and appreciation for their innate worth. People remember the important life lessons they learned from this coach who had their best interest at heart. The old adage rings true when we consider those who we choose to give our best efforts to, "I don't care how much you know, until I know how much you care."

We are seeing a common theme here, aren't we? These people who positively impact us tend to notice and nurture our strengths. They focus on what's strong in us, rather than on what's wrong. These coaches believe in us and bring out our finest moments. Much like a jeweler spots diamonds in the rough, a great coach, mentor, parent, grandparent, teacher, friend sees the potential within. It's as if these inspirational mentors shine a light on us that illuminates the best in our very hearts and souls!

Sometimes we are the ones who don't see the greatness deep within ourselves, therefore it's important to develop that awareness, and the ability to bring those strengths to the surface.

An example of bringing out greatness is the famous sculptor Michelangelo. In *9 Things You May Not Know About Michelangelo* by Evan Andrews, we learn the famous artist "was notoriously picky about the marble he used for his sculptures, yet, for his famous 'David' statue, he made use of a block that other artists had deemed unworkable. Known as 'The Giant,' the massive slab...was eventually abandoned... It had deteriorated and grown rough after years of exposure to the elements, and by the time Michelangelo began working with it in 1501, it already bore the chisel marks of more than one frustrated sculptor." But Michelangelo saw potential greatness within that slab of marble. Trusting his intuition and perseverance, he eventually crafted the discarded block into "one of his most luminous works."[60]

We are like that imperfect slab of marble. We may bear the marks of disappointments and failures, and yet within each of us, there is greatness waiting to be revealed. This attests to the power of seeing what's strong in ourselves and choosing to focus there, rather than on our flaws. This is authentic resilience.

As you learn to become your own strengths coach, you will shift your focus to your growth and untapped potential, rather than on your limits. Imagine for a moment how your life would change if you made a habit of focusing on your character strengths, such as your courage, perspective, kindness, gratitude, leadership, perseverance, teamwork, etc. You can learn to amplify, reflect and facilitate your strengths, encouraging yourself with strategies and solutions for moving forward in life, and positively impacting others by your example. Who doesn't want to show up each day contributing to solutions rather than being mired in problems?

Positivity Journal

- Recall once again your favorite teacher or coach and reflect deeply on what they did that brought out the best in you. Write it down in your journal with as much detail as possible.

Positivity Journal STRONG Questions

- How did you feel when you were in the presence of your favorite coach/teacher/mentor?
- What did you learn from them?

- How can you see yourself in this way, and bring out your own inner coach more consistently?
- How can you make a habit of likewise seeing and appreciating the strengths in others?

Share the Positivity!

Studies show that the best way to anchor what you are learning is to teach it to someone else within a day or so, while it is still fresh in your mind. If you want to internalize your insights thus far, find someone you trust, a friend, family member, or colleague and share your learnings with him or her.

CHAPTER THREE

MAKING MEANING OF HAPPINESS: WHAT WIRES TOGETHER FIRES TOGETHER

"It isn't what you have or who you are or where you are or what you are doing that makes you happy or unhappy. It is what you think about it."[61]

— Dale Carnegie

Every day of his life, Bill Shannon needs crutches to get around, due to a childhood hip deformity from Legg Calve Perthes disease. In Bill's own words from his video *Crutch*:

"Just imagine everywhere you go people say "sorry" "I'm so sorry" "oh sorry." After a while that can really affect you!"[62]

But Bill has learned to redefine his life experience. He skateboards and even break dances on crutches, posting his amazing creative expression on YouTube videos and TV news appearances that inspire countless people. Bill explains:

"Skateboarding and breakdancing...if you look closely...neither have defined techniques, it's all about individual style. So, you're building your own pathway. You're skating down the street ...you're relating to your

environment as it comes to you on an improvisational, freestyle basis. You are taking in what's thrown at you in the best way that you can, and you evolve your skills in that manner."[63]

Bill is an example of creatively defying odds, labels and assumptions. No one and nothing can take away the wholeness that he has discovered within. He has learned to intentionally evoke positive emotions in ways that are interesting, engaging and fulfilling for him—approaching life on his own terms. Bill's outlook inspires us to become active and resourceful participants in our own lives—developing greater capacity for really seeing and experiencing the good that is all around us. Bill makes his own, very personal meaning of the elusive and loaded word "happiness" in a way that baffles conventional understanding of happiness.

Making Meaning of Happiness

"Happiness is not the absence of problems, it's the ability to deal with them."[64]

— *Steve Maraboli*

The word "happiness" can be subjective and can take on many meanings for different individuals. Christine Carter, Ph.D. describes the scientific study of happiness in the video, *Happiness,* Gratitude Revealed by MovingArt, as follows:

> *"I use the word 'happiness' as a handle. The first thing—it's positive emotions. We may be talking about happiness, but really, we are talking about the physiological experience of an emotion that feels like happiness. We live in these cultures and these social structures—families, business, schools—that inhibit certain emotions and evoke others. We've spent an awful lot of time as a society looking at dysfunction and disorders. I've instead looked at the positive things—positive emotions—grit and resiliency—really with an eye toward*

what's in this that we can control? How is happiness a set of skills that we can practice?

I'm really hopeful that as we look at the scientific study of happiness what we will actually be leaning toward is the understanding that a happy life is full of a lot of different types of positive emotions— love and compassion and awe and astonishment and engagement and inspiration."[65]

It's interesting to note that the positive emotions described by Dr. Carter, and the positive emotions that Bill Shannon experiences while skateboarding and breakdancing, are all associated with strengths of character. We can learn from their examples that understanding how to use our character strengths more consistently not only builds our resilience, but also increases our positive emotions and ultimately our happiness.

As you consider Bill Shannon's and Dr. Carter's insights, let's revisit our inner coach, inner critic mindset. It's heartening to know that research shows our mindset is not fixed, but rather that our mindset can change and evolve, depending on where we choose to focus our time and attention. This is often referred to as neuroplasticity, which means that we can literally reshape and retrain our brains. You will learn more about neuroplasticity later in this chapter.

For this reason, the marks that you make on each of the arrows in the "Mindset Check" sections throughout this book need not remain where they are. When you choose to listen to your inner coach who invokes your best self, you are both inspired, and inspire others, to be more resourceful, creative and whole.

This is how to authentically move the mark further toward the right side—toward the inner coach spectrum. Developing an inner coach mindset is essential to boosting your resilience.

Take a moment to assess where you are today on the Mindset Check below, and to consider where you want to be over time:

INNER CRITIC	VS	INNER COACH
Focus on what's wrong		Focus on what's strong
Avoid/break commitment		Commit/follow through
Asking for help = weakness		Look for support
Avoid/control feelings		Understands feelings
Take everything on		Small consistent gains
Comparison mindset		Values mindset
Situation-driven		Choices-driven
Don't deserve celebrations		Celebrate growth

Coach vs. Critic Model, ©2014-2020, Authentic Strengths Advantage, LLC.
(Inspired by the following: Columbia University Coaching Certification Program Learner/Judger Model; Marilee C. Goldberg's, The Art of the Question 1998 p. 161-178).

Sketch Your Highs and Lows

Now, that you've revisited your mindset, let's do a new activity that will help you identify where you express or suppress your strengths. You are going to sketch your highs and lows for the past week or month. You can use crayons, markers, a pen or pencil. Sketching your highs and lows over the past week or month offers:

- A visual representation marking highs (using strengths) and lows (not using strengths) in recent situations.
- A creative illustration that helps you access your inner-knowing— your heart or conscience—not just your brain which often rational- izes behavior.

- An opportunity to revisit and reframe experiences in more productive ways, learning from the changes you want to make going forward.[66]

Below is an example of a person's highs and lows for the past week. In looking at this sketch they can identify strengths that are serving them well and also identify areas where they could use their strengths more consistently for better results. Your sketch doesn't have to look like this one. You can create yours with colored markers, drawn images, magazine clippings, etc.—as long as it is meaningful to you and helps you to see where you are thriving and where you are withering.

SKETCH YOUR HIGH & LOWS

- Past Week or Month
- Highs: Using Character Strengths
- Lows: Not Using Character Strengths

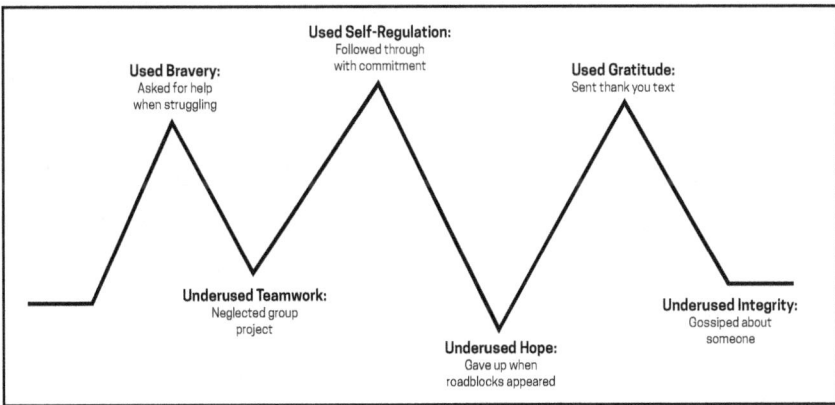

Life Sketch: Strengths Expression vs. Strengths Suppression, © 2014-2020 Authentic Strengths Advantage, LLC. (Inspired by the following: Columbia University Coaching Certification Program Life Map; Zeus and Skiffington (2003) The Coaching at Work Toolkit; Tichy (2002) The Cycle of Leadership: How Great Leaders Teach Their Companies to Win.

Highs

- Used *bravery* by asking for help when struggling
- Used *self-regulation* by following through with a commitment
- Used *gratitude* by sending a thank you text

Lows

- Underused *teamwork* by neglecting a group project
- Underused *hope* by giving up when roadblocks appeared
- Underused *integrity* by gossiping

Post-Traumatic Growth and the Slingshot Effect

"There have been many people for whom limitation, failure, loss, illness or pain in whatever form, turned out to be their greatest teacher. It taught them to let go of false self-images... It gave them depth, humility and compassion. It made them more real."[67]

—*Eckhart Tolle*

Although the valleys in the image above depict times of withering, occasionally a valley can represent a life challenge that has ignited significant strengths expression and growth as a response to the difficulty. In these instances, strengths we have not used much in the past are catapulted forward by life's hardships—when we are stretched to our limits. These post-traumatic growth experiences can be defining moments in our lives. I call this the "slingshot effect."

One of the most exciting areas of trauma research is in post-traumatic growth. The term was coined in the mid-1990s by psychologists Richard Tedeschi and Lawrence Calhoun at the University of North Carolina at Charlotte. According to Dr. Tedeschi, as many as 90 percent of survivors report at least one aspect of post-traumatic growth, such as a renewed appreciation for life. Whenever a group of people are traumatized, about 10 percent will develop post-traumatic stress disorder (PTSD), while 80 percent will return to their normal baseline within a few months. Another 10 percent will actually be stronger than they were before the trauma happened—those who experience post-traumatic growth.[68]

If you have been through a traumatic event, why not use all the tools at your disposal to increase your ability to not just recover, but to also grow and thrive after the experience?

Research suggests that post-traumatic growth is based on five factors that can help mitigate symptoms of distress, commonly known by the acronym "SPARK" and with the five listed factors below:[69]

1. A deepening of **S**piritual life, significant change in one's belief system, a new or stronger sense of meaning and purpose.
2. Seeing new **P**ossibilities because of the trauma or grief. New opportunities have emerged from the situation, opening up possibilities that were not present before.
3. Increased **A**ppreciation of life in general; better at appreciating each moment.
4. A change in **R**elationships or relating to others in more meaningful ways than before the trauma occurred. There is an increased sense of connection. People appreciate family and friends more.
5. Increased sense of **K**ick-ass personal strength. This is seen in expressions such as, "if I survived that, I can make it through anything!"

An example of post-traumatic growth is my dear friend Allyson Lyle, during her terminal battle with cancer. In her darkest hours, Allyson found her strengths propelled to new heights—a soaring assertion of her invincible spirit. In Allyson's own inspiring words:

"We seem shocked when life gets hard or unfair, and we beg a higher power to remove obstacles. We forget that opposition may be exactly what we need to progress. We think if we're not saved from our trials, we're not loved or we're not worthy. Actually, we just have different perspectives...and God's perspective has a wiser plan for us...I marvel at God's ability to create beauty out of hard things."

In a tender conversation with Allyson, she shared with me that the deep "valley" experience of fighting cancer called forth to new peaks some of her strengths—courage, perseverance, gratitude, spirituality, love—which served to fortify her through the biggest challenge of her life. Allyson tapped into these aspects of her highest self, in new ways that provided great comfort and resilience for her and her family. It is interesting to note that the strengths Allyson intuitively amplified are among those which have been shown to correlate to post-traumatic growth.

Those character strengths have been a source of immense fulfillment for Allyson—in turn profoundly inspiring many people with her unforgettable positive example that will live on for generations. Like a slingshot, we sometimes find ourselves "pulled back" and withering intensely, due to an extreme challenge. Then, we may reignite untapped strengths that propel our growth further beyond our expectations, often surprising ourselves and others.

Positivity Journal STRONG Questions

- Have you ever experienced the slingshot effect in your life by being propelled to new heights after a difficult valley experience (i.e. relationship challenges, divorce, financial stress, health issues, etc.)?
- Take a moment to recall it and describe the elements of your experience—what was it like? (If you feel safe, share your experience with

someone you trust, and how you were able to turn it into a positive learning experience.)

- What did you learn and how did you grow?

The Depression/Anxiety Epidemic

This chapter on cultivating more happiness in our lives would be incomplete without also discussing what happiness is not—stress, depression, and anxiety. The World Health Organization (WHO), estimates that stress related disorders, such as depression and anxiety, affect over 300 million people of all ages. It is the leading cause of disability worldwide.[70]

Both absenteeism—feeling too low to show up for school, work, or life in general—and presenteeism—being physically present but too energy-depleted to engage or accomplish much, take a toll on society.[71] Widely reported as a health epidemic for more than twenty-five years, stress, depression and anxiety have continued to increase. Depression and anxiety top the list of reasons students seek help from health services at their universities.[72]

Depression is different from usual mood fluctuations and short-lived emotional responses to challenges in everyday life. One of my colleagues, a marriage and family therapist, commonly sees children who complain of stomach aches. She explains that children don't have the vocabulary to call it anxiety or depression, but they know that their body hurts. Especially when long-lasting or with moderate or severe intensity, depression can become a serious health condition. Lack of support for people with mental health issues, coupled with a fear of stigma, prevent many from accessing the treatment they need to live healthy, happy, productive lives. This can cause the affected person to suffer greatly. At its worst, depression can lead to suicide. [73]

The statistics regarding suicide are the hardest to talk about. WHO estimates that each year approximately one million people die from suicide, which represents a global mortality rate of one death every 40 seconds. It is predicted that the rate of death will increase to one every 20 seconds. Suicide statistics among youth are the most alarming—it is now the leading cause of death among youth in many places around the world.[74]

It's more important than ever for us to create environments that support those who experience depression, anxiety, and/or suicidal ideation. Too many people suffer in silence—afraid of what others may think of them. Speaker, author and comedian Kevin Breel who personally deals with depression, shares these insights, *"We live in a world where if you break your arm, everyone runs over to sign your cast, but if you tell people you're depressed, everyone runs the other way. That's the stigma. We are so accepting of any body part breaking down other than our brains."*[75]

Research shows that the development of character strengths corresponds to increased resilience. [76] [77] Our resilience can help us weather life's storms, which can include the storms of mental health struggles.[78] You are not alone, there are medical professionals who can help you. To quote Kevin Breel once more, *"If you're going through it...know that you're sick, you're not weak; and it's an issue, not an identity."*

As I mentioned earlier in this book, building our resilience is only one part of the solution to this growing epidemic, but it is a vital part, nonetheless. The tools you are learning in this book are intended to add to your toolbox, rather than to replace any other tools, therapies or medications you are already using or may use in the future. These resilience tools are *not* intended to replace medical and mental health professionals that offer important tools specific to anxiety and depression. *(If you or anyone you know are experiencing anxiety, depression or thoughts of suicide, please seek professional help.)*[79]

Character strengths have been a source of strength during hard times for countless people. Character strengths build resilience and elevate our lives by providing a lens to focus on our positive attributes, and on those of others. Our resilience helps us withstand the inevitable tempests of life. Below is a moving story that was sent to me by a woman named Megan, who had read my prior books. In her own words:

"Reflecting on the past year, I am overcome with gratitude for my life. A year ago, I admitted myself to a treatment center for suicide prevention. It was a time of transparency. There was no hiding any longer. Things became so real so quickly for my husband, kids, parents, friends, siblings, in laws... and ME.

How many lives would have been forever changed if I had followed through with taking my life? It was a Monday. I remember that day like it was yesterday. The loneliness I felt even in a home with a husband and 4 lively children, not to mention a new puppy is hard to grasp. How could I feel so alone with so many people around me? Believe me it is possible.

So many things triggered me back then. Having an opportunity to share my story has helped me to think back to how I adapted to life after treatment and 8 weeks of therapy. The weeks and months it took me to feel normal again seemed like years. I had to relearn how to live again. It wasn't easy but it was worth it.

I took a strengths survey recently and have found parallels in my healing and the strengths I utilized to be resilient during that year. For example, during my 6 days in the treatment center I used my social intelligence to make friends and find connections, which aided greatly in my recovery. Together with other patients, we spent time in therapy rediscovering our strengths of gratitude and appreciation. I had previously been in awe of nature and grateful for my blessings, but those strengths had withered over time. I learned to again be present in the moment and to soak in all the beauty.

Spirituality is a huge strength for me. Even when I haven't felt my Higher Power's presence, I still have sought that connection. My spirituality was a big part in my healing, monumental in my survival.

Admitting myself to treatment opened up an opportunity to be real and honest, for the first time in a long time. It was refreshing to use my strength of honesty, as well as scary. During my healing I've learned to take responsibility for my feelings and actions.

My strength of curiosity helped me to seek learning and understanding of mental illness. I haven't stopped even to this day to better understand why I've experienced the things I have, and what I can learn from them. There is definitely a silver lining to my experience—it's made me more aware and empathetic of the struggles of others, and I hope to help others in similar situations."

Megan is just one of countless people who have struggled with mental health issues. Megan continues to grow from her experience, as she shares her encouraging story with family, friends and community groups.

Thoughts Affect Every Cell in Our Bodies

Thoughts have widespread effects throughout our bodies, and science is discovering that thoughts can either help or hurt our resilience and well-being. As Dr. Mark Hyman has said, *"Your mind affects your body. Your mental health affects your physical health. This in turn affects your mental health again. These are not separate systems. They are intertwined and interconnected in subtle and sophisticated ways you need to understand."*[80]

Left unchecked to fester in unhealthy rumination, negative thoughts can cause havoc on your body. One study that tracked almost 100,000 women in their 50s, 60s and 70s over an eight year span, demonstrated that pessimistic women had higher rates of heart attack and died earlier than more optimistic women.[81] Other studies reveal that people who develop more caring connections with others catch fewer colds, have lower blood pressure, and are at lower risk for heart disease, Alzheimer's disease, stroke, and some cancers.[82]

In addition, some studies have shown that, when we "harden our hearts emotionally," they harden physically as well. Research on heart patients has shown that when they experience negative emotions, the chambers of their hearts stiffen and contract.[83] Being a pessimist can, apparently, make you ill.

Hope and Optimism

On the other hand, research shows that hope (also known as optimism) is among the top strengths that boost resilience. For example, a 2019 research study, highlighted in a Harvard Business Review article titled *The Financial Upside of Being an Optimist* by Michelle Gielan, found that optimists experience 145 fewer days of stress each year than pessimists! Gielan summarized the study:

> *"an antidote to chronic stress is cultivating an optimistic mindset —and it serves us well over the course of our careers. We surveyed more than 2,000 people...the data clearly showed that optimists were significantly more likely to experience better financial health than pessimists, and engage in healthier habits with their money... the most compelling finding was how optimists felt, reporting that*

they stressed about finances 145 fewer days each year as compared to pessimists...Optimism is a lucrative investment beyond one's finances."[84]

Hope and optimism, it seems, can be a wise investment for both your well-being—and your financial health. But how does one develop such hope and optimism, among other positive emotions?

Richard Davidson, a neuroscience professor at the University of Wisconsin-Madison, has shown that monks who meditate on positive emotions such as loving-kindness and compassion emit more powerful brain waves and generate more activity in the part of the brain that is responsible for positive emotions. *"The brain is an organ built to change in response to experience,"* notes Davidson, Director of the Laboratory for Affective Neuroscience. *"We can change our brains by changing our minds."*[85]

The monks' sustained training in redirecting their thoughts and clearing their brains of negative emotions promoted an alpha-wave state of well-being. In other words, we can modify ordinary human suffering by learning to change our responses to experiences. He points out that studies based on tens of thousands of responses to surveys demonstrate that relationships only provide a happiness "bump." Similarly, money does not guarantee happiness after basic needs are met. Rather, we are learning that lasting happiness is activated by positive thoughts, a focus on our strengths, a sense of purpose, balanced emotions, and a connection to something larger than self. When you flip the switch in your thinking, your brain gets the message and sends out new signals.

STRONG Filter

So how important are our thoughts and emotions in influencing the experiences of our lives? Nearly 300 scientific research studies conducted on more than 275,000 people internationally show that when we are in a negative state, experiencing fear, anger and discouragement, our ability to solve problems decreases significantly. We literally take in less information, see fewer options to solving problems, remember less, have less patience and are more irritable, thereby straining relationships and decreasing our ability to influence situations.

In sharp contrast, when we focus on the positive, such as considering all that we are grateful for, we have more positive thoughts and the resulting positive emotions. Our feelings of faith, hope and optimism grow. Researcher Barbara Fredrickson calls this effect "broaden and build,"[86] which basically means that our problem-solving ability and intelligence literally increase after immersion in positive and enriching influences. Study subjects exposed to positive influences such as uplifting films, music, poetry, etc., consistently and significantly outperform their study counterparts who had been exposed to negativity.

Some negative thoughts, however, are necessary and even healthy for personal growth. Therefore, we need to learn how to tell the difference between "authentic" negative thoughts, which produce growth when worked through, and "debilitating" negative thoughts, which bring discouragement, despair, and disengagement. For example, a thought that produces some guilt or accountability (I *acted* badly) can be useful and can motivate us toward positive change. Whereas a thought that produces shame (I *am* bad) is debilitating and can spiral a person into despair, causing useless stress and suffering.

As if life's innate challenges are not enough, we often become our own worst critic as we entertain debilitating thoughts. For example, "I never measure up." "Nothing ever seems to work out for me." "I'm a loser." Recognize some of these? The part of our brains that is wired for survival in a hostile world kicks in. We tend to over-generalize and catastrophize events.

I've created a simple tool I call the STRONG Filter to help you distinguish between these two types of negative thoughts (and resulting emotions). Do the following exercise when you are in a safe and comfortable place. Using the STRONG Filter tool below, see if you can determine if a negative thought you experience is "authentic" or "debilitating." Based on the characteristics under each heading below, circle the words that apply to your negative thought so that you can easily see if most of the descriptive words you circled are under the "authentic" or "debilitating" category:

STRONG Filter Tool
Authentic
- Encourage authenticity, increasing your motivation for positive change and growth.
- Based on reasonable expectations, objective facts and truth.
- Increase your energy and confidence when you choose to make positive changes.

Debilitating
- Discourage authenticity, blocking your motivation for positive change and growth.
- Create unreasonable expectations. Use distorted facts, prone to self-deception.
- Decrease energy and confidence, often causing despair and disengagement.

So, the next time you notice yourself thinking a negative thought or experiencing a negative emotion, distinguish between authentic thoughts and emotions that, when worked through, produce growth, and the debilitating thoughts and emotions that produce discouragement, despair, and disengagement. Ask yourself, "What am I thinking/feeling that is based on unreasonable or irrational expectations?" "What am I thinking/feeling that is based on objective facts and truth?" (Many people find that just adding this "authentic" vs. "debilitating" filter can help them to sift through life's challenging moments.)

If you determined the negative thought or emotion was authentic, think of ways you can learn and grow from what this revealed to you. What positive actions will you take that will help you transform this into a beneficial outcome?

On the other hand, if you determined the negative thought or emotion was debilitating, it's important to connect with your inner coach by taking a few deep breaths and sending yourself compassion, then quickly shift your focus toward positive, empowering self-talk. The next tool, and following chapters, will give you more resources to do just that—to shift your perspective in a self-empowering way. Read on to discover how to replace such thoughts with positive and affirming thoughts...

STRONG Thoughts

"Try to pose for yourself this task: not to think of a polar bear, and you will see that the cursed thing will come to mind every minute."[87]
—*Fyodor Dostoevsky*

Earlier, we looked at the debilitating nature of negative thoughts. Learning how to quickly redirect negative thoughts in a positive way, rather than suppressing them, is one of the most effective ways to feel and perform better quickly. Research has also shown that peoples' attempts to suppress thoughts can actually result in a preoccupation with the very thoughts they are trying to suppress! This is a phenomenon referred to as a rebound effect.[88] In an experiment, people were told *not* to think about a "white bear." They were instructed to ring a bell each time they said or thought "white bear." Interestingly, when compared to a group that was told to think about white bears, the group that was asked to *suppress* white bear thoughts actually had significantly more thoughts on this topic! The researchers concluded that attempts at thought suppression had a paradoxical effect, suggesting that suppression might actually produce the very thought it is intended to stifle. Subsequent research has supported this notion and confirms repeated failure by people to successfully suppress unwanted thoughts.[89]

So, when you think, "I'm so stupid" vs. "I'm going to stop calling myself stupid," your brain really doesn't know the difference between the two thoughts and simply grabs hold of the word "stupid." What if you replaced the thought "I'm so stupid" with "I am capable, will work at this and will focus on my strengths." That's how to intentionally shift from your inner critic to your inner coach.

I suggest creating a mantra or phrase of your character strengths to use when negative thoughts arise. A woman I coached would recite a mantra every time she hiked as a way to dispel the negative, fearful, ruminating. She would say to herself, *"I am brave, perseverant, and hopeful. I see beauty all around me."* A key to getting rid of a negative thought is replacing it with something positive, such as focusing on your strengths.

The following is a simple, easy to remember, three-step process to help transform negative thoughts. First, ensure that you are in a safe and relaxed place before you try this tool. Now, recall a negative thought you have had in the past week, but something that you feel secure and comfortable recalling right now as you use this tool. Next, let's go through the three steps of the STRONG Thoughts tool as follows:

STRONG Thoughts Tool

Step 1: Observe

Observe how negativity makes you feel. "I'm so stupid!" "I can't believe I dropped the ball on that project!" "I'm a failure." Negative thoughts cause stress chemicals to be released in your body—e.g., muscle tension, faster heart rate, shallow breathing, sweating, dizziness, lack of awareness, foggy thinking, negative self-talk.

Contrast this with how differently positive thoughts affect your body—e.g., relaxed muscles, decreased heart rate, deeper breathing, energized, aware and focused, positive self-talk.

Step 2: Replace

Replace negative thoughts quickly with objective language that utilizes your strengths best suited to the situation. In other words, observe the situation as if you were coaching yourself and reminding yourself of all the ways your character strengths can help you better deal with or solve the issue.

For example, you are replacing a negative thought such as "I can't believe I dropped the ball on that project!" to "I am learning from this experience. I am using my strengths of (social intelligence, teamwork, honesty, perseverance, hope, etc.) to have a constructive talk with my (colleague, teacher, boss, friend, etc.) and take responsibility in a way that builds our relationship."

Step 3: Affirm

Affirm the authentic view of yourself. Close your eyes, take a few deep breaths, and visualize yourself using the strengths best suited to the situation that you just called forth. See yourself behaving in this higher, more ennobling and more productive way. Affirm these strengths in yourself until you feel differently about the situation and yourself. For example, visualize the details of the constructive conversation you will have and create in your mind the outcome you want.

Positivity Journal STRONG Questions

- How did that go for you?
- What did you learn from using the STRONG Thoughts tool and learning to quickly shift from a debilitating thought to an empowering thought (based on your strengths)?
- Which of your character strengths could you use to support others who may be struggling?

What Wires Together Fires Together

So how do we turn our new positive focus into a habit? Scientists are learning a great deal about our brain's ability to adapt and rewire. The old thinking was that our neurons and brain cells were limited and could not rebound after an accident or after a certain age. In recent years, neuroscientists have discovered the brain is much more changeable than hardly anyone expected. This phenomenon, known as neuroplasticity, demonstrates that there are concrete and provable benefits to exercising the brain for higher performance. And what we think about can literally change our brains.

We can steadily develop more productive thoughts by building our strengths the same way we build a muscle. The principle of regular exercise applies here: our new strengths-focused thoughts can be reinforced consistently, and they gradually become stronger day by day. When we "get real" and begin to look honestly at the link between our thoughts and behaviors, we can ask ourselves, "How is this serving me?" That one question prompts us to consciously choose strengths-focused thoughts and the resulting behaviors that serve our vision of our best selves. This leads us to live our lives consciously rather than by default.

Living consciously includes caring for oneself. For example, periodic "fasts" from negative news, life dramas, debilitating negative emotions, toxic relationships, etc.—whenever it's realistic to do so—can help us re-boot positive neural networks. Just like practicing self-care by avoiding toxins in favor of eating healthy food, we can give ourselves the gift of refraining from things that stress our nervous systems—choosing to instead immerse ourselves in positive influences, thus promoting resilience. We can re-wire negative neuro circuits into positive neural connections.

And when it comes to managing stress, it's important to note that getting out into nature can have profound beneficial effects. For example, multiple studies have shown that when people spend as little as 20 minutes outdoors, they report significantly elevated mood boosts, and even their blood pressure and other vital functions improve.[90]

Just like the athlete who works out a group of muscles over time to perform better in a sport, we can develop new neuropathways over time[91] that will improve how we show up in our lives—our relationships, our work, our health habits, and how well we stick to and accomplish any goal in general. One way to do this is by firing up the connection with our best self on a consistent basis, as you will see in the next section.

Best Self Experience

We are now going to do a fun exercise called Best Self Experience. This is perhaps the most energizing exercise I use with people, and I'm consistently amazed as I witness individuals come alive during this exercise. It's as if the recalling of their high-point moments infuses them with newfound confidence. This is an excellent way of reinforcing our brain's and our heart's neural connections to events that have made us feel empowered in the past. And more importantly, after understanding the key elements of past successes, people are filled with a powerful realization that they can re-create success and the accompanying positive emotions at will in their future. Invariably, as people recount their best self experiences, they recognize their strengths, sometimes as if for the first time!

So, are you ready to experience these insights for yourself? Think of a time when you contributed to a success or felt really good about something you accomplished, or simply felt that you were in the zone. Write down your 'best self" experience, including all of the important details, like a story with a beginning, middle and end.

Next, read your story and ask yourself, "What did you do to make this happen?" Consider any strengths you may have used in your past high-point experience and write them down. Recall the positive emotions that you experienced as you used your strengths, that you would like to feel on a more consistent basis.

Lastly, and most importantly, identify elements of the experience that *can be re-created to enjoy more high points in your future.* What can you take away from this best self experience that will help you recreate success at will going forward, and in other areas of your life? As you flex your strengths muscles in the future, note the strengths that have helped you most in feeling your best, and how you can use these strengths to boost your resilience, building on those past successes over time. (Another option is to do the exercise above verbally with someone you trust as a mutual sharing experience. If you choose this option, take turns sharing your best self experience, and see if you can spot which strengths were used in one-another's stories.)

For example, I vividly remember one of my best self experiences as if it were yesterday. It was my first opportunity to use strengths coaching with another person. I was humbled and filled with a desire to contribute meaningfully to this individual. I can only describe it as one of the most heart-filling and purposeful hours of my life. I found myself fueled by my strengths of teamwork, perspective, and kindness as I listened with sincere intent to be a conduit for growth with this person. Within that transformative hour, I was energized and experienced a deep and growing enthusiasm for my work, because I could see its positive impact on another human being. I realize now that I was bringing some of my top strengths to the coaching and this evoked my best self to come to the forefront. Fast forward several years—I continue to use the insights from this experience to re-create more highpoints in many aspects of my life.

Positivity Journal STRONG Questions

- How did it go?
- What top strengths did you use in your past best self experience(s)? How did they bring out the best in you?
- Recalling the principle of "what wires together, fires together," how could you apply your top strengths more consistently?
- Are there any strengths you are not currently using that were instrumental for past best self experiences? If so, why have you neglected those strengths and how can you bring them forward now?
- What if you could recreate best self experiences at will—how would that benefit you?

EMPOWERED
BY YOUR
STRENGTHS

*"And one has to understand that bravery is not the absence
of fear but rather the strength to keep going forward despite the fear."* [92]

—Paulo Coelho

*"I wanted to become educated
and empower myself with knowledge."* [93]

—Malala Yousafzai

CHAPTER 4

NO MUD, NO LOTUS: REFRAMING LOSS AND FAILURE

"If you feel lost, disappointed, hesitant, or weak, return to yourself, to who you are here and now, and when you get there you will discover yourself, like a lotus flower in full bloom, even in a muddy pond, beautiful and strong." [94]

—*Masaru Emoto*

Holding up a card from a woman whose husband—the father of their four-year old son—had suffered a stroke, my yoga teacher[95] reverently opened class. The card simply said: "No Mud, No Lotus, Embrace the Mud."

The remainder of class, we practiced yoga poses of strength in surrender—like the lotus flower that emerges victoriously clean above murky waters—representative of how each of us can overcome life's hard challenges. In many traditions, the lotus flower symbolizes purification of mind, body and speech; it is the spirit of awakening and letting go. It embodies resilience, as rain from dark clouds slides easily off its petals, and it opens itself to the sunshine that follows.

In each pose, we practiced mindfully observing and making peace with the darkness beneath the lotus—our fear, sadness, anger, and other difficult emotions so that we could release them. We experienced the visceral lotus within our own bodies.

Embracing the muddy, murky waters of loss, failure, or disappointment that each of us encounters in life is easier said than done! How do we cultivate our own metaphorical lotus flowers and emerge triumphantly from the darkness, you may ask?

We can draw strength from examples of people who emerged triumphantly from these murky waters and shifted their focus to what they "have" instead of what they "lost."

An example is blind architect Chris Downey. He began to lose his sight two days after surgery to remove a brain tumor, and on the third day, it was completely gone. Yet, despite the painful challenges that ensued, Downey claims he never once considered giving up his work in architecture. According to Downey, at the age of 45, waking up blind and with no sense of smell (also lost in the surgery), was *"quite frankly, really terrifying."* But, when interviewed about the resulting development of his architectural skill to design buildings with much needed accommodations for the blind, he replied, *"I'm absolutely convinced I'm a better architect today than I was sighted."* [96]

Perception Colors Everything

"I've missed more than 9,000 shots in my career. I've lost almost 300 games. Twenty-six times, I've been trusted to take the game-winning shot and missed. I've failed over and over and over again in my life. And that is why I succeed."

—*Michael Jordan*

Michael Jordan, perhaps the greatest basketball player of all time, has modeled for the world that setbacks are part of success.[97] What if we stopped considering our setbacks as set-ups for failure? What if we could see that some deficiency is often part of an overall proficiency?

Some of the world's greatest thinkers and leaders were told that they would never amount to anything or were labeled due to disabilities. Sir Richard Branson, founder of more than 100 companies in his Virgin Empire and one of the world's great philanthropists, has dyslexia and performed poorly in school, dropping out at the age of sixteen.[98] Albert Einstein is said to have performed poorly in traditional schools and was allegedly homeschooled by his mother.[99] These divergent thinkers used their problem-solving skills to dream up groundbreaking ideas and solutions.

Perception colors everything in our inner and outer world, from obsessively comparing ourselves to others on social media—never feeling like we are enough—to reframing loss or failure in a way that is for our highest good. Through the power of "story" we can learn to reframe our difficulties in ways that better serve us —understanding how post-traumatic stress can be transformed into post-traumatic growth. This is precisely what the blind architect Chris Downey did—he wrote the rest of his own story—after his fateful diagnosis.

Comparanoia and Social Media

"Insecurity comes from comparing our out-take scenes with everyone else's highlight reel."

—Anonymous

Excessive comparing is a non-productive perception that can color everything in our world. Mark Twain once said, *"Comparison is the death of joy."*[100] All people compare. For example, people compare athletic ability, financial status, possessions, looks, etc.

When comparison turns from perceptive discernments to discriminating judgments that rank things, it becomes a fear-based pursuit that separates people into categories rather than uniting them. When we look for what makes us better or worse than someone else instead of looking for uniting factors such as what we can learn from another person, we contribute to the illusion that we are more different than alike.

With this kind of thinking, we reaffirm the fallacy that human worth can be distilled into comparisons. Ultimately, "comparanoia," a trendy, made-up word that means excessive comparing, is destructive in its consequences. Someone must be better because they have more and someone must be worse because they have less or what they do or are is perceived as "less than."

Comparing our own progress or success with others' successes has been characterized as "keeping up with the Joneses," based on a comic strip that originated in the U.S. in the early 1900s. In it, a never-seen neighboring family was portrayed as having a bigger house, greener lawn, better furnishings, more success at work, nicer children and an enviable relationship.[101]

Today, instead of comic strips, we have social media. Every culture has its own version of social envy, and social media now plays a large part in trapping people into striving for things they don't really need, but think they want because those things are perceived as status symbols. There is a manipulative component in social media, that left unchecked, competes for our own sense of autonomy.[102] [103] Even worse, a growing obsession with how many "likes" we get on Instagram, Facebook, or Twitter derides our sense of self-worth in a subtle, yet corrosive way.

In her book, *The Future of Happiness*, author Amy Blankson offers insights, *"Technology, at least in theory, is improving our productivity, efficiency, and communication. The one thing it's not doing is making us happier... knowing that technology is here to stay and will continue to evolve in form and function, we need to know how to navigate the future to achieve a better balance between technology, productivity, and well-being... By rethinking when, where, why, and how you use technology, you will not only influence your own well-being but also help shape the future of your community."[104]*

Comparanoia, in social media and in life, is fueled by an irrational and insatiable need to be perceived as "perfect." Let's take a deeper look at perfectionism in the coming section.

Perfectionism

Striving for your best is motivating. Striving for perfectionism is demoralizing. Perfectionism is not the same thing as the pursuit of excellence. Psychologist Dr. Thomas Greenspon explains the distinction between perfectionism and striving for your personal best. Greenspon states, *"Perfectionism is more than pushing yourself to do your best to achieve a goal; it's a reflection of an inner self mired in anxiety."[105]*

Below are some common pitfalls to perfectionism:
- anxiety/depression
- shame: feeling "less than"
- overly focusing on personal flaws/mistakes
- feeling unworthy: low self-compassion/self-acceptance[106]

One thing that debilitates a perfectionist is a fear of failure. Here Greenspon observes:

"Perfectionistic people typically believe that they can never be good enough, that mistakes are signs of personal flaws, and that the only route to acceptability as a person is to be perfect. A perfectionist often sees anything less than perfect as failure, and often would rather give up or not try than risk experiencing 'failure.'"[107]

This perception fuels the anxiety, shame and/or depression that perfectionists tend to feel when things don't run smoothly. In extreme circumstances, perfectionism and fear of failure can be connected with eating disorders and even self-harm. (*If you are experiencing any of these health issues associated with perfectionism, please seek professional help.*)

Sometimes, experiences we perceive as failures are opportunities that signal that our inner critic is in the driver's seat rather than our inner coach. When we turn up the volume on our inner coach, and learn to silence our inner critic, we may discover that our failures can be the turning points in our lives, revealing what our true purpose is. But we have to be willing to look at the message of the failure and put it in the context of our long-term goals and values, so that we can grow from it.

By reframing failure, we can choose to see the experience as an opportunity to learn and grow, thus helping us reach for our highest level of performance. It's no wonder that the TEDx Talk, *What I Learned from 100 Days of Rejection* by Jia Jiang has amassed millions of views.[108]

People around the globe are fascinated with how to overcome fear of failure, which has roots in fear of rejection. Jiang has used his greatest fear to move himself forward. You never know when a setback could put you ahead. That's living in the realm of possibility rather than in an arena with a penalty box.

Take a moment to assess where you are currently on the perfectionism Mindset Check below, and to consider where you want to be:

INNER CRITIC	VS	INNER COACH
I have to be perfect.		I am doing my best.
There is only one right way.		There are many possibilities.
I need to be told what to do.		I can figure it out on my own.
Feedback = I did it wrong.		Feedback = opportunity to grow.
Failure = I'm not good enough.		Failure = I am learning.
Fear needs to be avoided.		I can act even when afraid.
What if I make a mistake?		Mistakes are part of progress.
What went wrong?		What went right?
I can't do it right.		I can master this with practice.

Coach vs. Critic Model, © 2014-2020, *Authentic Strengths Advantage, LLC.*
(Inspired by the following: Columbia University Coaching Certification Program Learner/Judger Model; Marilee C. Goldberg's, The Art of the Question 1998 p. 161-178).

Attitude of Gratitude

An antidote to comparanoia and perfectionism is the attitude of gratitude. Christine Carter, Ph.D. explains, *"I see gratitude as a route to a happy life, and a skill that we can practice in order to not just cope with life's difficulties, but to embrace those difficulties, and then let the positive emotions emerge from within those."*[109]

Research overwhelmingly shows that people who practice gratitude consistently report a host of physical, mental, and social benefits. For example, people who write a gratitude list of their blessings each day report higher levels of happiness and life satisfaction. A great time to do this is first thing in the morning or before going to sleep at night. Consider that while you sleep, your brain rests, recovers, creates, has insights, and solves problems. Therefore, the last thought you have before falling asleep each night is significant in many respects. And also reflect for a moment on how the thoughts you experience first thing in the morning can positively or negatively influence your day. It makes good sense to practice some form of a gratitude mindfulness practice to shift all your mental, physical, emotional, and spiritual focus and resources in your favor. Another option is to mentally list what you are grateful for when you are faced with the temptation to compare yourself to others.

In the words of filmmaker, Louie Schwartzberg:

> *"Practicing gratitude does not ignore the harsh realities of life; in fact, it accepts them, then encourages us to identify some amount of goodness in our life. Looking a little deeper into where this sense of goodness comes from, we can see that much of this appreciation stems from external sources. Gratitude can humble us and help us acknowledge that other people—or even higher powers, if you're of a spiritual mindset—gave us many gifts, big and small, to help us achieve the goodness in our lives.*[110]

I've heard some positive psychologists call gratitude the "mother of all character strengths" because of its immense, positive effect on all aspects of our lives, including our mental, physical, and emotional states, as well as our relationships with others. Take the time each day to reflect on all that you are grateful for, even if you have to begin with the basic necessities of life that sometimes go overlooked, like clean drinking water, etc.

Positivity Journal

- Write 5 things for which you are grateful. Write these down in a colorful or artistic way and post them somewhere you will be continually reminded of them. (One young man whom I coached after his suicide attempt (while he was in the care of medical professionals) placed his gratitude list on his bathroom mirror, so that he would read it upon awakening and before going to sleep.)

- Using a piece of paper, a card or your phone, spend the next five minutes writing a note to someone in your life for whom you are truly grateful. Be as descriptive as you can. Hand this note, text it, or read it to that person.

Reframing Failure

"Owning our story can be hard but not nearly as difficult as spending our lives running from it."

—Dr. Brené Brown[111]

If we're going to talk to ourselves about what we have done, why not be encouraging instead of punitive? Why not complement our progress, instead of picking apart our mistakes? The challenge is to grow from our disappointments and failures instead of letting them shrink us. Let's learn from an inspiring woman, Tiffany, through her story of reframing "failure":

"I recently was asked to participate in a focus group to assist in the creation of a support class for people who are in the midst of divorce. I was asked because I had been through a divorce, and I went as a favor to a friend. An interesting thing happened when I arrived. The participants were swapping divorce stories—who left whom, how old the kids were, how old the 'new' spouse/partner is, the financial toll incurred, the emotional fallout, etc. As I listened, I was surprised that I felt like an outsider. I wasn't sure how to tell my story (if I was asked) because my story didn't feel like part of my identity anymore. I couldn't share feelings of injustice or righteous indignation. I couldn't tell the story from a wounded place because I wasn't wounded anymore.

To be fair, I could have been right at the center of that conversation even just a year ago. I've told my story with as much drama as anyone and, in reality, it ranks up there with the best of them in terms of having been 'wronged.' But in that moment, listening to those stories, I realized how differently I see it now. I've mentally reframed it in such a way that it doesn't define me anymore. It's just part of my life journey—a left turn in the road when I thought I would be turning right. Turns out that turning left led to some amazing experiences. Turning left helped me use strengths I didn't even know I had.

For years while teaching at the university, when I introduced myself to my classes at the start of each semester, my first words were 'I'm Tiffany. I'm divorced. I'm a single mom...' These days, I start with 'I'm Tiffany. I'm a mom. I have two amazing kids...' My divorce is no longer who I am. And when I look back at it in the rearview mirror, I don't see disaster, but rather a well-worn road full of life experiences that have helped shape who I am today."

Revisiting the life stories that we have been telling ourselves for years—looking at our life experiences through the lens of character strengths and reframing experiences in ways that better serve us can be cathartic and profoundly healing. Research shows that stories are a powerful catalyst for personal growth.[112] A person's own life stories can yield powerful insights that can serve them going forward.[113]

Positivity Journal STRONG Questions

- Recalling Chris's story earlier in this chapter of excelling in his career after becoming blind, what did you learn that impacted you most? What character strengths did Chris use?
- Now consider Tiffany's story; what elements provided helpful insights for you? What character strengths did you see Tiffany tapping into?

- And finally, in the story of Douglas and Walter, what were the key differences between the two men's approaches? Why do you think they had very different outcomes? What character strengths did you see Douglas using?

Curiosity and Creativity

Research shows that several strengths are directly related to resilience, among them curiosity and creativity. For example, when we use our creativity or our curiosity to learn from and reframe our failures, these strengths help us bounce back from the failure.

One of the hallmarks of withstanding life's storms is the ability to see beyond your current circumstances. The strengths of curiosity and creativity have been shown to help you look outside of your current circumstances and to envision positive things that your future might hold. For example, sometimes we think our current circumstances will last forever. To counter this, focusing on activities that build curiosity and creativity may help you to look beyond the clouds where the sun is peeking through.

Building your strengths of curiosity and creativity serve as a powerful antidote to lessen the fear of failure, and in turn, shift us out of the damaging cycle of comparanoia and perfectionist thinking. Here are four strategies for unleashing your curiosity and creativity:

- Positive Emotions — Curiosity and creativity are much more likely to occur when we are open to new ideas and new experiences. Dr. Barbara Frederickson, who studies positive emotion, suggests that positive emotions are evolutionarily adaptive because they trigger a broadening of our mental state.[114] Examples of how to evoke positive emotions could be to listen to your favorite music or read something inspiring before engaging in a task in which you want to use your creativity or curiosity.

- Positive Mood — Study participants in a happy mood out-performed participants in a negative or neutral mood on a task requiring a creative solution.[115] Similar to evoking positive emotions, some examples of eliciting a positive mood could be to recall something or someone that you are grateful for, or to engage in a pleasant activity before a creative endeavor.
- Energized Focus - Focus and hard work is often a prerequisite for creativity. In order for an idea or product to be considered creative, it typically has to be complete. An example of this is making the commitment and following through to diligently work on your creative project or task.
- Time Management - People are much less curious and creative when they are under time pressure. Managing time well allows space for creativity and curiosity to thrive. An example of this might be setting aside ample time in your day for creativity to flow, rather than rushing through creative tasks.

Practicing these four strategies can build your strengths of creativity and curiosity, thus making you more resilient in the face of setbacks and more open to new experiences and ultimate successes!

Positivity Journal STRONG Questions
- How can I reframe a failure I've struggled with in the past and write a new ending to my story, in a way that best serves me?
- How can I grow from the situation(s) I'm currently facing? What am I learning?
- How could curiosity and creativity help me when I feel overwhelmed, discouraged or hopeless due to a life challenge?

Post-Traumatic Growth
When we are resilient, we can find purpose and meaning within life's "losses" as well as life's "successes." Understanding our character

strengths can increase our confidence in our ability to deal with challenges that come our way. No one can predict the future, but we often create undue stress, excessively worrying about what "might happen." While we cannot predict the future, we can choose to focus on our strengths, thus increasing our confidence and ability to deal with whatever the future brings.

Identifying with your strengths can build your resilience to remain strong wherever you go and regardless of what happens to you. People like Chris Downey, the blind architect we learned about previously, are examples of not only resilience, but also of post-traumatic growth. Research is showing that resilience and post-traumatic growth correspond with the following character strengths (among others):

- Improved relationships (kindness, love)
- Openness to new possibilities (curiosity, creativity, learning)
- Appreciation of life (appreciation of beauty, gratitude, zest)
- Personal strength (bravery/courage, honesty, perseverance)
- Spiritual development (spirituality)[116]

In one study, bravery was strongly related to the recovery of life satisfaction after physical illness[117], and to post-traumatic growth.[118] Resilience involves the development of such courage, defined as the capacity to deal with situations when we feel fear or hesitation. People who develop bravery do not shrink from threat, challenge, difficulty, or pain, and are better able to face adverse situations with increased resilience.[119]

Dr. Seligman's work with the U.S. Army offers valuable insights into how character strengths relate to post-traumatic growth, in his words:

"On one end are the people who fall apart into PTSD, depression, and even suicide. In the middle are most people, who at first react

with symptoms of depression and anxiety but within a month or so are, by physical and psychological measures, back where they were before the trauma. That is resilience. On the other end are people who show post-traumatic growth. They, too, first experience depression and anxiety, often exhibiting full-blown PTSD; but within a year they are better off than they were before the trauma...[120]

More than 900,000 soldiers have taken the VIA Survey. The resulting database has enabled positive psychologists to answer questions like: Do character strengths help protect against PTSD, depression, and anxiety? Does a strong sense of meaning result in better performance? Can optimism spread from a leader to followers? In these scenarios and more, character strengths had a positive effect. Seligman said, *"We...can draw lessons from this approach, particularly in times of failure and stagnation...we are helping to create an army of Douglases who can turn their most difficult experiences into catalysts for improved performance."* Basing your self-concept on your character strengths builds your resilience to remain strong wherever you go and regardless of what happens to you.[121]

Building Resilience

"Imagine each challenge as an opportunity to elevate rather than to exhaust. That's resilience. By harnessing strengths, you provide a pathway into what's right and good in self and others. It's an invitation to embrace all of your experience— knowing what it means to be fully alive, fully human!"

—*Megan McDonough*

Different strengths can promote resilience in distinctive ways. Below is a model I've developed, inspired by the research of Martinez-Marti and Ruch[122], that can help you see how each of your character strengths can play a vital role in increasing resilience. A key ingredient in building resilience is to anchor your self-concept in the authentic strengths that define your uniqueness. Understanding your strengths can increase your confidence in your ability to deal with challenges that come your way. It is possible to cultivate gratitude and even humor, among other strengths, in the midst of life's hardships.

As you review the model below, recall the times you have used the corresponding strengths in each category for similar purposes. Connecting this model to your own life experiences will bring it to life for you and help you to intentionally build your resilience going forward:

Dimensions of Resilience Model

1 **Meaning Strengths**
Create connections to something beyond self, inspiration/meaning in adversity

2 **Emotional Strengths**
Provide energy, determination, and social support to face challenges successfully

3 **Strengths of Restraint**
Maintain will to persevere, regulate emotions/behaviors during difficulties

4 **Intellectual Strengths**
Help find solutions through the gathering/ use of new information and approaches.

5 **Interpersonal Strengths**
Encourage healthy relationships with others: i.e. friends/family/community.

Dimensions of Resilience

ASA Dimensions of Resilience Model © 2018-2020, Authentic Strengths Advantage, LLC. (Inspired by the following: Martínez-Martí, María Luisa, and Willibald Ruch. "Character Strengths Predict Resilience over and above Positive Affect, Self-Efficacy, Optimism, Social Support, Self-Esteem, and Life Satisfaction." The Journal of Positive Psychology, 2016).

For example, emotional strengths, which include bravery, hope, humor, love, social intelligence, and zest can provide individuals with the energy, social determination, and social connectedness necessary to face adversity.

Strengths of restraint, which include honesty, persistence, perspective, prudence, and self-regulation can boost resilience by maintaining the will to accomplish goals in difficult situations, regulating emotions and behaviors in ways that promote positive adaptation while being careful about one's choices.

Intellectual strengths, which include creativity, curiosity, love of learning, and open-mindedness can boost resilience because they involve the acquisition of information and the use of this information in new and effective ways, facilitating problem-solving.[123] This group of strengths might also help people see life in general as an interesting experience, including the negative experiences, helping them approach life in a more engaged way. In addition, they might encourage resilience by thinking things through and examining them from all sides, broadening the perspective on a given situation[124], and being able to discern the nature of a situation. Providing individuals with a more accurate perception of the stressor might help individuals downplay certain adverse situations and diminish catastrophizing, facilitating problem-solving.

Interpersonal strengths which include fairness, forgiveness, kindness, leadership, humility, and teamwork can promote resilience through healthy relationships with others and group activities. Strong, healthy social networks have been shown to promote resilience, and health in general.

And finally, meaning strengths, which include appreciation of beauty and excellence, gratitude, and spirituality promote a sense of connectedness to something beyond self. They provide inspiration and meaning in the midst of adversity, which increases resilience.

Your Story: Victim or Victor?

"While victimization creates dependency and distrust, accountability creates interdependence and trust," says Stephen M.R. Covey in *The Speed of Trust.*[125] When a loved one, friend or colleague takes responsibility, it encourages others to do the same. But sometimes people get stuck in the victim role and don't move ahead. It takes imagination to envision something different and better than the limiting stories we have been telling ourselves our whole lives, whether they are echoes of others' voices or our own inner critic. You may have heard the acronym FEAR, which maps to

False Evidence Appearing Real. Often the stories we have internalized are not based on reality, but on someone else's distortion. Choosing a new, more accurate story to tell yourself, stepping forward to call upon your strengths of character, defuses victim mentality. Amplifying a positive voice gives power and energy to our authentic self, guiding us to the heart of all matters.

But some suffering in our lives is not necessarily a negative thing. *"Suffering is a great equalizer. You have a choice to let it make you 'bitter' or 'better',"* says my friend Sam Bracken. *"That one letter makes all the difference in how you approach life."*

Who would have thought that when Sam's mother said to him at age fifteen, "I don't want you anymore; you get in the way of my partying—you have to leave," that her abandonment of him would turn out to be his chance to become a victor? A family from his church took him in, which allowed him a glimpse of what a normal home life looked like. He took his childhood suffering and used it to inspire others who had also suffered hardship. As a motivational speaker and author of *My Orange Duffel Bag: A Journey to Radical Change,* he is on a mission to help homeless young people, high-poverty youth, and teens aging out of foster care, see that they can change—no matter their circumstances.

It's important to be real, and acknowledge our story, but at some point, we must shift to focusing on our wholeness to build a new and better story. You don't have to stick to the script that others have written for you.

Defining Our Own Stories

"When we deny our stories, they define us. When we own our stories, we get to write the ending."[126]

—*Dr. Brené Brown*

I did not look forward to a long stay at my mother's home after my brother's untimely death. I felt such a deep sadness and emotional vulnerability—it had not been long since my father's passing. My mother's bouts with debilitating illness had sometimes caused our roles to be reversed when I was a child. Not wanting to burden her with my childhood worries and adolescent challenges, I had learned to avoid my pain and suppress my emotions. I had kept my youthful insecurities to myself.

But after the catharsis of the funeral, I decided to look for all that I could appreciate and embrace about my childhood. I knew that I loved my mother deeply, that she had done the best she could, and that there were so many things to admire about her. I also knew that the time had come to let go of my expectations and embrace the growth my childhood had provided me, reframing my story. Although I recognize that some people have had much more difficult childhood experiences than me, in that moment I was able to see my mother through a new lens. We were now two adult women holding the sorrow of our loss together.

I opened my eyes and saw a spry, energetic, intelligent woman who loves animals, reading, gardening, and cooking. I recalled the time a wild squirrel ate peacefully out of my mother's hand. She had a genuine goodness and strength about her. She was an interesting woman, a different woman than the one lodged in my consciousness, the mother of my childhood. I enjoyed our time together without judgment.

At times when I had looked into the dark tunnel of my childhood, I felt like a train was coming at me and the only safety was cringing against a wall. This time the light was not from a locomotive bearing down on me; it was the sun shining through the other end of the tunnel. I followed the light and walked out of the past into a different place. That's where I found my wonderful mother.

My mother had done the best she could with what she had been given. The trap that I fell into is a common one. It's seductive to blame people, circumstances and events—to get stuck in the regrets. I realized that now as an adult woman I could look back on those hard times through a more accurate, appreciative and positive lens. Sometimes, from our deepest wounds comes our greatest gifts.

Flexing and Building Your Strengths

Reframing loss and failure sometimes can call for building a "less-used strength." This may feel a bit challenging because it takes you out of your comfort zone. It requires flexing a muscle you haven't flexed in a while, but you may be surprised as a lesser strength becomes an important and powerful tool in your life. Or, you may choose to exercise a "top strength" to increase your positive mindset and resilience. I've included some strengths-building strategies for you below (based on the VIA character strengths-building activities on their website).

Positivity Journal

Take a few minutes to identify a strength you would like to build to help you reframe a loss or failure, or simply to increase your resilience. Then choose a strengths-building activity (or create your own) that you will do over the next week. Read the list of suggested strengths-building activities and choose one or two to focus on that you resonate with.

Ideas for Building Authentic Resilience:

Appreciation of Beauty and Excellence

Noticing and appreciating beauty, excellence, and skills for example, in nature, art, mathematics, science, and in everyday experience.

- Go to a museum and pick out a piece of artwork or a display that has aesthetic value and touches you because of its beauty.
- Take a walk with a friend and comment on something pleasing to look at.
- Attend a concert and enjoy the sound for its musical value. Or pick music you enjoy and listen to it appreciatively each night. Or ask a friend to recommend the most beautiful music he or she enjoys.
- Keep a journal and record something nightly from your day that struck you as beautiful or skillful.
- Find something that is pleasing to you in aesthetics or value, such as a scene in nature, an object or a physical activity, and draw inspiration from it throughout the day.

Bravery

Not shrinking from threat, challenge, difficulty, or pain; speaking up for what is right even if there is opposition; acting on convictions even if unpopular; includes physical bravery.

- Introduce yourself to someone new.
- Stand up for someone you agree with, even if you are outnumbered by people with opposing views.
- Take action in a situation that you have been avoiding.
- Do one small thing daily that pulls you out of your comfort zone.
- Speak up for an unpopular idea you believe in.

Creativity, Ingenuity and Originality

Thinking of novel and productive ways to conceptualize and do things.

- Keep a journal, draw/paint a picture, or write a poem.
- Submit a piece to a literary magazine or newspaper.
- Decorate/change your work or living space into a new creative design.

- Find a new word each day and use it creatively.
- Change your profile on social media to reflect your creativity.

Curiosity

Taking an interest in ongoing experience for its own sake; finding subjects and topics fascinating; exploring and discovering.

- Ask questions (in meetings, with friends, at school, at work, etc.).
- Discover new places.
- Explore the stacks and/or tables in the library or bookstore. Pick a book or magazine that interests you and spend some time skimming it.
- Eat something new that you would not have tried otherwise.
- Go to a lecture or watch/listen to a speaker online about something you find fascinating.

Fairness

Treating all people fairly and with justice; not letting personal feelings bias decisions about others; giving everyone a fair chance.

- Allow someone to speak their peace while keeping an open mind and not passing judgment.
- Stay impartial in an argument between friends despite your beliefs— help mediate for a peaceful resolution by encouraging each person to be fair with one-another.
- Notice when you treat someone based on a stereotype or pre-conception; resolve not to do it again.
- Resolve daily to treat others the way you would want to be treated.

Forgiveness

Forgiving those who have done wrong; accepting the shortcomings of others; giving people a second chance; not being vengeful.

- Think of someone that you found hard to forgive. Try to see the situation from their perspective.
- Keep a journal of all the ways you forgive self and others. Only include positive statements of how you are forgiving, releasing, and letting go of past grievances.
- Make contact with someone who has upset you in the past. Let them know that you forgive them, or simply be kind to them so that they know you have let it go.
- When someone does something that you do not understand, try to understand his/her best intentions rather than fixating on their actions.
- Give people the "benefit of the doubt" by being slow to judge and quick to forgive.

Gratitude

Being aware of and thankful for the good things that happen; taking time to express thanks.

- Each morning before stepping out of bed, make a mental note of 3 things you are grateful for and that you will appreciate that day.
- Every day, thank someone for something that you might otherwise take for granted (e.g., thanking the janitor who cleans a public building).
- Keep a record of the number of times you use the words "thank you" in a day. Over the course of a week, try to double the number of times that you say those words.
- Call or text a co-worker/partner/family member/friend each day and thank him/ her for something you appreciate.
- Keep a journal, and each night, make a list of three or more things that you are truly thankful for. (Your list can be as basic as indoor plumbing, food, clothing, etc.).

Honesty

Speaking the truth; presenting oneself in a genuine way; acting in a sincere way; being without pretense; taking responsibility for one's feelings and actions.

- Refrain from telling small, white lies to others, including to yourself.
- Evaluate your values and actions and see if they align. Commit to taking action to be in alignment where needed.
- If you misrepresent the truth, admit it and apologize right away.
- At the end of each day, identify something you did that was attempting to impress people, or to put on a show. Resolve not to do it again.
- If you do or say something not in accordance with your values, sincerely apologize and make a commitment to behave in accordance to your values going forward.

Hope

Expecting the best in the future and working to achieve it; believing that a good future can be achieved.

- Keep a journal, and every night, record a decision you made that day that impacted you positively.
- When you are in a bad situation, turn it around to see the optimistic side of it. You can almost always find some good in a situation, such as looking at the glass "half-full" instead of "half empty."
- Create a daily, realistic goal. Note your success at the end of the day and remind yourself that you can continue to create consistent, small victories each day.
- Collect quotes about hope. Print those which you find meaningful and display them where you can view them often.
- When you notice the negative self-talk of your inner critic, counter it with positive self-talk and uplifting thoughts from your inner coach.

Humility

Letting one's accomplishments speak for themselves; not regarding one-self as more special.

- Don't talk about yourself at all for a full day.
- Don't post anything about yourself on social media for a week. Spend that week only commenting positively on others' posts.
- Find a way in which someone you know has a talent different than yours. Show appreciation to that person.
- Look for ways to compliment others rather than seeking compliments for yourself.
- Find ways to include other people in projects you would normally excel in and share the credit.

Humor

Liking to laugh and tease; making others smile and laugh; seeing the lighter side of situations.

- Make a daily effort to make someone smile or laugh.
- Learn a joke and tell it to your friends.
- Watch something on TV or on a device that you find funny.
- When in a tense situation, look for the humor in it to lighten the mood.
- Learn a magic trick and perform it for your friends.

Judgment and Open-mindedness

Thinking things through and examining them from all sides; not jumping to conclusions; being able to change one's mind in light of evidence; weighing all evidence fairly.

- Go to a multi-cultural event.

- Advocate for and discuss an issue from the side opposite to your personal views.
- Hang out with someone who is different from you in some way.
- Go to a different spiritual or religious setting from your own belief system.
- Pick something you believe and make a list of other perspectives.

Kindness

Doing favors and good deeds for others; taking care of them.

- Leave a large tip.
- Do a random act of kindness every day. Make it anonymous if possible.
- Be a listening ear to a friend. Ask them how their day was and actually listen to the answer before telling them about your own day.
- Send a kind text to a different friend/family member/colleague each day for a week.
- Pitch in with your time and resources to help someone in need (e.g., friend, family member, colleague, stranger).

Leadership

Encouraging your group to achieve while maintaining good relations; organizing and completing group activities.

- If leading a group, treat everyone with respect and express appreciation for their contributions.
- Organize a study group, get together, or team project.
- Lead by example—practice aligning your values, words and your actions daily.
- Volunteer to lead a group if given the opportunity.

- Find something you are passionate about and join an organization/group/club related to that passion. Be willing to lead in any way you are asked.

Love

Valuing close relations with others, especially when sharing and caring are reciprocated.

- Tell your partner/sibling/parent/friend that you love them.
- Send a loved one a message to say that you were thinking about him/her.
- Give a loved one a big hug.
- Write a nice note where someone you love will find it sometime during the day. Do this in a new place, or for a new person, every day.
- To increase your self-compassion and self-love: write down your top 5 strengths and post them, or read the *Authentic Strengths* book or blog.

Love of Learning

Mastering new skills, topics and bodies of knowledge; related to the strength of curiosity but, also includes the tendency to add systematically to what one knows.

- Discover one new place where you live every day.
- Ask a question to learn something new from a colleague or friend.
- Daily, read a chapter of a book on a topic that you want to know more about.
- Google a new topic you are interested in and learn more about it.
- Watch a TED Talk or listen to a podcast about something you find intriguing but haven't found the time to learn about.

Perseverance

Finishing what one starts; persisting in a course of action in spite of obstacles; taking pleasure in completing tasks.

- Finish work ahead of time.
- Notice your inclination to procrastinate on a task that requires effort, and choose to complete the task.
- Plan ahead—use a calendar for projects and assignments.
- Set a STRONG Goal and stick to it.
- In the morning, make a list of things that you want to get done that day that could be put off by rationalizing delays. Make sure to get them done that day.

Perspective

Ability to provide wise counsel to others; having ways of looking at the world that make sense to oneself and to other people.

- Write down a new, meaningful quote each day.
- Consider teachings from wise leaders or wisdom literature before responding to a friend seeking advice.
- Think of the wisest person you know—note some of their strengths and try to incorporate them into your daily life.
- Look up inspiring people in history and learn their views on important issues of their day and/or find a significant quotation that they said.
- Reflect on your perspective on various topics and how to communicate your perspective in a way that makes sense to yourself and others.

Prudence

Being careful about one's choices; not taking undue risks; not saying or doing things that might later be regretted.

- During a conversation, think twice before saying anything. Weigh the probable effect of your words on others.
- Think about the motto "better safe than sorry" at least three times a day. Try to incorporate its meaning into your life.
- Before you decide to do something important, reflect on it for a moment and consider if you want to live with its consequences 1 hour, 1 day, or 1 year later.
- Always wear a seatbelt when traveling in a car, always wear a helmet when doing sports that recommend helmets, etc.
- Consider risks and rewards when making decisions.

Self-Regulation

Regulating what one feels and does; being disciplined; controlling one's appetites and emotions.

- Clean or organize your living space. Every day, pick up whatever mess you made during the day.
- Make a resolution to not gossip. When you feel the urge to talk about someone, remember your resolution and stop yourself before you talk.
- Exercise four days each week (if you don't already do this).
- In the evenings, make an agenda for the following day. Stick to that agenda.
- For one week, choose to eat only healthy food.

Social Intelligence

Being aware of the motives and feelings of other people and oneself; knowing how to adapt to social situations.

- Meet one new person each day by introducing yourself or interacting in some way.
- Go into a new social situation and try to participate.

- Develop your self-awareness by reflecting on what motivates your behavior.
- Whenever you talk with someone, seek to understand how they see the world differently than you.
- When you encounter someone eating alone or doing an activity alone, be friendly and invite them into your group.

Spirituality

Believing in a higher purpose and meaning of the universe; knowing where one fits within the larger scheme; having beliefs about the meaning of life that shape conduct and provide comfort.

- For five minutes a day, relax and think about the purpose of life, and where you fit in.
- Reflect on the things you can do to improve the world or your community and make a list that you will work to accomplish.
- Explore different religions in a respectful manner. You can do this by going to a library, looking on the Internet, or asking your friends about their religions.
- Invest in a book of affirmations or optimistic quotes. Read a few every day.
- Spend a few minutes a day in mindfulness, meditation or prayer.

Teamwork

Working well as a member of a group or team; being loyal to the group; doing one's share.

- Volunteer.
- Take on added responsibility within an organization you are already a part of.
- Pick up litter that you see on the ground.

- Clean an area of your home which is used by all.
- Organize a get together for a group of your friends, family or colleagues.
- Do your share in a group/team project.

Zest

Approaching life with excitement and energy; not doing things halfway or halfheartedly; living life as an adventure; feeling alive and activated.

- Go out of your way to become more involved and enthusiastic in a cause you support.
- Join a new club, sports team, or group you are excited about.
- Do something because you want to, not because you feel obligated to do it.
- Get a good night's sleep and eat healthfully to give yourself more energy during the day.
- Do something physically vigorous during the day.

Strengths-Based Mindfulness Practices

A powerful way to boost your resilience is to use strengths-based mindfulness practices. A mindfulness practice has been defined as: "a way of paying attention...in a particular way: on purpose, in the present moment, and nonjudgmentally...Bringing one's complete attention to the present experience on a moment-to-moment basis."[127]

Research has shown the benefit of infusing character strengths with mindfulness and meditation. Dr. Ryan Niemiec asserts: *"There is a powerful, albeit hypothetical, synergy between character strengths and approaches to mindful living, such as mindful eating, driving, working, walking, speaking, and listening, in which each mutually enhances the other and creates opportunities for personal transformation."*[128] You will be introduced to simple mindfulness practices and meditations through-out this book, such as the one below.

I call the mindfulness practice you are about to do an "embodied positive psychology practice" because it reconnects you with your body and your breath, deepening what you are learning in this book as you relax.

Researcher Barbara Fredrickson describes the embodiment of positive psychology: *"For just as neuroscientific studies show that positive emotions open your perceptual awareness, kinematic studies ... show that they also open your torso, literally expanding the (rib) cage in which your heart sits. When your mind and body are infused with good feelings, those feelings lift and expand your chest, a subtle nonverbal gesture that makes you more inviting to others, more open for connection."*[129]

And Megan McDonough asserts: *"Philosophers, psychologists, and even artificial-intelligence researchers who study the embodied mind contend that the body shapes cognition. Or, to put it more simply, the body shapes what we think and how we feel—and, by extension, how we act."*[130]

The following mindfulness practice is helpful for reframing failure. Find a quiet place where you will not be disturbed to simply sit and experience the uplifting words and calming breathing techniques below, letting them lift your mood and spark your hope:

Morning Positivity: 5 minutes (also available on audio)

Today, as the sun rises, it glows with endless possibilities.
Breathing in, I become aware of my breath and find my center.
Breathing out, I relax my body into the present moment.
Breathing in, I embrace this opportunity to begin anew.
Breathing out, I let go of the past, releasing fully.

I fill myself with unlimited potential, feeling my lungs expand.
As I breathe mindfully, I ease into my authenticity.

I see myself contributing in meaningful ways.
I envision my positive interactions with others.

Using all of my senses, I literally experience the real me.
Focusing on the positive, what will I do, what will I say, how will I feel?
I linger in these elevated emotions, feeling gratitude for a new day.

I place my hand on my heart and notice it expand.
I am reborn in this day—my authentic self has emerged.
It is time to live my best life, sharing my strengths with others.
My highest and best self now steps into the world.

Evening Positivity: 5 minutes

Tonight, as the sun softly sets, it invites me to rest and relax.

Breathing in, I settle into my body.

Breathing out, I release all stress, letting go.

Breathing in, I acknowledge all that I am grateful for today.

Breathing out, I send my thanks back to the world.

Breathing mindfully, I open my heart to receive.

I recall the times I connected to my authenticity today.

And the ease I felt being genuine using my strengths.

I set an intention for restful, peaceful sleep.

I am capable, resourceful and whole.

I am compassionate to myself and others.

I am in harmonious, uplifting relationships.

I am the creator of my life and my own decisions.

CHAPTER 5

SURRENDERING TO FREEDOM: MINDFULNESS AND SELF-COMPASSION

"If there is truly nothing that you can do about the here and now, surrender to it. Surrender is not weakness, there is great strength in it."[131]

—*Eckhart Tolle*

It was a sunny day as Diane drove to do her customary banking. She had to do a double take when she saw $500.00 was missing from her account. She was informed that someone had taken it from the ATM at her bank. They take photos of people when they withdraw money, so the bank researched and found the photo of the thief. It was Diane's son.

Diane's jewelry disappeared that same day. She went to a local pawn shop and sure enough, her jewelry was there. The store manager knew her son and told her that he had pawned the jewelry. The manager quietly whispered that he suspected Diane's son, a talented young construction worker with a beautiful family, was addicted to opioids. Diane felt as if she was living a surreal nightmare, and she left the pawn shop dazed.

As the reality sunk in, she experienced a myriad of emotions—anger, hurt, disappointment, fear, despair—she felt crushed. She confronted her son and they both cried. He wrote her a letter that night, admitting that he needed help and that he wanted to get well.

The coming months of recovery were gut wrenching. Diane's son lost his job, his marriage and his family. Standing in line to apply for a recovery program in their rural town, another person in recovery asked, "Did you start with Vicodin? I'll bet everyone in this line started with Vicodin after an injury working in construction." Her son nodded in solemn agreement.

Fast forward two years—not only did Diane's son survive, he is working on his credential to teach high school, has a good paying job, a nice home, and is remarried. Diane now has five lovely grandchildren from his blended family.

In her words, *"I attribute my son's recovery success to developing the character strengths of love, bravery, perseverance, hope, spirituality and love of learning. He is now very involved with his family, and in his church playing drums, singing and studying scriptures. Each member of our family has learned self-compassion in the process.*

I believe that my husband and I contributed to our, and our son's resiliency, because we truly 'surrendered' to the reality of the situation, enabling us to do the work of healing. Our character strengths of honesty, hope, forgiveness, love and gratitude were and remain our lifeline. Although this took a heavy toll on our family, in the end, we surrendered to a higher consciousness—the deep gratitude that our son survived and is in recovery."

Self-Compassion Builds Resilience

"Interestingly, the one thing perfectionists are decidedly not perfect at, research shows, is self-compassion."[132]

—*Dr. Thomas Greenspon*

When we deal honestly with our negative emotions, we can extend genuine compassion to ourselves. This enables us to feel cared for, accepted and secure. We are then able to shift our focus to our strengths and employ them in finding solutions. The self-produced feelings of well-being and safety deactivate the body's threat system, calming down the amygdala and mitigating the release of stress chemicals—increasing the production of positive chemicals as a counterbalance.[133]

Positive psychologists Kristin Neff's and Christopher Germer's research on self-compassion[134] is showing that a healthy way to manage unavoidable negative emotions is to acknowledge them while practicing self-soothing techniques. This can soften negative emotions, eventually losing their debilitating grip. Neff and Germer identify three components of self-compassion:

The first component is "self-kindness," which entails being kind and understanding toward ourselves when we suffer, fail or feel inadequate, rather than ignoring our pain or flagellating ourselves with self-criticism.

The second is "common humanity," which is recognizing we are all human, none of us is perfect, and everyone experiences loss or failure at some time in his or her life. Our frustration with not having things exactly as we want is often accompanied by an irrational sense of isolation—as if we are the only person suffering or making mistakes. This is simply not so and reminding oneself of this can be a source of comfort.

And the third component is "mindfulness." Self-compassion requires taking a balanced, mindful approach to our negative emotions so that our feelings are neither suppressed nor exaggerated.[135]

Mindfully Experiencing Negative Emotions

"Gradually, study after mind body study, carried out with the most careful scientific protocols, produced incontrovertible evidence that the mind can indeed influence—and heal—the body."[136]

—*Herbert Benson, MD*

As we've learned thus far, everyone experiences pain—thus negative emotions are an unavoidable part of life. Emotion literally means "energy in motion." Emotions are often experienced like a wave, they can be powerful as they build and crest, but they typically don't stay at their height, they eventually flow back to normal. When we experience negative emotions, we may not know how to deal with them, stuffing them (like damming a river). In these situations, they can become stagnant and toxic, and the emotion levels, like water levels behind a dam, can remain high.

A key to managing negative emotions is to first mindfully observe them. Mindfulness (the practice of being aware of your body, mind and feelings[137]) teaches us to become the "watcher" of the present moment, fully engaged in our lives without stuffing, judging, shaming, hiding from, lashing out at, or resisting the uncomfortable moment that has presented itself. This shifts us quickly from the primal, fear-focused part of our brain to the more evolved, higher brain, where the solutions can be created. Because fear robs us of essential energy and clarity to solve our challenges, mindfulness can help us find our center—the place where our strengths reside, which is energizing and promotes resilience.

Being mindful leads to truthful, authentic living. It is the first step in transforming our negative emotions and creating a healthier outlook. When we deal honestly with our emotions, we can extend compassion to ourselves. We can learn to experience and express our feelings in an emotionally intelligent way that serves us, without harming ourselves or our important relationships.

Mindfully experiencing a negative emotion does not mean we don't prefer, hope for, or work toward something better. It is not a passive approach to life. Rather, being mindful allows us to experience hard moments such as conflict, loss, stress or failure—to learn and grow from these experiences—rendering them less acute and more manageable. And more, it helps us work through our afflictions while centered in our highest self, so that we begin to experience the whole of life more peacefully. As Dr. Ryan Niemiec has said:

> *"To merge character strengths and mindfulness is to bring a deep awareness to our best qualities and to use these abilities to improve our awareness of all aspects of our lives. Mindfulness and character strengths deepen one another. To practice using character strengths with mindfulness is to be intentional and conscious about noticing and deploying your best qualities."*[138]

Connecting to Emotions

Allow

There is no controlling life.
Try corralling a lightning bolt,
containing a tornado. Dam a
stream, and it will create a new
channel. Resist, and the tide
will sweep you off your feet.
Allow, and grace will carry
you to higher ground. The only
safety lies in letting it all in —
the wild with the weak; fear,
fantasies, failures and success.
When loss rips off the doors of
the heart, or sadness veils your
vision with despair, practice
becomes simply bearing the truth.
In the choice to let go of your
known way of being, the whole
world is revealed to your new eyes.

by Danna Faulds
Used with permission, from her book Go In and In[139]

A monk once wrote the following equation: Pain x Resistance = Suffering.[140] The more we resist negative emotions by assaulting ourselves with all the "should haves," "could haves," or "would haves" in a situation, the more we suffer. Does this sound familiar? "I should have known better." "I could have made a better choice." "If she hadn't pushed my buttons I would have responded differently."

In contrast, connecting to and objectively observing our negative emotions enables us to process them, deflating much of the power they exert. Practicing mindfulness in this way of "connecting" to the present reality, cultivates a deeper awareness of ourselves, learning to better self-regulate. This approach strengthens our relationship with self and others, ultimately making us more effective and content.

Recall the STRONG Filter that we learned previously—it helps us filter between authentic and debilitating thoughts and emotions. Some negative emotions are authentic and even healthy for personal growth. It is natural to mourn the loss of someone dear to you, to feel guilt when you do something you know is wrong, or disappointed when things don't go your way. When we suppress authentic negative emotions, they can grow stronger beneath the cover we have placed, and eventually surface in other parts of our lives.

The ancient teaching of the Two Arrows helps us to avoid the "second arrow" of extended suffering, falling prey to rumination, bitterness, or despair, what I call the "debilitating" negative emotions.[141] It is like being shot with an arrow, and right afterwards being shot with a second and more debilitating one. Thus, we can see the distinction between pain on the one hand, and our self-imposed suffering in response to the pain, on the other. How we experience pain can agonize and debilitate us, like the second, more lethal arrow.

In our instant gratification culture, perceiving this distinction between the two arrows has become blurred because as soon as we feel discomfort, we tend to reach for some external fix (food, shopping, alcohol or drugs, technology, etc.) to alleviate the discomfort. There are many ways that we avoid the present moment. These may include denying, rationalizing, or trying to push our feelings into the background. Or we may try to handle our pain by projecting onto others, getting lost in self-pity, torturing ourselves with guilt, and so on. Once we become familiar with our evasions, we can become more intimate with the deeper feelings we seek to evade—like fear, despair, anger and shame. To acknowledge these painful emotions requires courage and determination, but it is the first step to transforming them. Transformation occurs after we first embrace our situation as it is.

Self-Care

"Self-care is how you take your power back."

—*Lala Delia*[142]

An example of self-care comes from a woman who shared with me a breakthrough experience she had in dealing with recurring negative emotions. She had accompanied her teenage daughter on a performing tour. Her adolescent memories of being the lonely outcast resurfaced when several chaperones on the trip turned out to be a tight-knit group who had known each other for years. Exacerbating her insecurity was her desire for her daughter to feel proud of her. Throughout the entire trip, she felt like she just didn't fit in as she repeatedly failed to break into the group. *"It felt just like high school all over again,"* she told me later.

On the ride home, she was seated next to one of the moms she had tried to befriend. *"At last, a chance to connect,"* she thought. At that exact moment, the woman excused herself and moved up to an empty seat in the midst of a group of moms several rows ahead.

Left alone in a row, she struggled not to take it personally and buried herself in her book. As she listened to the other women laugh and

136

share stories, she physically felt her heart close and harden defensively. *"Just let yourself feel your loneliness"* she heard from within. She felt the piercing ache of exclusion, followed by compassion for herself, which gradually transformed into self-care and self-love, filling her with peace.

After savoring the feeling, she felt a confidence inspiring her to join the group and was welcomed into the conversation. Relating the story, she said, *"I didn't stuff my emotions like I had many times before. I allowed myself to feel their full depth, and I experienced resolution. I had mourned, and I was comforted."*

This time she did not run away from what she was feeling, drowning the discomfort in distraction. She challenged herself to be present in the moment, to face her fear of exclusion, experiencing it so that she could ultimately transcend it. By doing so, in that instance she overcame a pattern of thinking that had held her hostage for years.

The "Undoing" Effect of Positive Emotions

Have you ever been overcome by a negative emotion, only to be surprised at how quickly your negative emotion dissipates when a genuine positive emotion becomes the new focus? Maybe it was an inspiring quote you stumbled across that helps you to see your situation in an empowering new light, an unexpected phone call from a loved one that opens your heart, your favorite song playing on the radio that stirs inspiration within? How did that happen? What if you could learn to "undo" negative emotions when needed?

Research on the "undoing effect" of positive emotions suggests that people can improve their well-being by evoking positive emotions at opportune moments to cope with negative emotions.[143] Scientists tested this undoing effect by first inducing a negative emotion in study participants by assigning a time-pressured speech—with just a few minutes to prepare. They were led to believe that their speech would be videotaped and evaluated by their peers. This speech task induced anxiety along with increases in heart rate, peripheral vasoconstriction, and blood pressure. Then the scientists randomly assigned participants to view one of four films. Two films elicited mild positive emotions (joy and contentment), a third served as a neutral control condition and a fourth elicited sadness. In three independent samples, participants who watched the two positive emotion films exhibited faster cardiovascular recovery than did those in the neutral control condition. Participants in the sadness condition exhibited the most delayed recovery.[144]

Inducing a positive emotion can loosen the hold that a negative emotion has gained on a person's mind and body. For example, if you are feeling rejected, you can cultivate the emotions (and character strengths) of gratitude and hope as you intentionally focus on other positive aspects of your life. This helps you learn to self-regulate and to bring your best self to the forefront—strengthening your emotional health, your relationships with others—rendering you more productive and fulfilled. As Barbara Fredrickson's research on the undoing effects of positive emotions has shown, *"broadened mindsets carry indirect and long-term adaptive benefits because broadening builds enduring personal resources, which function as reserves to be drawn on later to manage future threats."*[145] Thus positive emotions not only have an undoing effect on negative emotions, but also broaden and build our personal resources—providing us with a reservoir of strength to draw from—when subsequent challenges arise.

Creating What You Really Want

I will never forget the time I was invited to teach refugees and aid workers in Africa with the International Rescue Committee. I did a creativity exercise with this group that I had done countless times before in my workshops with diverse cultures, but this time I was surprised with the results.

I asked the participants to look at a paper cup placed in front of them, and to work with one other person to identify as many creative uses for that paper cup that they could think of. Then I timed them for 90 seconds.

I was amazed to witness an explosion of resourceful uses for the paper cup that I have never witnessed elsewhere after decades of doing this exercise. Each dyad doing the exercise literally came alive with energy! They examined the cup from all possible angles, looking at how it diffused light by holding it up to a light bulb, throwing the cup in the air or rolling it to carefully observe its movement qualities, attaching it to other items in the room, drawing on it, cutting it up and creatively using its parts for dozens of surprising purposes, and even placing the cup on their heads, etc. They doubled the highest number of creative uses I had ever observed in any other country!

At the conclusion of the exercise, the entire group reflected on what they had just experienced. They explained that when given the opportunity, materials or tools, they were eager and passionate to improve the quality of their lives—leveraging their creativity and their resourcefulness. One of them then showed me how he had repurposed a used plastic liter soda bottle into sandals by cutting holes into the halved soda bottles and threading the rope through the holes. Another person displayed how she had collected rubber bands and discarded pieces of cloth, then carefully fashioned them into a functional soccer ball by tightly wrapping the cloth and binding it neatly with the rubber bands. Because they had very little, they literally lived from a place of heightened awareness and gratitude for all that they had.

What if we followed their lead—opening our minds and hearts to see our challenging situations with fresh eyes so that we could create a positive new perspective? We might be surprised to notice resources and strengths we hadn't noticed before. The solutions to our difficulties could be hiding in plain view if we could only shift our perspective.

Let's next look at how to use the principles we've just explored of "connecting," "caring for self" and "creating what we want" in a simplified tool to address our negative emotions.

Connect-Care-Create Tool

I have synthesized evidence-based techniques and research findings to manage negative emotions into an easy to remember, three-step tool below, that I call: "Connect-Care-Create." This tool can help you process common negative emotions associated with disappointments, losses or failures. (*Some negative emotions, like those rooted in mental health issues, substance abuse, abusive environments, etc., require the help of medical professionals or therapists. Please seek appropriate help.*)

- First, because your brain tends to exaggerate an event and get stuck in an endless cycle of rumination, this process begins with focusing on your body as you connect to the emotion, which helps stop the cycle by giving your brain something new to focus on.
- Second, it prompts you toward self-care and self-compassion by helping you accept that negative emotions are a part of life, recognizing that you are not being "singled out."
- Third, this process helps you transform a negative emotion by using your creativity/resourcefulness and your character strengths as a lens to address the issue, thus creating a new positive emotion/perspective to undo the effect of the negative emotion.

In practicing this tool, people report a sense of relief, liberation, and a freedom from rumination that opens them to real growth. The most encouraging part of this approach is that we can learn to productively process negative emotions. After all, you are the one person in your life that is always around when you are feeling negative emotions, so why not learn to deliver an antidote? Identify a negative emotion that you feel safe exploring at this time and let's take a few minutes to experience this tool as follows...

Connect — Find a quiet place where you can feel relaxed and will be uninterrupted. Get into a comfortable seated position and take a few calming breaths. Become mindful of a negative emotion you are feeling or have felt in the past that you feel safe connecting to now. Notice all aspects of the emotion without judging it, shaming it, or avoiding it. Just let yourself observe it objectively, in a gentle, self-compassionate way. Name the emotion without blaming anyone or anything, just try to identify the emotion. For example, if you're feeling anxious where in your body do you feel the emotion most (your stomach, shoulders, heart, back, lungs, etc.)?

Care — Practice self-care. Relax the area where you are holding the negative emotion (your stomach, shoulders, heart, back, lungs, etc.) and with each breath imagine it dissolving like an ice cube in warm water. Send yourself compassion, reminding yourself that everyone experiences difficulty, loss, mistakes and failure. Reassure yourself that all will be well, that you will give yourself the resources and support you need to get through this experience, taking the steps to better the situation.

Create — Leverage your creativity and resourcefulness as you identify a character strength(s) to help you "undo" this negative emotion, creating a positive shift in perspective so that you can learn and grow from this experience. What new positive emotions are you noticing now...hope, forgiveness, love, perspective, kindness, self-regulation? Observe the negative emotion gradually dissipate and lose its power over you, as new positive emotions are created in its place. Take time to linger in this positive new emotion and let it soak into your awareness, to build your resilience going forward.[146] [147] (It's helpful to identify a positive ritual you will do to celebrate the emancipating feeling of releasing the negative emotion, such as taking a walk in nature or a favorite physical activity, listening to uplifting music, reading something inspiring, writing down the emotion then throwing it away, celebrating with someone you trust, etc.—whatever tends to genuinely lift your spirit.)

Positivity Journal STRONG Questions

- How did that experience go for you? What did you learn?
- Which of your strengths help you increase your self-compassion and self-care?
- Which of your strengths help you "undo" negative emotions, shifting your focus to create a positive new perspective?
- How will you apply your insights next time you experience negative thoughts and emotions?

Mindfully Savor the Present

"If you are depressed, you are living in the past.
If you are anxious, you are living in the future.
If you are at peace, you are living in the present."

—Unknown

This quote, often attributed to Lao Tzu but of unknown origin, sums up the general ideas of mindfulness and self-compassion very well. Mindfulness and self-compassion have gained momentum during the last decade. These practices have been researched extensively and show many benefits for increasing well-being, including improving immune function, increasing gray matter density in the brain, and increasing positive emotions while decreasing negative emotions.

There is some awareness, however, that should be applied when using mindfulness techniques, as Ed Halliwell cautions in an article in *Mindful* magazine: *"If you experience depressive episodes, you'll need to pay close attention to the types and doses of mindfulness practice you use and consider seeking the aid of a therapist or psychiatrist who can assess your unique needs."*[148]

If you feel comfortable to doing so, spend the next five minutes using your senses to pay attention to the present moment. Really see, hear, and feel the present moment. Look around the room you are in—you may find many things you have never noticed before. Or, close your eyes, and try to notice things you typically don't pay attention to. Maybe it's the sound of the wind, or footsteps, or the rain, or birds outside.

Positivity Journal

Choose an activity from the list below, or come up with your own activity to focus you on the present moment. Then write in your journal about what you noticed during that mindful state that was interesting, beautiful, motivating or uplifting to you.

1. Focus on restorative breathing (this simple technique can be found online).
2. Enjoy a snack or meal while mindfully eating. Plan on some extra time to eat, and slow down to appreciate each sensation. Chew slowly and deliberately, paying close attention to the texture/taste.
3. Engage in Progressive Muscle Relaxation (This simple technique can be found online).
4. Try Mantra Meditation (This simple technique can be found online).

5. Practice Loving Kindness Meditation.[149] Bring attention to your breath, then turn your attention to yourself, focusing on loving, forgiving, and kind thoughts. Visualize what you like about yourself. Move your attention to a close friend or family member. Send loving thoughts to them. If time permits, you can then focus on humanity at large. Close with a positive affirmation, such as: "May all beings be peaceful, happy and free."

6. Choose an activity you do regularly, like a household chore, and make it a mindful pursuit.

7. Use a reminder to center yourself such as making your phone or laptop background a calming scene. Each time you notice this reminder, stop and take a moment to bring yourself to the present. Quiet your mind, bring your attention to your breath and stay there for a minute or so.

8. Use your wait time for a bus or a meeting to start. Practice a mini version of an exercise above.

9. Focus on your feet. While you walk around your home, school or office, make your movement mindful by noticing the sensation of your feet moving against the ground.

Self-Compassion is Surrendering to Freedom

My friend Jane sent me this moving story, illustrating her surrender and ongoing practice of self-compassion raising a child with a disability:

"The nurse had just brought my newborn baby back from the nursery where she had been under lights to treat jaundice. I held the tiny bundle in my arms and looked down at my daughter's sweet face. She had a little nose and perfect mouth with dainty princess lips. She was beautiful, and I was soaking her in. 'Your daughter has some features that could be a concern.' The words shattered my moment of new mom

bliss. Suddenly, the pure joy I felt was pierced by confusion then intense fear. In an instant, what I hadn't seen before was painfully clear. My daughter had Down syndrome.

When you are a young, healthy, first-time mom who gives birth to a child with Down syndrome, suddenly life doesn't feel as safe or as simple. It was the moment I first realized that joy and pain are not far apart. I felt a new vulnerability and an overwhelming fear that I was totally unprepared to be her mother. That's when my husband whispered to me that our baby girl 'had stolen his heart.'

From that moment on I have followed his lead, finding the good in the bad. Instead of focusing on my fears, I look for moments of love, hope and a little humor when life gets hard. The same attributes I've come to discover are among my top character strengths. Looking back I see that my love for my daughter gave me the courage to put her on a giant, yellow school bus at age three and send her across town to a pre-school for special needs children. Years later I stood back and watched as she learned to navigate city buses and commuter trains on her own, so she could become independent. And that humor I mentioned helps diffuse moments of frustration. Like when my daughter cleans the house and I can't find anything. Not car keys. Not my purse. Not important papers. But hey, at least my kitchen is spotless. And hold onto hope because of my daughter, too. She is full of more love, laughter and happiness than I thought possible and she never doubts herself or her place in this world. It is clear to me now that raising a daughter with a disability has helped me tap into my character strengths and use them to deal with life's challenges.

I remember wishing early on that my daughter's disability wasn't so easy to see. But the physical features I worried would make her look different and single her out, tend to trigger kindness and compassion from strangers. And when your child's first steps, first words, first everything is a struggle, her successes are sweeter, too. Looking for a bright side does not protect me or my daughter from heartache, but it helps me make sense of things I can't change, and this surrender brings me freedom.

While I would do anything to make her life easier, I wouldn't change what happened. Twenty-six years later I continue to learn that life's most precious gifts are unexpected. Like the unconditional love from a child who has grown into a strong, beautiful young woman who is just like her dad and sees the good in everything and everyone."

Jane surrendered to freedom from regrets—a newfound freedom to live in the moment—with no guarantees, yet joyfully surpassing her expectations.

As you endeavor to increase your own self-compassion, you may want to take a few minutes to find a quiet, safe place to do the following mindfulness practice:

Self-Compassion: 8 minutes (also available on audio)

Find a quiet place where you won't be disturbed,
and get into a comfortable, relaxed position.
Connect to the present moment, relaxing fully
as you take a few deep, centering breaths.

Closing your eyes, set an intention
to practice self-compassion in this moment.

Now, calmly observe any negative emotion you are feeling.

Serenely notice all aspects of the emotion without judging,
shaming, or avoiding it.

Just let yourself observe it truthfully and objectively,
while being kind to yourself.

Name the emotion without blaming anyone or anything.

For example, if you are feeling anxious,
where in your body do you feel the sensation most?

Are you noticing it in your stomach, shoulders, back, neck, chest?

Care for yourself by relaxing the area where you have been
holding negative emotions.

Place your hand on the location with a healing intention, inhaling fully.

As you exhale, imagine releasing the emotion and see it dissolve
like an ice cube in warm water.

Continue inhaling and exhaling mindfully,
detaching from the emotion, letting it go.

Send yourself compassion, acknowledging everyone
experiences difficulty—it's part of being human.

Reassure yourself all will be well.
You will give yourself the support and self-care you need.

Identify a positive practice to release negative emotions such as...

Exercising, talking to someone you trust, listening to uplifting music,
reading, enjoying nature...

Now visualize doing this and the positive emotions it will evoke.

Create what you want for yourself in this moment.

Recognize your ability to respond to emotions in resourceful new ways.

Identify a character strength such as hope, perseverance, bravery,
forgiveness, love, gratitude...

That can help you transform negative emotions now and in the future.

Breathe in as you create a positive perspective,
expand your vision and embrace your growth.

What new emotions are you feeling now—
optimism, perspective, energy, abundance?

Notice the old emotion has dissipated and lost its power
as new positive emotions were created in its place.

Celebrate this new shift in perspective by treating yourself
to something enjoyable today.

Take a moment to recognize what gives you joy in life.

May you be happy, healthy, peaceful and free.

CHAPTER 6

AUTHENTIC MOTIVATION: THE TRANSFORMATIVE POWER OF THE WORDS "I AM"

"The words [I am] which you consistently use to define who you are and what you are capable of, are holy expressions... Teach your outer self to accept the unlimited power of your inner spirit and the things you place in your imagination can become true for you."[150]

—*Dr. Wayne Dyer*

A friend of mine who has struggled with weight-related health issues once told me, *"You overhear someone commenting that you have gained weight and then you say to yourself, 'I am fat. I am an out of control eater. I am unable to get healthy.'"*

As my friend pointed out, in that moment of saying "I am" he had just taken the next step into solidifying someone else's limited opinion of him. By saying "I am"—my friend had given that person's comment great power over himself. But now, with his newfound awareness, my friend was shedding the power of that old memory like someone sheds a smothering winter coat on a sunny day, and replacing it with affirming, new "I am" statements.

When we inadvertently use such powerful words as "I am" negatively in a sentence, we plant our feet in a disparaging reality, giving those negative thoughts and emotions legs. We must learn to observe our reactions to situations, instead of reinforcing beliefs that don't serve us. For example, when blindsided by someone else's comment, or our own inner critic language, we can stop for a moment and mindfully notice our sensitivity to such ideas. From this place we can access our higher brain which objectively sorts through potentially damaging self-concepts, using the tools we have learned thus far in this book. This can take the power away from the negative things we and others think, feel or say. Choose very carefully when you use definitive language such as "I am."

But why do the words "I am" carry such immense power? There is a universal sacredness in the words "I am." These words are central to wisdom literature from around the world. It doesn't matter if you resonate with a particular religious tradition, the important thing is to recognize that you have great power within, and to choose to align with it. This is where your own potential resides—the greatness within that elevates you to your highest self.

"I am" has no split with self. "I am" is present, here and now. "I am" goes beyond "I hope" "I will" "I plan to" "I want to." By understanding the immensity of these words in creating meaning (good or bad), we can see the link between our thoughts and words, and our own resulting life experiences.

Your Sacred Inner Life

"Those who have not found their true wealth, the radiant joy of being and the deep, unshakable peace that comes with it, are beggars, even if they have great material wealth. They are looking outside for scraps of pleasure or fulfillment, for validation, security, or love, while they have a treasure

within that not only includes all those things but is infinitely greater than anything the world can offer." [151]

—*Eckhart Tolle*

The Oxford dictionary defines the word "sacred" as something that is considered to be "holy"—something "very important" and to be treated with "great respect." These are empowering guidelines for how to use the words "I am" when referencing oneself.

Dr. Rick Hanson, neuropsychologist and author of *Hardwiring Happiness,* describes the importance of honoring the sacred in our lives:

> *"I think each one of us — whether theist, agnostic, or atheist — needs access to whatever it is, in one's heart of hearts, that feels most precious and most worthy of protection. Imagine a life in which nothing was sacred to you — or to anyone else. To me, such a life would be barren and gray."* [152]

Remember when I mentioned our "spiritual DNA" earlier in this book? Our character strengths are, in many respects, our sacred inner self—the highest expression of our humanness. A deep human need is to be understood and seen for our potential—our best intentions within. It's empowering to reconnect with our true nature—where we feel ease, peace, wholeness. In this reacquaintance to our inner highest attributes, we can enjoy a liberation of our authentic selves. This is why it's imperative that our language reflect who we really are. Consider for a moment the 24 character strengths, and you will recognize that which is highest and most noble within:

Gratitude, Creativity, Honesty, Love, Curiosity, Kindness, Fairness, Teamwork, Forgiveness, Leadership, Humility, Social Intelligence, Hope, Love of Learning, Perspective, Bravery, Perseverance, Humor,

Judgment/Open-Mindedness, Zest, Spirituality, Prudence, Self-Regulation, Appreciation of Beauty and Excellence.

Each of these strengths of character, those innately virtuous aspects of ourselves, are worthy of our great deference and safeguarding. This is the dignity and self-respect within each of us that cannot be taken away. As Mahatma Gandhi said, *"No one can take away our self-respect if we do not give it to them."*[153] It's encouraging to note that each time we use the words "I am" we have an opportunity to create our self-concept, yet again, in a way that best serves us.

Dr. Hanson goes on to explain the psychology of sacredness:

"Opening to what's sacred to you contains an implicit stand that there really are things that stand apart in their significance to you. If you're like me, you don't stay continually aware of what's most dear to you. But when you come back to it — maybe there is a re-minder, perhaps at the birth of a child, or at a wedding or a funeral, or walking deep in the woods — there's a sense of coming home, of 'yes,' of knowing that this really matters and deserves my honoring and protection and care."[154]

Words Create Worlds

"Language is central to our experience of being human, and the language we speak profoundly shapes the way we think, the way we see the world, the way we live our lives."[155]

—*Lera Boroditsky*

What inner and outer worlds have you created—what are the results you have sown through your thoughts and words, creating your self-concept over the years? Have you been influenced by limiting, or even toxic beliefs about yourself that have not served you? This can be illustrated by looking at common everyday tweets. Dr. Martin Seligman's research on how our language affects well-being is intriguing. Researchers reviewed language in tweets by categorizing 45,000 words in the English language into positive (i.e. great, grateful, interesting, discovered, fabulous) and negative (i.e. stupid, hate, various obscenities) tweets. Over 80 million tweets in 1,200 counties in the eastern United States were included in the study. More heart attacks occurred in the counties where more negative words were tweeted.[156]

Words create meaning in our lives, as has been shown by research in many disciplines, including the field of Appreciative Inquiry. In fact, the tagline for the Center for Appreciative Inquiry is "Words Create Worlds." This new field, associated with positive psychology, has been defined as a "co-evolutionary, co-operative search for the best in people, their organizations, and the relevant world around them."[157]

The good news is that you can make the shift to create the life experiences you want in your life, now and in the future. "I am hopeful." "I am grateful." "I am courageous." "I am lovable and loving. "I am perseverant." "I am forgiving of myself and others." "I am kind to myself and others." "I am honest and real." "I am creative." All of these are character strengths we can call upon to evoke our best self, our noble core

In 2013 I had the pleasure of interviewing the late Masaru Emoto on an hour-long Skype call. He is perhaps most well-known for having researched the effects of different words on water. In 2008, Emoto published his findings in the Journal of Scientific Exploration, and his books are widely circulated in over 45 languages, having sold millions of copies. During our discussion, Emoto explained his research and his findings—what he believed was evidence that human consciousness has an effect on the molecular structure of water.[158] He told me that he had come up with the idea to take photos of water crystals after the water was exposed to specific kinds of music or written words. Words such as 'thank you' or 'love' or 'gratitude' formed lovely symmetrical hexagons. But water that was exposed to negative words or phrases such as 'you fool' or 'war' produced ugly, misshapen crystals. As a result of much research, he had come to believe that water indeed has the capacity to memorize and transfer information.[159]

Considering that our bodies are predominantly made up of water,[160] it follows that sound and intention conveyed in words may have a profound effect on each of us and on our lives as well. The late Louise Hay had these words to say about Emoto's work, *"It's a perfect example of how our thoughts affect our bodies and our world. Say loving words to water and it smiles; be angry at water and it shrivels. Since we are mostly made up of water, can you imagine how our minds and bodies react to the thoughts and words we use?"*[161]

Quantum physics also draws correlations between thoughts, words, intentions, and how their energy affects us, and our well-being.[162] [163] As Dr. Joe Dispenza, researcher and author explains, *"If you're viewing your life from the same level of mind every day, anticipating a future based on your past, you are collapsing infinite fields of energy into the same patterns of information called your life. For example, if you wake up and you think, 'Where's my pain?' your familiar pain soon appears because you expected it to be there."*[164]

And one need not search far for timeless wisdom and insights showing connections between our language, intention, and the manifested world. Consider Native American leader, Chief Seattle Duwamish, who said, *"When you know who you are; when your mission is clear and you burn with the inner fire of unbreakable will; no cold can touch your heart; no deluge can dampen your purpose,"*[165] and also a contemporary Buddhist teaching, *"Words have the power to both destroy and*

heal. When words are both true and kind, they can change our world."¹⁶⁶
And the Bhagavad Gita points to the sacredness of the creative power of
the words "I am," "*I am the beginning, middle, and end of creation.*"¹⁶⁷
Many enduring philosophies the world over point to our language and
thought patterns as a creating force in our lives.

Sonic Healing

I had the good fortune of meeting Dr. Joan Borysenko and hearing her
thoughts on embodied positive psychology. Dr. Borysenko, a licensed
psychologist and instructor of medicine at Harvard Medical School, has
spent years in clinical research and co-founded the Harvard Mind Body
Clinic with Dr. Herbert Benson. I asked her about her work and what
energizes her most at this stage in her life. She came alive when she talked
about the mind-body-spirit connection to resilience.

Dr. Borysenko has posted many YouTube videos in which she describes the beneficial effects of different modalities, among them one
that she calls "sonic healing"—employing sound therapy through music, hymns and chanting. In her words, *"In every tradition there is some
kind of sacred music...and that's a gateway that brings people into an
altered state...and that's where I think meditation and music overlap...
you're present and you're in a reverie...something very special happens."*¹⁶⁸

On another occasion, I attended a sound healing lecture at Canyon
Ranch, one of the most respected wellness centers in the world. Canyon
Ranch has been at the forefront of expanding the concept of integrative
well-being by introducing a comprehensive professional approach, with
a staff that includes registered dieticians, board-certified physicians, exercise physiologists, licensed therapists and other highly skilled staff. They
understand the mental, emotional, physical and spiritual connection to
well-being, and host leaders in their fields from many countries, including sound healers.

So, what does sound, vibration, and energy have to do with resilience? The use of sound vibration through uplifting words and music to set positive intention for our lives has been used since ancient times—and carries on to this day. What are the words you choose to say to yourself and others, and what type of music do you choose to listen to? Do these choices build you and others up, or bring you and others down?

Anyone who has attended a yoga class has likely heard the "OM" chant. This Sanskrit sound is now commonplace throughout western culture. An explanation for the origins of the "OM" chant is: *"If at first there was nothing, the very first thing was a sound vibration, and from there everything sprang into existence and the material world was born."*[169] Likewise, we are constantly creating reality with our own words and the energy we put out, and with the energy we choose to surround ourselves with. As Nikola Tesla, inventor and visionary, once said, *"If you want to find the secrets of the universe, think in terms of energy, frequency and vibration."*[170] We are part of this universe Tesla described, and we are influenced by sound and energy.

My experiences have led me to not only choose my words carefully, but to also evaluate the messages, music and entertainment that I take in. I now try to immerse myself in sounds and energy that lift me and help create positive neural pathways. As we learned earlier, what fires together wires together—thus positive, lasting change involves creating the conditions for new resilient circuits to form—promoting our well-being.

Positivity Journal STRONG Questions
- What are your "I am" beliefs?
- What would you change in your beliefs to make them more positive and empowering?
- What do you consider sacred or precious to you?

- Which of your character strengths express the parts of your inner self that you most value?
- How would everything you think, do, and say change if you first considered what is sacred or precious to you?
- How is a knowledge of your highest self a refuge for you during life's storms?
- What one thing will you do differently to bring more positivity into your life?

Authentic Motivation

I've witnessed many breakthroughs when people come to understand the "why" behind their actions. It all comes down to belief systems and motivation. What are your "I am" beliefs? Are they empowering you with sustainable sources of intrinsic motivation, or are you motivated by unsustainable sources outside of yourself? Understanding this can be a game changer. Choosing "I am" strengths motivation will provide you with authentic, sustainable motivation that gets you the most effective results. It's less about what you do, and more about *why* you do what you do—your belief systems about yourself and the world.

So what drives you? To help you better understand what motivates your actions, I have developed the Authentic Motivation Grid below, inspired in part by the work of Dr. Paul Gilbert, and my friend, Liz Patterson, among other research.[171] This grid is a tool that helps people connect the dots from their motivation and corresponding actions to the results they are getting. As you develop an awareness of what has motivated your past and present behaviors, going forward you can intentionally choose to focus on the most productive motivation that will produce the best results for you.

The goal is to recognize when you are being motivated by your character strengths (the sustainable, upward spiral) vs. counterfeit motivation (the unsustainable, downward spiral). The three counterfeit motivations depicted on the model below are alarm, overachieve, and apathy. For example, the alarm quadrant is characterized by fear and stress; the overachieve quadrant is characterized by perfectionism, comparanoia and constantly needing to prove one's self; and the apathy quadrant is characterized by an utter lack of motivation such as languishing hopelessness, helplessness and avoidance. In sharp contrast, the strengths quadrant is a source of sustainable motivation because here you are tapping into your intrinsic motivation—you are connected to what you truly value—your strengths of character that enable you to bring your highest and best self forward. It is from this place that you are empowered to make your authentic contributions in all areas of your life, and to build the healthy and satisfying relationships that you most desire. As you review the Authentic Motivation Grid, ask yourself this question: Is your motivation getting you the results you want?

Authentic Motivation Grid

ALARM Motivated by Fear: External	STRENGTHS Motivated by Authenticity: Internal
• Threatened by Competition/Others • Blame/Critical • Fight/Flight/Freeze/Please • Pressure/Strain/Stress • Anxiety/Worry • Lack Trust in Relationships • Downward Spiral/Unsustainable	• Appreciate Strengths in Self/Others/Competitors • Confidence/Best Self • Autonomy/Transparency/Vulnerability • Creativity/Flow/Focus • Meaning/Purpose • Build Trust in Relationships • Upward Spiral/Sustainable
Result: Stress	**Result: Contribution**
OVER-ACHIEVE Motivated by Comparison: External	APATHY Not Motivated
• Diminish/Disempower Others • Perfectionism/Comparanoia • Workaholic/Ego-Driven • Distraction/Overwhelm • Unprincipled Competitor • Guarded/Calculating in Relationships • Downward Spiral/Unsustainable	• Diminished by Others • Hopeless/Helpless • Exhaustion/Burnout/Check Out • Apathy/Don't See or Seek Solutions • Insecurity/Shame/Paralyzed by Competition • No Energy in Relationships • Downward Spiral/Unsustainable
Result: Proving Self	**Result: Avoidance**

Authentic Motivation Grid, ©2014-2020, Authentic Strengths Advantage, LLC. All rights reserved.

Everyday Examples of Motivation

Let's now take a good look at the Authentic Motivation Grid and consider what will consistently motivate you to reach your highest "I am" potential, and also notice what may have gotten in the way for you in the past. Below are some real-life examples of how any of these quadrants might surface in our lives...

If you are motivated by "alarm," the equivalent of fear, you may only do tasks or projects because you worry about a bad review or negative feedback. For example, you may procrastinate until you fear that the deadline is on the horizon, then go into stress mode to get it done. Over time you may get burned out by this type of fear-based motivation. The result is chronic stress. This is not sustainable.

If you often compare yourself to others, then you are likely spending time in the "over-achieve" quadrant. This is where perfectionism, or what I call the "comparanoia mentality" plays out. An example of how this can show up in your life is that you may only give your best efforts to a task in order to "outdo" another person, or group, that you tend to compare yourself with. Over time, you may feel discouraged that your efforts/projects/work are not "perfect" or "better than others." This pressure to constantly over-achieve will likely drain you. The result is that you carry the self-imposed, heavy burden of constantly needing to "prove yourself" again and again. This is not sustainable.

If you are continuously living your life in the previous two "alarm" or "over-achieve" quadrants, you may begin to feel "burned out." You may find yourself listless and "checking out" of opportunities or obligations when they present themselves. Over time, this can take a toll on your future goals, and on your relationships. The result is avoidance—of school, of work, of relationships, or of life in general. Yet again, this is not sustainable.

Let's now look at the "strengths" quadrant. Here you are motivated by your own authenticity, your own unique character strengths expression. If you are using your top strengths consistently, you are probably experiencing satisfaction from being your best self. You find ways to infuse your authentic strengths into your tasks, work, projects, relationships—and this is likely very motivating for you. This is the *sustainable* upward spiral, because your motivation is intrinsic—it comes from inside of you!

Live as if Life Happens *for* You, Not *to* You

There are many stories of people who tap into this sustainable source of intrinsic motivation. It's an affirming approach to life—living life as if it happens *for* you, not *to* you.

The breakthrough phrase of "life happens for me, not to me" is gaining traction around the world, as it flips a switch in the thinking of countless people. From self-help sites to world-class athletes, to Tony Robbins, search this phrase and you will find dozens of articles. Why is this resonating broadly with so many? Take for instance the story of Tony Robbins and his mother, written and posted on his website by Tony Robbins' staff:

> *"As he's shared, she was violently abusive to him. But she also loved him dearly. If he's going to blame her for the pain and suffering she caused, then he also must blame her for the beauty in his life. He blames her for the wonderful wife he has. He blames her for his capacity to feel and to care. He blames her for his insatiable hunger to end suffering for any human he can. If she had been the mother he had wanted, he wouldn't be the man that he is today."* [172]

People who espouse this outlook have learned to push aside their fear by seeking the help that they need to heal and to move forward.

They choose their "I am" statements intentionally, living with the conviction that life will work better if they are optimistic and engage in creating their future. They have learned how to call forth strengths such as hope, perseverance, creativity and bravery—to mention a few. When asked what was instrumental in accomplishing the seemingly impossible goal of eight gold medals at the 2008 Olympics, Michael Phelps responded that he only allowed in positive thoughts and reframed negative feedback from naysayers into fuel for his accomplishment. He taped articles to his locker about how it would be impossible for him to win eight gold medals and used them for inspiration to energize him to do something new and unthinkable.[173] No one can say he didn't practice to get his body in shape for the challenges of the Olympics. But, equally as important, he visualized himself achieving those eight gold medals. Make it your goal to harness the power of life happening *for* you, not *to* you, by visualizing how you want your life to be! How could you use the motivating effect of your strengths to create the conditions for life to happen *for* you?

Where You Look is Where You'll Go

Visualization is key to living life "as if it happens for you." My friend Marissa, an avid mountain biker, shared an interesting insight with me. She noticed that the more she feared hitting a rock while riding her bike, the more she focused on the rocks, and the more she hit the rocks! She decided one day to change her focus and to look for the smooth paths, instead of watching for the rocks. She found her ride was much smoother. She literally went where she looked! Marissa was on to something that many great athletes have long discovered—the power of focus and visualization.

One such athlete is Noelle Pikus-Pace, who won the silver in the skeleton event in the 2014 Winter Olympics. Noelle lives not far from my home and I have watched her rebound from devastating injuries over the years, before she finally achieved her Olympic dream. Careening down an unforgiving track, head-first at 78 miles per hour, is not for the faint of heart. When Noelle was asked what makes the most difference in a successful ride, she said, "It's what direction you are facing. You go where you look."[174] That quote made me smile, because that simple statement is true in building resilience. What we set our sights and our hearts on becomes the trajectory for our lives.

There's a popular saying I love to use as a learning tool: *what we choose to focus on grows.* What if we applied this principle of focus to the powerful words "I am"? We can choose to focus on what's best in ourselves and in our lives (our strengths), and start seeing strengths in others as well, and that new focus will grow and become our new life path. Conversely, we can choose to focus on what's wrong with ourselves and our lives and that list will grow as we are myopically transfixed on all of our own imperfections and on the faults of others. *So, where do you want to go in your life?*

Visualization Promotes Resilience

We add fuel to our strengths focus with the process of visualization—a mental rehearsal that has been successfully used by world-class athletes to invoke vivid, extremely detailed mental simulations of their goals from start to finish.[175] Visualization gained popularity when the Soviets made visualization their competitive advantage in sports in the 1970s.[176] World champion golfer Jack Nicklaus once said, "I never hit a shot, not even in practice, without having a very sharp, in-focus picture of it in my head."[177]

Here's an easy to try example of visualization: visualize yourself placing a lemon wedge in your mouth, biting into it and drinking the juice from it. Did you pucker, did your salivary glands go into full gear, did you tense up, even though it was just an imaginary experience? That is a physical example of the power of visualization.

Studies on the brain are revealing that thoughts can produce similar mental and physical processes as actions. Scientists are learning that mental imagery affects our motor control, perception, attention, planning, and memory.[178] Therefore, real performance training occurs in the brain during visualization. We are learning that mental simulations can increase motivation, confidence, and enhanced performance.[179]

I have found that one of the most important behaviors that contributes to success is getting crystal clear on what we really want to create in our lives. Visualize what would improve your life and the lives of others—then visualize using your strengths to create those outcomes. Essential to this visualization process is evoking and experiencing the positive emotions you would feel with the desired outcome. I encourage you to linger in the positive emotions this creates for you—savoring and internalizing the new emotional state.[180][181] Once you practice these new skills of focus and visualization, you can keep your eye on the "good life" you are creating for yourself."

STRONG Visualization Exercise

Step 1: Visualize yourself successfully using a character strength(s) best suited to a challenging situation. For example, imagine yourself using hope and bravery (courage) to bounce back after a setback. (It's helpful to review your character strengths report and choose a strength(s) to focus on here.)

Step 2: Invoke a clear mental picture utilizing as many of your senses as possible. Visualize your environment, including sights, sounds and smells, who will be there, what you are wearing, etc. You can combine this visualization with self-talk, such as, "I am hopeful and brave as I face each new day." Linger in the positive emotions this creates for you.

Step 3: Practice this visualization at least once each day. A powerful time to visualize is during exercise, upon arising in the morning or going to bed at night, or any time you are in an environment conducive to focus. (By the way, if you visualize before you go to bed at night, your body and your subconscious mind marinate in those thoughts throughout your sleep.)

Whole Life Well-being

"We are embedding health and well-being at the heart of our business strategy because our people are our greatest asset, and we recognize that a healthy, happy and committed workforce is vital to our business success."[182]

—*Alex Gourlay, Co-Chief Operating Officer,*
Walgreens Boots Alliance, Inc.

In caring for the most foundational elements of your being on a regular basis — mind, body, heart, and spirit, you honor your wholeness. You don't just haphazardly pay attention to the parts of your life that are currently screaming out for attention, instead you proactively nurture your being. And as CEO Steve Flanagan has pointed out, the benefits don't just reside with you, but also radiate out into all of your relationships and even into society: "Improving the health and well-being of our employees...offers a 'win-win' all around. Employees benefit from better support for their health. Companies benefit from less absence and improved productivity. And society benefits from improved public health."[183]

Our energy is just as interdependent as our global economy has proven to be. Neglecting one key area of our overall self throws everything else off kilter. "Connection," "interdependence," "networks," and "systems" are buzzwords of the twenty-first century. Your overall success in improving your resilience depends upon addressing the many aspects of your being—mind, body, heart (relationships), and spirit—paying attention to the integrated systems that comprise your well-being. The benefits of taking a comprehensive approach to your well-being (nurturing your mind, body, heart and spirit) are exponential.

For example, the mind responds to stimulation and learning by developing skills and capabilities. Education helps maintain mental focus and sharpness, as well as supports critical and creative thinking. To function, the body has basic needs that must be met; shelter, nutrition, rest, and recovery time. The healthier you are physically, the more engaged you will be and the better you will perform. The heart desires love, trust, respect, and is the seat of wisdom. This translates to relationships, friendships, networks, groups, or customers. And the spirit is that part of us that hungers for meaning and purpose, a cause greater than self.

Paying attention to and making the most of your strengths is associated with a number of positive health behaviors such as promoting feelings of well-being, living an active life, pursuing enjoyable activities, engaging in healthy eating, and valuing physical fitness. While self-regulation had the highest associations overall in a recent study, curiosity, appreciation of beauty/excellence, gratitude, hope, humor, and zest also displayed strong connections with health behaviors.[184]

Furthermore, strengths have been highly correlated with well-being subscales of self-acceptance and purpose, as well as good physical and mental health.[185] In yet another study, the people who made strong use of their strengths experienced greater well-being, which was related to both their physical and mental health. Strengths usage was a unique predictor of well-being.[186]

Use Your Strengths to Recharge

"The key to resilience is trying really hard, then stopping, recovering, and then trying again."[187]

—*Shawn Achor and Michelle Gielan*

In a Harvard Business Review article, *Resilience is About How You Recharge, Not How You Endure,* researchers Shawn Achor and Michelle Gielan offer compelling evidence for the benefits of recharging the important facets of ourselves. As parents of a young child, they describe their frenetic work life, coupled with the constant demands of parenthood, as a recipe for burnout. In their words:

> *"Based on our current research, we have come to realize that the problem is not our hectic schedule...the problem comes from a misunderstanding of what it means to be resilient, and the resulting impact of overworking. We often take a militaristic, 'tough' approach to resilience and grit. We imagine a Marine slogging through the mud ...We believe that the longer we tough it out, the tougher we are, and therefore the more successful we will be. However, this entire conception is scientifically inaccurate.[188]*

Arianna Huffington has been on a compassionate crusade to help people see the wisdom in recharging. With sincere concern for the welfare of others, she shares her own story of working massive hours building the Huffington Post website, in her book *Sleep Revolution.* While juggling the phone and emails at the same time, she passed out from exhaustion, waking up in a pool of blood with a broken cheekbone and a lacerated eye. Huffington points to the irony *"We sacrifice sleep in the name of productivity, but ironically our loss of sleep, despite the extra hours we spend at work, adds up to 11 days of lost productivity per year per worker."[189]* In addition, it's common knowledge that stress and sleep deprivation significantly increase our susceptibility to infectious diseases[190]. Why create the best odds to stay healthy and productive? It's an investment in ourselves.

So how do we care for the many aspects of our being? The answer is to consistently take the time to recharge. And to be motivated to recharge, we must see it as a critical investment in ourselves, acknowledging that without stopping to recover we lose the very ability to continue or to contribute to others. Going full steam each day without recovery can backfire, as we learned from Arianna Huffington.[191] According to Achor and Gielan *"If you really want to build resilience, you can start by strategically stopping. The very lack of a recovery period is dramatically holding back our collective ability to be resilient and successful. And lack of recovery —whether by disrupting sleep with thoughts of work or having continuous cognitive arousal by watching our phones —is costing our companies $62 billion a year (that's billion, not million) in lost productivity."[192]* In other words, stop to recharge the areas of your being that get depleted. Take the time to schedule breaks, investing in your well-being.

You can increase your motivation to recharge your mind, body, heart, and spirit by enlisting your strengths in activities that replenish these important aspects of yourself.[193]

For example, if you have a top strength of "appreciation of beauty and excellence," your body recharging activity could be hiking or running outside in the beauty of nature. If you have a top strength of "teamwork," your mind recharging activity might be to organize a book group to discuss new insights from the book being reviewed. If you have a top strength of "leadership," your heart recharging activity could be to organize an outing to get to know more people in your neighborhood. And if you have a top strength of "kindness," your spirit recharging activity might be to reach out to someone who is having a bad day. The more you connect your energizing strengths to activities that recharge you, the more likely you will enjoy and continue the positive behaviors.

Whole Life Thriving

When you consider the words "I am" what comes to the forefront for you? What are your deepest values? What motivates you? What is your vision, your unique legacy? How can you empower it with your character strengths? The answers require introspection and the courage to shape your own future by designing your life instead of passively letting it be determined for you. The result will be a powerful sense of meaning and purpose.

Poet and lecturer David Whyte, while conducting a workshop for AT&T employees about giving up "personal vision" and "sacred desires" to profit a company, had a memorable experience. Reportedly, a woman in his workshop wrote a poem with the following words: "Ten years ago...I turned my face for a moment...and it became my life."[194] In essence, this woman was describing living her life unconsciously—just going through the motions. This poem strikes a familiar chord with people who have put their dreams on hold. For example, how many people show up for work just to watch the clock until quitting time, and only come alive on the weekends when work is over.

Why do we postpone joy? "I'll be happy when..." or "If only..." are common ways we do this. We sometimes look away at momentary distractions or settle for immediate but empty gratification, as the years fly by. We must instead turn our faces toward our vision, dreams, and what we cherish most deeply—the deeper "I am" within. Only when we are authentic with ourselves can we make this exploration. And when we connect with our authentic selves, we harness the power of living in the now, mindfully present. Think about it this way, if you're not happy in your personal life, it will impact how you show up elsewhere—at work, at school, as a spouse, as a caregiver, etc. And the converse is true. If you're not happy in your life outside of your home, it will affect how you act when you walk through the door at the end of the day, how you show up in your relationships, how you feel physically, mentally, spiritually and emotionally. But when you practice self-care and continually recharge all aspects of your being, this benefits others as well. You can make your best contributions to others by bringing your whole self to all aspects of living—your work and personal life are parts of the whole person that you are.

Positivity Journal STRONG Questions

- Where do you experience joy?
- Where are you postponing joy?
- What "perfect" conditions are you waiting for before you allow yourself to be happy?
- Based on your last answer, what two things can you do in the here and now to increase your happiness, and your life satisfaction?
- How will you regularly recharge your Mind (mental)?
- How will you regularly recharge your Body (physical)?
- How will you regularly recharge your Heart (relationships)?
- How will you regularly recharge your Spirit (sense of meaning/purpose)?

Below are affirmations that you may find helpful as you build your resilience (Or, you can take some time to create an affirmation of your own). Choosing affirmations that inspire you and repeating them morning and night can become an empowering ritual:

- "I am authentic."
- "I am creative, resourceful and whole."
- "I am free to be me."
- "I am supported."
- "I am hopeful."
- "I am courageous."

Below is a mindfulness practice to close this chapter. Find a quiet place where you will not be disturbed to experience it:

Positivity Reset: 5 minutes
Breathing in, I take a moment to reset,
becoming aware of my breath and find my center.

Breathing out, I release any tension
as I connect to the present moment.

Breathing in, I recall my strengths of character
that have empowered me in the past.

Breathing out, I see myself sharing my strengths with others.

Breathing in, I relax into my authenticity.

Breathing out, I feel the power of my
unique contributions to the world.

Breathing in, I see and appreciate the strengths in others.

Breathing out, my gratitude fills the space I am in.

I am revitalized and my mind is clear.
I am living from my strengths today.
I am creative, resourceful and whole.
I am resuming my day with renewed, positive energy.

ENGAGING
YOUR
STRENGTHS

"There are two ways of exerting one's strength: one is pushing down, the other is pulling up."[195]

—*Booker T. Washington*

CHAPTER 7

THE WISDOM OF FORGIVENESS
AND THE
BRAVERY OF BOUNDARIES

"Forgiveness is not the misguided act of condoning irresponsible, hurtful behavior. Nor is it a superficial turning of the other cheek that leaves us feeling victimized and martyred. Rather, it is a finishing of old business that allows us to experience the present, free of contamination from the past."[196]

—Dr. Joan Borysenko

"Daring to set boundaries is about having the courage to love ourselves, even when we risk disappointing others."[197]

—Dr. Brené Brown

Marc uncharacteristically awoke before his alarm rang. He had made this work trip from Brussels to his home in the US more than 200 times. Arriving at the airport, a few security questions at check-in, boarding passes in hand, he left the counter. Marc made an exception that day and stopped at a bookstore where he never stops. As he took out his wallet to pay, a numbing explosion rocked the hall. In disbelief, Marc saw the terrified eyes of the cashier.

175

"I turned to see the ceiling collapse and windows explode. Within seconds the entire hall was engulfed in dust and debris, lights were replaced by emergency lights... screams of so many people running filled the air. Then the second bomb exploded. I felt as if I was in a nightmare. I texted my wife and children—that I didn't know whether I would make it and that I loved them all very much...The crying, screaming, running in the hall was intense. The debris covered all and the dust formed a thick fog. I could barely see...Finally, we were being led out, running along the destruction onto the tarmac...I saw bloody clothes—children's socks and pants soaked with blood. I cried while running, knowing that these bombs had done much savage destruction. About a thousand people gathered, many crying, hugging, looking for friends and relatives. A grandfather telling his wife that he didn't find their grandson...

I left the parking lot and walked stunned toward a nearby coffee shop and ordered some coffee. I realized I had no money—my wallet was gone. In the café, I watched the news, crying as I saw many people had died, more were injured, and there was another attack in the subway. People in the cafe were crying, shaking, including the Muslim owners of the Café. They were genuinely as shocked and devastated as we were. No need to pay for the coffee, they said.

Days later, when I was finally able to fly back home, I walked slowly to the counter, looking everywhere for signs of danger, overly aware and sensitive. In a somber ritual, I bought once more the magazines I lost in the bomb explosion. The fact that I went to buy them, I believe, may very well have saved my life. For the first hour of the flight I could not refrain from crying. The stress and tension needed an outlet. I prayed and remembered the victims, many young. Why them? Why not me? Later I understood that survivor guilt is one of the more difficult hurdles to overcome with post-traumatic stress.

In the year that followed the trauma, I began to suffer from physical ailments and sought medical help. At my wife's request, I eventually hired Fatima as my coach for various reasons. When Fatima asked me if perhaps the physical issues I had been experiencing might be anchored in a deep anger, and even hatred of the attackers, I could see this as a real possibility. Try as I may, the thought of forgiving the attackers was excruciatingly difficult. Then she suggested something that opened the door of possibility for me. During a guided mediation she prompted me to see the attackers as children—to envision the innocence of their youth and their innate goodness. I worked to see them using their strengths of character as little ones. This was the first time that I could see their 'humanness' and I must admit it melted my hard shield of anger. This has allowed me to see with new eyes people who have been indoctrinated with hate and radicalism in their young adult lives.

My heart began to soften, and I could feel my body letting go of the various symptoms that plagued me after the terror attack. I released the resentment and unspeakable pain, and even the hatred that had been thrust into my heart without my permission. All began to dissolve as I experienced the miracle of forgiveness. I came to understand that trauma manifests as fixed memories in our brains. Through writing about what I had learned from the trauma, it lessened the rigidity of the memory, toxic emotions were released, and I reframed the experience in a way that has better served me.

Every human being has 'their' moment when the call of death will come. For unknown reasons, Brussels wasn't mine. While it seems unfair that I survived and much younger people did not, it also meant to me that my role on earth is not yet complete, encouraging me to use my remaining time wisely. I have been able to help others who have lost loved ones. I have felt 'called' to speak to Belgium law-makers to help all victim's families, regardless of whether they are Belgian citizens or not.

And, throughout my coaching as I used my strengths—kindness, appreciation of beauty and excellence, spirituality and gratitude have helped me in the healing process. In addition, I chose to build my strength of bravery after learning of its high correlation to building resilience—the development of this strength has helped me overcome the anxiety that often accompanies Post Traumatic Stress.

Two years later I continue to thrive mentally, physically, emotionally and spiritually. My character strengths fuel my passion for life as I take joy in expressing them with my beloved wife, my family, friends and co-workers."

I share Marc's inspiring story with his permission. During the time I coached Marc, I was privileged to witness his breakthroughs. I'm not sure who learned more, however, Marc or me. His example of courage, integrity, kindness, forgiveness, and more continues to influence me to this day. Marc lives his life on the high ground of interdependence, and his relationships with his wife, children, friends and colleagues continue to flourish because of this.

Forgiving and Letting Go

To many of us, forgiveness is tantamount to surrendering a battle. But once we realize that we contribute to our own suffering by holding on, we can see the wisdom in letting go. I once heard someone say, *"Holding on to anger is like taking poison and expecting the other person to die."*[198] Letting go is freeing.

Sometimes in life we have to let go of a monumental, festering hurt, or it can be something more benign like an opinion or an expectation that is not working. We hold on tight and fight for what we think we "need." Then if we lose, we hold a grudge or sabotage progress to show we don't agree with the outcome. Your inner coach can guide you beyond this limiting level of perception. The sooner we forgive and free ourselves to move on, the less likely we are to become or remain a victim. Shining a light on our dark and negative thoughts can lessen the shadows they cast and free us to go on with our lives. As Eva Kor, Auschwitz survivor, wisely counsels, *"Forgiveness is really nothing more than an act of self-healing and self-empowerment. I call it a miracle medicine. It is free, it works and has no side effects."*[199]

Research shows that forgiveness can improve our resilience, reduce our stress levels, lower our blood pressure, lessen gastrointestinal and other bodily pains, boost our immune system—benefitting our well-being.[200] In addition, forgiveness has been linked to increased positive emotions, especially when we forgive someone close to us.[201] Juxtapose this to holding a grudge, which has the opposite effect overall.[202]

Forgiveness also builds relationships because when we let go of hurt or disappointment, we are more likely to cooperate with others. Forgiveness increases trust in our relationships, bringing us closer together and stopping the toxic downward spiral that can lead us to walk away from important relationships.[203] And most importantly, forgiveness elevates everyone to experience life on a higher plane. We are inspired to be more forgiving when others extend forgiveness to us.

Unpacking Forgiveness

Dr. Everett Worthington, founder of the REACH Forgiveness Program, collaborates with researchers around the world to study the connection of forgiveness to resilience, and is now researching forgiveness as a public health issue with colleges and communities. He identifies two types of forgiveness:

> *"The first type, decisional forgiveness, is a decision to treat the other person as a...valuable person. People can make a sincere decision to treat the other person differently and still feel bitter, resentful, hostile, full of hate, angry, or fearful at being hurt again. This is emotional unforgiveness, which suggests that there is a second type of forgiveness—emotional forgiveness. This is the gradual replacement of those unforgiving emotions until one has eliminated all the negative through empathy, sympathy, compassion, or love. If the person who hurt us is a stranger (i.e., someone who robbed us) or someone we don't want to continue to interact with (e.g., an ex-spouse), getting rid of negative emotions is considered complete emotional forgiveness. When the other is...a partner, friend or family member...we usually keep adding positive emotions until we reach a net positive emotion toward them."* [204]

In earlier years, Dr. Worthington noticed with amazement that couples who came to him for therapy improved their relationships through forgiveness. In his words, it "eventually boiled down to partners forgiving each other for past harms." [205] He later developed an emotional forgiveness intervention [206] that he said was *"put to a test when my mother was brutally murdered in 1996 and I forgave the young man who did it."*

Forgiveness is often difficult, and when we are tested and rise to the challenge, it strengthens us. That strengthening helps us bounce back in the wake of disasters and traumas."[207]

Forgiving the Unforgivable

Throughout history there have been people who walk forth with unexpected acts of deep and abiding compassion and forgiveness. One such event was after the 2006 mass shooting of children in an Amish schoolhouse in Pennsylvania. The gunman stormed into the rural one-room schoolhouse shooting ten girls, killing five. The shooter wasn't Amish—he worked in the tiny community as the milk truck driver.

Not that any shooting "makes sense," this was inconceivable, unimaginable, reprehensible—there are not words to describe it. The response of the Amish was, also, unimaginable. On the day of the shooting, within hours, members of the affected community went to the shooter's widow's home to comfort her, her parents and children, and to express their forgiveness for the shooter. The community even donated money to the shooter's family—retaining their humanity in the midst of savage circumstances.[208] Given the immensity of this act of forgiveness, we can find in it peace, comfort and inspiration to let go of our own grievances. Some people have the misconception that forgiveness is weakness and a denying of oneself. That can't be further from the truth. Forgiveness requires great strength of character, self-awareness, self-control, and dignity.

A towering example is holocaust survivor Eva Kor, who forgave the Nazis during the 50th anniversary of the liberation of Auschwitz. In her words:

"I stood by the ruins of the gas chambers with my children...I read my document of forgiveness and signed it. As I did that, I felt a

burden of pain was lifted from me. I was no longer in the grip of hate; I was finally free. The day I forgave the Nazis, private-ly I forgave my parents whom I hated all my life for not having saved me from Auschwitz. Children expect their parents to protect them; mine couldn't. And then I forgave myself for hating my parents."[209]

Sometimes forgiving oneself can be our life's most epic battle. The quote of Jesus, *"love thy neighbor as thyself"* draws our attention not only to others, but it teaches that an equal respect and caring must be extended to oneself. I coached a man who struggled with forgiving him-self for self-destructive substance abuse in his youth. He was stuck in regret and came to see that it was getting in the way of showing up fully for his young family years later. In recognizing this, he dedicated time to researching forgiveness and turned some of those same healing practices toward himself. He began repeating these words to himself several times each day: "I forgive myself. I forgive others" and he gradually let go of the self-inflicted pain. He is now thriving in his personal and work life.

Grace and Forgiveness

In the landscape of human healing, grace and forgiveness are often spo-ken in the same breath. Yet they are not interchangeable. Forgiveness is the act of letting go—a conscious release of resentment or retribution toward someone who has caused harm. Grace, by contrast, is the un-earned, often unspoken gift, extended in the absence of any merit. For-giveness is transactional in nature: it responds to wrongdoing. Grace, on the other hand, simply is—a gift offered freely, often inexplicably, and sometimes even in silence.

And yet, these two are not at odds. Grace may precede forgive-ness—it may even make forgiveness possible. Without grace, forgiveness can feel like a moral obligation or spiritual performance. But when forgiveness is saturated in grace, it becomes more than release, it becomes restoration.

In trauma work, particularly among survivors of deep violation, this distinction matters. Suggesting forgiveness too soon can feel like pressure. But grace—true grace—never forces, never insists. It simply waits. It says: You are still whole. You are still loved. That is why grace is often more healing than forgiveness: because it offers restoration without condition.

In the end, perhaps grace is the soil, and forgiveness the flower. One is the mysterious force that sustains life; the other, the choice we make to let something bloom where once there was only pain.

The How of Forgiveness

"You will begin to heal when you let go of past hurts, forgive those who have wronged you, and learn to forgive yourself for your mistakes."

—*Author Unknown*

Dr. Fred Luskin, a leading researcher on forgiveness, directs the Stanford University Forgiveness Project, and uses forgiveness therapy with people around the world, including those who suffered the attacks on the World Trade Center on 9/11. His work and his book *Forgive for Good*,[210] have helped people in their personal lives, and also in corporate, medical, legal and religious settings.[211] Dr. Luskin has beautifully summed up the myriad benefits of forgiveness as follows: *"The practice of forgiveness has been shown to reduce anger, hurt, depression and stress, and leads to greater feelings of hope, peace, compassion and self-confidence. Practicing forgiveness leads to healthy relationships as well as physical health. It also influences our attitude which opens the heart to kindness, beauty, and love."*[212]

Below is a summary of the 9 steps to forgiveness that Dr. Luskin offers on his website, used with his permission. I also suggest accessing his website for more resources at https://learningtoforgive.com/9-steps/

1. *Know how you feel and be able to articulate what about the situation is not OK. Tell a trusted couple of people.*
2. *Make a commitment to yourself to do what you have to do to feel better. Forgiveness is for you and not for anyone else.*
3. *Forgiveness does not necessarily mean reconciliation with the person that hurt you, nor condoning of their action. What you are after is to find peace.*
4. *Get the right perspective on what is happening. Recognize that your primary distress is coming from the hurt feelings, thoughts and physical upset you are suffering now, not what offended you or hurt you two minutes — or ten years — ago.*
5. *At the moment you feel upset practice a simple stress management technique to soothe your body's flight or fight response.*
6. *Give up expecting things from other people, or your life, that they do not choose to give you.*
7. *Put your energy into looking for another way to get your positive goals met than through the experience that has hurt you, instead of mentally replaying your hurt.*
8. *Remember that a life well lived is your best revenge.*
9. *Amend your grievance story to remind you of the heroic choice to forgive.*[213]

Everyday Authentic Forgiveness

"Forgiveness of the present is even more important than forgiveness of the past. If you forgive every moment, allow it to be as it is, then there will be no accumulation of resentment that needs to be forgiven at some later time."[214]

—*Eckhart Tolle*

There are many opportunities throughout an average day to use this empowering character strength of "forgiveness." When a loved one speaks sharply, when a colleague takes credit for our work, when someone cuts in line in front of us, when our dinner arrives late and cold at our restaurant table, etc. This does not mean that we don't speak up in the moment, but it does mean that we refuse to be held hostage by negative emotions. As Buddy Hackett famously said, *"While you're carrying a grudge, the other guy's out dancing."* [215]

After extensively studying the latest research on forgiveness, I have synthesized the best thinking I could find, and combined it with my understanding of character strengths, into this easy to remember, visual tool below. I call it the Authentic Forgiveness tool and it is my sincere hope that more of us will take the time to give ourselves the gift of forgiving others—and forgiving ourselves as well. Take a moment to review it and envision using it in specific situations going forward. Consider any resentments that you may have been holding onto that if let go, would enable you to reclaim your personal power and your inner peace:

Authentic Forgiveness Tool

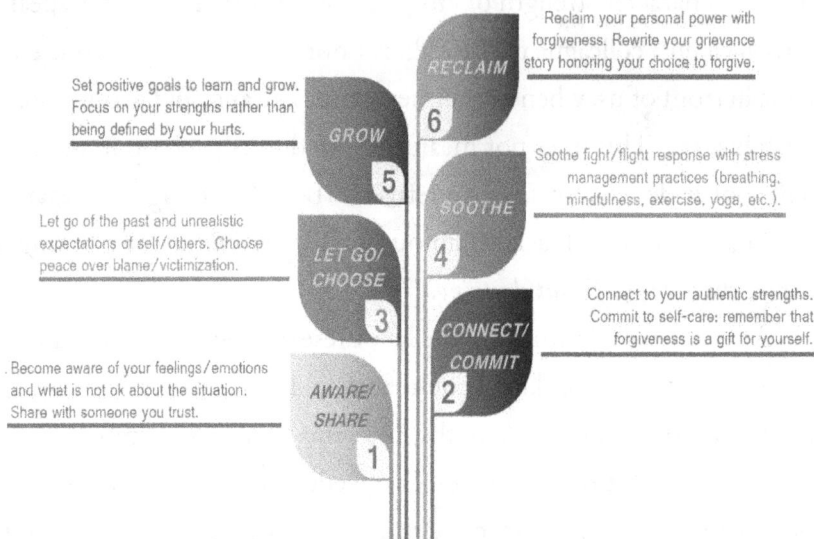

Reclaim your personal power with forgiveness. Rewrite your grievance story honoring your choice to forgive.

RECLAIM

Set positive goals to learn and grow. Focus on your strengths rather than being defined by your hurts.

GROW

6

5

Soothe fight/flight response with stress management practices (breathing, mindfulness, exercise, yoga, etc.).

SOOTHE

Let go of the past and unrealistic expectations of self/others. Choose peace over blame/victimization.

LET GO/ CHOOSE

4

3

CONNECT/ COMMIT

Connect to your authentic strengths. Commit to self-care: remember that forgiveness is a gift for yourself.

. Become aware of your feelings/emotions and what is not ok about the situation. Share with someone you trust.

AWARE/ SHARE

2

1

Inspired by the following: Luskin, Dr. Fred, The Stanford Forgiveness Project: Effects of Group Forgiveness Intervention on Perceived Stress, State and Trait, Anger, Symptoms of Stress, Self-Reported Health and Forgiveness, Forgive for Good, 9 Steps (2006); Saffarinia, Majid and Mohammadi, Narges and Afshar, Hamid (2016) The role of interpersonal forgiveness in resilience and severity of pain in chronic pain patients. Journal of Fundamentals of Mental Health); REACH Forgiveness of Others by Everett Worthington.

When we use this tool, our ability to communicate our boundaries and preferences in a way that others will honor can be greatly increased. This willingness to forgive in the moment and continually let go of resentment throughout our day frees us to think more clearly from a place of strength. Author and teacher Eckhart Tolle has explained: *"Through forgiveness... allowing the present moment to be as it is, the miracle of transformation happens not only within but also without... You dissolve discord, heal pain, dispel unconsciousness."*[216] People tend to regard boundary setting as the opposite of forgiveness and love, but we can only forgive and love others when we love ourselves, as you will see in the coming section...

The Bravery of Boundaries: Courage to Love Oneself and Others

"When people set boundaries with you, it's their attempt to continue the relationship with you. It is not an attempt to hurt you."[217]

—*Elizabeth Earnshaw*

No exploration of the character strength of forgiveness would be complete without an understanding of the character strength of bravery. As Stephen Covey often taught, one must balance courage with consideration.[218] This means that one must look out for one's own needs (using bravery/courage), as well as the needs of others (forgiveness/compassion).

In their book, *The Psychology of Courage: Modern Research on an Ancient Virtue*, Cynthia Pury and Shane Lopez help us understand courageous actions and how they are related to prosocial behaviors.[219] Bravery balanced with compassion can build relationships—and resilience. As we practice forgiveness of self and others, letting go of past grievances that no longer serve us, our boundaries often come into focus. We find ourselves examining what works for us and what doesn't. This self-awareness is foundational to cultivating resilience in one's life.

Millions of people resonate with Dr. Brené Brown because of her common-sense wisdom. She provides this straightforward definition of boundaries: *"simply our lists of what's okay and what's not okay."* Brown asserts that it makes sense for all ages in all situations to set healthy boundaries, in her words:

> *"When we combine the courage to make clear what works for us and what doesn't with the compassion to assume people are doing their best, our lives change. Yes, there will be people who violate our boundaries, and this will require that we continue to hold those people accountable. But when we're living in our integrity, we're strengthened by the self-respect that comes from the honoring of our boundaries, rather than being flattened by disappointment and resentment."[220]*

A couple of my favorite tips that Brown offers, and that I have applied in my own life in setting boundaries, may appeal to you as well. One is to "rehearse" what you will say in common situations, such as "I can't take that on" or "My plate is full." Another is to "make a mantra" using a tangible reminder. Brown shares her own mantra, "I need something to hold on to—literally—during those awkward moments when an ask hangs in the air. So, I bought a silver ring that I spin while silently repeating, 'Choose discomfort over resentment.' My mantra reminds me that I'm making a choice that's critical to my well-being—even if it's not easy."[221]

In an interview with psychologist and boundaries expert Dr. Chad Buck,[222] Huffington Post Senior Wellness Editor Lindsay Holmes lists what she calls the "life-changing power of establishing a clear-cut view of what you're willing to tolerate."[223]

As Dr. Buck asserts, *"Research has shown that people with less effective limits or boundaries are more likely to violate the boundaries of others, as well...Without a boundary, we absorb the stress around us, and our own psychological resources get drained."* So, doesn't it make sense to not only consider how we want to be treated by others, but also to take inventory of our own ability to be a good friend and partner to others? This is not a selfish act, because it is a two-fold, compassionate effort: peacefully communicating our own healthy boundaries, while also honoring the healthy boundaries of others. Below are the *"10 Great Things that Happen When You Set Boundaries"* that I have summarized with Dr. Buck's permission:

1. You are more self-aware.
2. You become a better friend and partner.
3. You take better care of yourself.
4. You are less stressed.
5. You are a better communicator.

6. You start trusting people more.
7. You are less angry.
8. You learn how to say "no."
9. You end up doing things you actually *want* to do.
10. You become a more understanding person.

Interestingly, Dr. Brené Brown has reported being shocked by her research findings that the most compassionate people she interviewed were also the most boundaried.[224] Brown writes in her book *Rising Strong*, "*Compassionate people ask for what they need. They say no when they need to, and when they say yes, they mean it. They're compassionate because their boundaries keep them out of resentment.*"[225] After reading Brown's book, I reflected on the most compassionate people I've known in my own life. It was a revelation for me to recall the many times I have witnessed caring, yet boundaried people, gently set clear expectations with me and with others. They are examples to me of how to balance the strength of bravery with the strength of kindness (compassion). And we can all learn to do so as well.

Real Life Boundaries

"*It was a slow process, but a polite 'no' soon entered my vernacular ... And something miraculous happened: my personal life followed suit. ... People respond well to honesty, to reality. They understand. And so with those no's, YES sprung back up everywhere. Funny how that works.*"[226]

—*Lena Dunham*

Thinking about boundaries is one thing. Following through on setting healthy boundaries in a compassionate way is quite another. But there are countless inspiring stories of people who have done just that with grace—understanding that being assertive, rather than aggressive builds the type of relationships they want in their lives, because they have laid the foundation for trust. Dr. Buck has suggested *"Expressing your limitations to others means you're trusting them to handle those emotions you're conveying."[227]* And it doesn't have to be an overwhelming, drawn-out process, *"Communicate rather than anticipate or expect that other people will respect or understand your limits. Setting a boundary doesn't require a long, convoluted justification."[228]*

Below is one such story that my colleagues, Karina and Chris Whetstine, have shared with me. They are founders of an organization that helps blended families thrive, using the tools in this book, among others, in their toolbox. Studies have shown that second marriages, especially when blending families, face an uphill battle for successfully staying together.[229] Karina and Chris help blended families to flourish, including how to set healthy boundaries.[230] In their own words:

> *"Our blended family life for the first four years consisted of survival mode—we were stuck on repeat. Daily 'marriage encounters' as we called them, faced with the reality of day-to-day living: unhealthy boundaries, co-parenting issues, scheduling changes, financial responsibilities, first day back after exchange day, different ways of doing everything, navigating mom/dad and stepmom/stepdad relationships. Add emotional hurts, and guilt driven parenting to the list. Although our days were sprinkled with efforts to create a positive family identity, the chaos was louder. It became our normal. We had reached a breaking point.*
>
> *This was the pivotal moment we needed to make necessary changes and create the happy marriage and family life we so desired. When we married, we had said forever, no matter what our future looked like. At our breaking point, forever seemed like a very long time. We*

were committed, but would this be an amazing journey, or would it be just enduring? We wanted better, we wanted more.

Excessive calls and disruptive conversations controlled the dynamics of our home life until we decided to teach others how to treat us. We finally recognized that healthy boundaries, where none had existed, were a necessary part of a thriving life. In doing this we took our first steps toward a new future, from a loving place. Our driving statement was 'love is a choice, love is a verb.' Most of all, it meant we write our own story. Being the recipients of negative emotions and demanding situations did not stop automatically. What did stop was the constant feeling that someone else was in the driver seat of our life. We realized we always had a choice! It was when we acted as though we did not, that unhealthy situations were activated.

It was a huge step to move forward in bravery — to be strong and courageous and act with love. We were committed to our vision and leveraged each other's strengths. It was a process. We chose not to respond in the moment and carefully considered how we would respond to any request. We kept it simple — 'thank you for asking, we will discuss and follow up with you.' No more fearing what others would say or do.

We knew establishing boundaries would be an adjustment to others, but we forged ahead to respectfully create our life-giving space. It meant using bravery, forgiveness, perseverance, and love, over and over, to create the home life we wanted. These strengths in action eventually resulted in the outcomes we desired. Our emotions were no longer functioning on overdrive, in response mode to what was being directed toward us, or around us. We came to understand that being respectful and choosing based on values, regardless of what was happening, did not equal being defenseless targets. Creating boundaries carved the healthy space we needed to build our relationships. It required developing a toolbox of strengths.

Our boundaries provided what we were missing all along, a healthy space to protect what mattered most to us—our 'this is us' team—comprised of his, hers, and ours. Keeping our eyes up, our spirituality provided the ultimate resilience factor needed to expect the best, even while experiencing the worst. It kept our focus on love, commitment, and believing that we could have something better than our current reality. It positively influenced our perspective, words, thoughts, and emotions—and beautifully blended our family."

We can all learn from Chris and Karina's journey, as they continue to maintain the boundaries they created over ten years ago. Based on their experience and the experiences of many other people who have volunteered their stories, boundaries require being able to communicate what is okay and what is not okay. Simply put, creating boundaries means teaching people how to treat you. It is essential to know how you will communicate these needs with others going forward and what your new behaviors will look like to maintain your newly formed boundary. You have to be prepared to deal with the aftermath of individuals who do not care to make positive changes in the relationship and who may never change. Below is a tool I created that incorporates the latest research on boundaries. Consider the three steps below if you are needing to create healthy boundaries in your own life:

Authentic Boundaries Tool

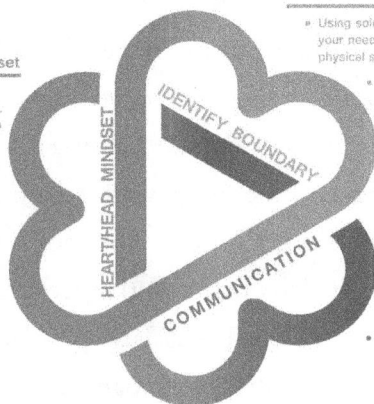

Step 2: Identify Boundary
- Using solution-focused questions, clearly identify your need for the healthy psychological and/or physical space that this boundary will create.
- With self-compassion, an open mind, and a peaceful heart, identify the desired/needed boundary.

Step 1: Heart/Head Mindset
- Acknowledge your worth and right to set healthy boundaries. Grant permission to yourself to create personal limits.
- Which character strengths can you bring forward to help you set this boundary?

Step 3: Calm Communication
- Calmly communicate in a safe/comfortable place with "I" messages that take personal responsibility and don't vilify others.
- Identify character strengths you can use to communicate new expectations and to create healthy behaviors.

Inspired by the following: Dr. Henry Cloud and Dr. John Townsend, Boundaries (2017); Buck, Chad, Establishing Effective Personal Boundaries, Vanderbilt University Faculty and Staff Health and Wellness (2015, 2016); Pury, Cynthia, and Shane Lopez. The Psychology of Courage: Modern Research on an Ancient Virtue. The Psychology of Courage: Modern Research on an Ancient Virtue. Washington, DC, US: American Psychological Association, (2010); Dr. Brené Brown "3 Ways to Set Boundaries." Oprah.com; and Lindsay Holmes "10 Great Things that Happen When You Set Boundaries." Huffington Post. April 4, 2016.

As Karina, from the previous story, stated in an email to me, "the Authentic Boundaries Model is invaluable within the blended family/co-parenting world—creating healthy boundaries is absolutely necessary for blended families. Given that about 60-70 percent of blended family marriages end in divorce (about twice as many of overall marriages),[231] for many couples it is essential in moving forward in a positive way."

Boundaries at Work

A man named Howard shared with me his example of setting boundaries with colleagues at work. When he would talk to his colleague Janice, she would share everything she could that was negative. It affected Howard and his relationships with other people at work. He talked with Janice about it, and he decided to set a boundary by gently explaining to Janice that he would not continue having conversations if they were always negative. Janice continued in her normal way, however, when she was negative about others, Howard would respectfully change the subject or politely move toward ending the conversation. Although Janice continued her behavior, Howard did not waiver. Howard identified and created what he wanted to have in his work relationship with Janice. Over time, Janice has learned how to communicate with Howard differently. This has resulted in a better working relationship not just for Howard and Janice, but the change has also positively impacted their work group as a whole. Through his boundary setting, Howard has sent a compassionate and effective message to Janice about how to treat him and others.

Positivity Journal

- Is there someone or some situation that you could benefit from forgiving?
- Take the time to write a forgiveness note, but you need not send it. That's entirely up to you. Sometimes just writing it out on paper can help you release resentment, then you can throw it away.
- What steps do you need to take to let go now? Perhaps it will be a process over time for you? (For example, it took time for many people to forgive the events of 9-11.)
- Feel the positive emotions of letting go flow through you—for example, are you experiencing freedom, peace, contentment, ease, equanimity, love, etc.?
- Savor these new positive emotions as they "undo" any past negativity you have been holding onto.
- Spend some time identifying your own healthy boundaries.

- Balancing your bravery with compassion for others, how can you peacefully express your boundaries to the people in your life when the situation requires it?
- You may want to also call forth some of your strengths, i.e., social intelligence, kindness, teamwork, perspective, fairness, etc. as you plan in advance how you will handle challenging interactions.

CHAPTER 8

AUTHENTIC CONNECTION: THE HIGHER GROUND OF INTERDEPENDENCE

"A human being is a part of the whole...He experiences himself, his thoughts and feelings as something separated from the rest, a kind of optical delusion of his consciousness. This delusion is a kind of prison for us, restricting us to our personal desires and to affection for a few persons nearest to us. Our task must be to free ourselves from this prison by widening our circle of compassion to embrace all living creatures and the whole of nature in its beauty." [232]

—*Albert Einstein*

From Individualism to Authentic Connection

Fierce independence is often praised in modern society. Look around you—in the news, in magazines, in politics, in communities, on social media, and you will see movements to separate self, or one's particular group, from others. But this disconnection can come at a high cost, as is evidenced by growing tension and the resulting stress, anxiety and depression. [233] Although it's healthy and necessary to care for and honor

197

oneself, the advice to always first "look out for number one," continually putting self before others, can take its toll on relationships and communities, as well as dimming our own spirits through this myopic view. Dr. Barbara Fredrickson in her book, *Love 2.0: How Our Supreme Emotion Affects Everything We Feel, Think, Do, and Become,* explains the price we sometimes pay when we lose connection with others: *"One unfortunate side effect of rugged individualism can be a thick cocoon of self-absorption that all but blinds you to the concerns, gifts, and welfare of others."*[234]

How do we break out of this confining cocoon? The attention we place on the virtues of others can lower the divisive walls of race, religion, gender, politics, class, etc., because we see the human being, rather than the label. In addition, appreciation (or gratitude) has been shown to consistently produce positive emotions,[235] which expands our ability to notice the many facets of others, and even to see and recognize their unique facial characteristics. So, rather than classifying them into a particular "other" group—we see the individual. [236] This is one way to inject positivity into our relationships, our communities, and the world at large. Dr. Fredrickson continues, *"Becoming more aware of the inherent value of positivity resonance can help you break free from this life-limiting cocoon. Indeed, study after study suggests that positive emotions, in and of themselves, unlock your ability to really see other people. When feeling good, then, you're far more likely to approach each new person as an opportunity for connection and growth."*[237][238]

Appreciating the character strengths in each other can bring people and communities together—and can even heal past wounds. I received this email (condensed below) from a college in Romania that I have worked with. Their faculty, staff and students have begun using many of the principles in this book. This email summarizes this move from individualism to authentic connection:

"We live in a world where many believe it is easier to judge, criticize, punish and see the weakness in others. A world where the mentality of scarcity is taught and even though we connect to different devices and technologies, we have begun losing signal for connections with other human beings.

We have built a school in Romania that challenges the paradigms that many of the adults in our school grew up with. We believe in a community that continuously evolves and sees the value of synergy...We model empathy, wholehearted apologies, value the teachable moments and strive to live a life of courage and consideration. We recognize that change is inevitable, and that we must work from a place of authenticity, integrity and responsibility.

We have been implementing cultural change with leadership principles and well-being interventions for healing from our country's past...the lens of working with our character strengths is giving us the motivation to become a school of transformation for our students, parents, teachers and staff..."

—Ruxandra Mercea, Executive Director,
Transylvania College, Romania

Elevating Relationships

Perhaps my most valuable insights from the many years I worked with the late Stephen Covey came from witnessing his commitment to seek the higher ground of interdependence. In his words:

"Interdependence is a far more mature, more advanced concept. If I am physically interdependent, I am self-reliant and capable,

but I also realize that you and I working together can accomplish far more than, even at my best, I could accomplish alone. If I am emotionally interdependent, I derive a great sense of worth within myself, but I also recognize the need for love, for giving, and for receiving love from others. If I am intellectually interdependent, I realize that I need the best thinking of other people to join with my own."[239]

Expressing gratitude and appreciation for the strengths in others does not diminish the self, but rather builds people, relationships, families, communities and organizations. Gratitude and appreciation are "social emotions" because these positive emotional states enhance relationships and invite us to see how we've been supported and affirmed by other people.

When we strive to develop what is noble and best in ourselves, others will catch the vision and want to do the same. In fact, when we use our characters strengths, it has been shown to inspire others to rise to the example that has been set, to match the tone of the behavior: *"In many if not most cases, onlookers are elevated by their observation of virtuous action. Admiration is created more than jealousy because character strengths are the sorts of characteristics to which most can—and do—aspire. The more people surrounding us who are kind, or curious, or full of hope, the greater our own likelihood of acting in these ways."*[240] All benefit when someone acts in accordance with his or her strengths and virtues.

Remember Ben Zander, the orchestra conductor we learned about earlier in this book? He encourages his musicians to "lead from every chair." Sometimes an individual can feel like "second fiddle" to someone else's outstanding qualities. As your own strengths coach, remind yourself there is no such thing as second fiddle with strengths. An orchestra, a relationship, a family, a team, are all made up of unique elements that work together in order for the whole to be at its best. We must learn to neither overshadow nor compare, but instead to appreciate strengths that allow one-another to elevate our contributions to the whole.

Learn to Spot Strengths

Your resilience increases not just by developing an awareness of your own strengths, but also when you learn to recognize and appreciate character strengths in others. This not only gives you a renewed positive sense of yourself, but it also provides a boost to the relationships in your life, in turn creating greater satisfaction for all. It is an act of generosity to spot strengths in others, and it's a gift that keeps on giving. The old model of personal growth was magnifying weaknesses under a microscope so defects could be addressed and performance improved. The new model is to hold up a mirror to strengths, to take the best that is already there, to notice it and leverage it. Practice keying into these observable verbal and non-verbal cues that become apparent when you or others are engaging strengths:

Verbal Cues	Non-Verbal Cues
• Clearer Speech	• Increased Energy
• Faster Pace	• Improved Posture
• More Direct Communication	• Increased Eye Contact
• Larger Vocabulary	• Eyes Light Up
• Stronger Voice	• Increased Animation

I love receiving emails like the ones below from people who have increased their strengths spotting abilities, or have been "seen" for their strengths:

"It feels good to be recognized by others for who we are at our core; and when people make the effort to see these parts of us, we feel closer to them and more likely to return the favor by seeing what's best in them."

—*Edwin Boom, Netherlands*

"I have begun to see strengths in people all the time. Last week while paying for my parking space, the parking lot attendant raced over to me because my work bag was hanging a little into the driveway. She had a sense of urgency, and you could tell she was very diligent in her role. My immediate thought was that she was high in prudence (caution) and that my car would always be very safe in her car parking lot. Perhaps if I were not a strength spotter, I'd see her urgency and actions differently!"

—*Jane Wundersitz, Australia*

Clash or Collaboration?

I'm certainly not suggesting that everything in life is always positive. Let's be real—no relationship is free of the occasional clash. Trust me, like everyone I've had my moments of yelling at my kids because they didn't do things "my way." I've felt frustrated with others, or been on the receiving end of the anger and frustration of others.

The "dance" in relationships can get out of rhythm and we may clumsily start bumping into each other. Sometimes, this can even come about because we are using our strengths and they collide with the strengths of others. Let's say one of my signature strengths is "love of learning." I may assume that everyone loves learning as much as I do and drone on in conversations, *ad infinitum.* I might lose sight of the fact that my team member is biting his nails. He will interject, and I'll

202

feel that he's cutting me off, and I'll be offended. Differences of opinions and even differences in which character strengths we value most can sometimes put us at odds with one-another. The following are some common strengths clashes:

- Bravery vs. Prudence (e.g., a brave person might want to quickly move forward on a decision, while a prudent person may want to research all aspects of the decision first.)
- Zest vs. Self-Regulation (e.g., a zestful may push to stay out late at a party, but their self-regulated partner may argue to get home so they can sleep well before work.)
- Creativity vs. Judgment (e.g., a creative person might find it fun to explore radical ideas, however their colleague may want to use judgment to hone down the options.)

Sometimes the dance that goes on between us and others can be downright painful when someone steps on our toes. Other times it is poetry to behold. So, how do we develop the ability to dance fluidly with people in ever-changing circumstances? An important aspect of learning to get along well with others is knowing how to turn a "strengths clash" into a "strengths collaboration."

Misunderstandings can be avoided if we understand our differences and respect one another's strengths at the onset, developing awareness about how we can come together and collaborate. Since all character strengths are positive, we don't have to be embarrassed about any of our strengths. But we do have to learn to appreciate one another's character strengths.[241] It's like a good potluck meal—which takes everyone bringing something different to the meal to make it successful.

Again, I recognize that negative things happen. People fall short. We get disappointed and frustrated with ourselves and with others. We shouldn't ignore problems as they occur. But we do want to increase our awareness of the ratio of positives to negatives overall. Research shows that the ideal praise to criticism ratio is 5 to 1—meaning for every negative comment a relationship benefits from at least five praise comments.[242]

Achieving this requires paying attention to what is going well. When people put their character strengths into action, and we appreciate their use, connection most often results. When people feel connected, they will shine and in turn illuminate those around them. We can see more strengths expressed by others when we brighten the environment with our own strengths and appreciate the strengths of others. One's positivity can be a guide—like a lighthouse—that will illuminate the way for others to activate their character strengths as well.

Take Back Your Remote Control

When we experience a "strengths clash" it can feel like the person we are clashing with is literally "pushing our buttons." Sometimes we behave as if the other person has a remote control dictating our negative behavior. We get our buttons pushed and act without thinking, regretting the behavior later. Let's explore how we can use our character strengths to regain control of our own emotions, and in the process increase our emotional intelligence, beniefitting our relationships.

The following simple, three-step tool I developed helps people gain better self-control over automatic negative reactions. Thoughtfully consider the following three steps and take back your remote control!

Take Back Your Remote Control Tool

Step 1: Recall a situation where you consistently get your buttons pushed and tend to respond from a critic mindset (e.g., losing your patience with others, passive-aggressive behaviors, lacking self-discipline, jumping to conclusions, quickly taking offense, reacting from fear, etc.).

Could there be a clash of strengths here? How can you shift your reaction and learn to value the differences in this other person's strengths?

Step 2: Identify strengths being expressed by the other person and why their strengths may be colliding with yours. Consider how appreciating one another's strengths could improve the situation. Identify a strength(s) that you could use to respond more effectively next time—that could be a source of connection rather than division. How can you respond differently, in a way that leverages your own character strengths and that serves you better in the future? (e.g., using your strengths of love or kindness or perseverance to increase your patience; using your strengths of self-regulation or social intelligence or fairness to choose your words and actions wisely.

Step 3: Respond in a way that helps create the positive outcome(s) you most desire. List the positive outcomes of responding in this new, strengths focused way? Who and what would be positively affected/impacted? (e.g., improved relationships with others, greater sense of peace, less stress, accomplishing more of what you start, greater fulfillment overall?)

Respect is "To Look Again"

Your choice to appreciate the strengths in others can build a bridge of understanding and respect between your differences. Respect comes from the Latin word "spectare," which means "to look," so to respect another is "to look again," showing deference to the uniqueness of another human being. And when we extend such respect to others, people often respond in a similar manner—viewing us in a more positive light as well, looking for our best intentions.[243] This is important, because we tend to judge others according to their actions, but we tend to judge ourselves according to our intentions. But no one can see within our minds or hearts for our highest intentions, unless of course, we share them, or they learn to spot our strengths and to key into what matters most to us. The reverse is also true.

Positive Contagion vs Psychic Pollution

"Dare to connect with your heart. You will be lifting not only yourself and those you love and care about, but also the world in which you live."[244]

—*Doc Childre, HeartMath Founder*

Have you ever walked into a room and even before you looked around, you could feel the tension and other negative emotions—in a work meeting or at the dinner table? And the reverse is also true, a negative mood can be lifted by opening oneself to positive surroundings. The Institute of HeartMath has shown that the energy we emanate from our hearts, our body's most powerful oscillating organ, can be felt by, and even influence others. The magnetic field produced by the heart is more than 5,000 times greater in strength than the field generated by the brain, and can be detected up to 10 feet beyond the body in all directions, if not further.[245] If we are emanating fearful, angry or malicious thoughts and emotions, then we are impacting not only ourselves, but others as well.[246] Ultimately, we are responsible for our own inner world, which can influence our outer world.[247]

Positivity begets more positivity. In fact, positivity is contagious.[248] When you are positive with another person, he or she is more likely to return the favor. So, looking for the best in a situation or in others creates an upward spiral of positivity, leading to higher cognition and to higher performance. Over 100 research studies conducted globally have shown that when people are exposed to positivity, they see more solutions in puzzles, score higher on cognitive tasks and remember more informa-tion[249] The key is to become the catalyst that puts the upward spiral into action. As Dr. Tal Ben-Shahar puts it: *"When you appreciate the good, the good appreciates."*[250] If each of us is waiting to be appreciated by others, guess what? We will always be waiting to be appreciated by others! The game changer is to begin appreciating the people in our lives and extend-ing the positivity first.

Studies show that the most productive teams are able to communi-cate respectfully with one another and to create an atmosphere of positiv-ity and openness. Achieving this appreciative atmosphere requires a con-sciousness of looking for what's going well—again, changing perspective from "what's wrong" to "what's strong"—catching the positives as they occur and not letting them slip by without acknowledgement.[251]

Dr. David Cooperrider is at the forefront of new and exciting re-search that shows that what you focus on literally grows. His work in the field of Appreciative Inquiry is being used to bring about the best in teams around the world. He has even worked to create understanding between countries that have been at war for years.[252] Dr. Cooperrider defines "positive organizations (or communities)" as having developed the ability to:

1. Consistently see and engage human strengths.
2. Create new alignments of strengths to make weaknesses irrelevant.
3. Refract human strengths such as compassion and wisdom out into society and the world.[253]

Research has shown five strengths are highly related to life satis-faction. These strengths are hope, gratitude, zest, love, and curiosity.[254] These same strengths may be important to group satisfaction to the de-gree that the group finds opportunities for expressing these strengths. Given that positivity is contagious, satisfaction can spread through the community, team, or family because these particular character strengths are prevalent in the group culture.

We are all connected, therefore we can all contribute to the well-being of the whole. In the words of Rollin McCraty, Ph.D., HeartMath Institute's director of research who is heading up the Interconnectivity Research Project, *"I believe humanity is at a unique point in its evolutionary history of consciousness. We now have an opportunity and the intelligence to make more empowered choices to create a cooperative and harmoniously connected world."*[255]

Authentic Connection: Be a Contribution

One reason many New Year resolutions fail is because they are focused only on "self." When we also consider how our goals benefit others, we increase our motivation. We are social by nature—we thrive when those around us thrive. If I see myself as being a "contribution" to others, in addition to accomplishing a goal for myself, then whatever I do is powered by something larger than myself. Creating value and fulfillment for the recipient of my contribution in turn creates value and fulfillment for me, launching a positive upward spiral. It's the law of reciprocity—what goes around comes around.

Be a Contribution:

- Fills you with meaning and purpose
- Energizes your goal as you use your strengths
- Serves as an antidote for unproductive competition and comparison
- Creates value and fulfillment for the recipient of your actions and thus you!

For example, if your goal is to improve your health, ask yourself, "Why do I want to do this?" Which is more compelling: losing weight to look better, or becoming healthy so that you have more energy to participate in activities with those you love? Learning to love, value, and take care of yourself is a powerful growth experience and motivator. As you begin to truly value yourself, you will also begin to see how you can be a contribution to others, which then makes getting and staying healthy deeply compelling. The TV show, The Biggest Loser, is a great example of this. Notice the people who are most successful in accomplishing their weight loss goals on the show. Most often they are the ones who first recognize their own self-worth, and then discover how to be a contribution to others through building relationships, being their best self, and living a life of meaning and purpose. They think about how weight loss will allow them to be around to see their kids grow up, to inspire their loved ones to get healthy, to better enjoy activities with loved ones, or to have the energy to contribute to others. Instead of anchoring their goals in what they must "give up" such as favorite foods, they anchor their goals in what they will "gain," such as energy, longevity, enhanced relationships and meaningful contributions to others.

When we work from the desire to make things better not only for ourselves, but also for others, obstacles seem to vanish, and unpleasant tasks become more pleasant. Those negative, critical, judging internal voices, and our inner critic's ranting, fall away. We notice what we can give, and that focus becomes a freeing and joyful experience.

I remember the first time I shared these concepts on television. As I drove to the TV station, my clammy hands gripped the steering wheel and I could feel my heart pounding in my chest as I mentally reviewed what I would say. I took a couple of deep breaths, and I said out loud, *"Fatima, just 'be' a contribution today. Think only about helping people today and everything will fall into place."*

That small adjustment transported me from fear of failure to simply wanting to get helpful information across to people. Like everyone, I get caught up in everyday pressures to perform, but when I'm immersed in using my strengths to contribute, the performance anxiety melts away and I get the deep satisfaction that comes from giving to others — the world becomes a much less complicated place.

Mindset Check

Consider the mindset you bring to your relationships with yourself and others—are you creating what you really want in your relationships? Take a moment to do the mindset check below, assessing for yourself where your mindset currently is:

INNER CRITIC	VS	INNER COACH
Competitive		Cooperative
Individualistic		Teamwork
Threatened by differences		Values differences
Defensive		Dialogue / Feedback
Entrenched		Seek common ground
Afraid of change		Dynamic / Growing

Coach vs. Critic Model, ©2014-2020, Authentic Strengths Advantage, LLC.
(Inspired by the following: Columbia University Coaching Certification Program Learner/Judger Model; Marilee C. Goldberg's, The Art of the Question 1998 p. 161-178).

Notice the first two mindsets listed on the left: competitive and individualistic. A common question I am asked is whether there is anything inherently *wrong* with being competitive or individualistic, if one is behaving in a principled way?

The answer is "no," there isn't anything inherently wrong with principled competition or individualistic pursuits. The important question here is *"when is it appropriate?"* For example, these two mindsets could be appropriate in sports, in some business settings with competitors, etc.

However, do you think it is appropriate to bring a competitive or individualistic mindset into a relationship, such as with a friend, a loved one, a colleague, or someone on your team? Invariably people tell me that relationships are not well-suited to competition or individualistic attitudes. Rather, relationships thrive when cooperation, teamwork, and mutual respect are the guiding mindsets.

Mindset is everything. A powerful part of the learning process is to check your mindset as you embark on the journey of coaching yourself or others. Some people still carry the outdated, misguided view that coaching is about critiquing, and correcting weaknesses, so that in the process improvements can be made. But as we learned earlier, the critic mindset on the left side of this slide focuses on "what's wrong" with a person or a relationship, which is demoralizing and deflating. Notice the stark difference in the coach mindset on the right side of this model.

You will learn that bringing a "coach" mindset to the table, focusing on "what's strong," will generate the best results and strengthen relationships. In other words, when you focus on yours and others' strengths you become a builder and a motivator.

Positivity Journal STRONG Questions

- Referencing your top character strengths, how are you using them now to shift your mindset towards your inner coach as you work to improve your relationships?
- How is your mindset changing as you proceed through this book— what new tools are you learning to help you turn up the volume on your inner coach?
- As you make an effort to consistently use your strengths, what positive changes do you notice in your life?

- What mindset do you think is most suited for fulfilling and productive relationships?

Striving Together

"Alcoholics Anonymous is a group where everybody stays anonymous, nobody has a title, there are no leaders...I have people in my own family who have struggled with addiction and I go with them and sit there, and I get shivers down my back to be in the presence of people who all they want to do is help each other."

—*Dr. Wayne Dyer*

When we make a habit of looking for the strengths in others, it opens up a cooperative new world for all, even expanding our understanding of competition. The original meaning of the verb "to compete" is "competere," which means "to strive together."[256] The fallacy of competition at all costs, as often portrayed in pop culture and the media, is contributing to the disconnection many people feel from others. It's imperative to shed light on this misconception and to offer a new, holistic and sustainable model of building resilience in community with others. This can build our relationships and positively shift our collective experience, opening our hearts to others.

For example, humility is often an underrated strength, but one necessary for healthy relationships and building resilience. Although we live in a celebrity-obsessed world, great power can be found in humility. Says Stephen Covey: *"People who are truly effective have the humility and reverence to recognize their own perceptual limitations and appreciate the rich resources available through interaction with the hearts and minds of other human beings."*[257]

Today however, many of us think of competition in terms of rivals and contention. Photographer Kevin Garrett suffered a mild traumatic brain injury when his car was struck from the rear on his way to a pho-to shoot.[258] David Johnson, another photographer Garrett had met at a workshop, learned about the car wreck and that Garrett was having dif-ficulties. He cleared his schedule and flew from his studio in New York to help Garrett learn how to use some new equipment.

Professional photography is known to be a cutthroat business and, over the years, Johnson and Garrett have gone on to compete directly for jobs at times. They've astonished some of their clients by recommending each other for jobs, loaning each other equipment, and sharing names of crew members in a business where people jealously guard every aspect of their business.

If we could see those around us as co-creators in our growth, gravi-tating toward them and learning that another's star quality doesn't dim our own brightness, we might learn that we can all shine more brilliantly together.

Strengths Authenticity

When we are living inauthentic lives, unable to express our unique char-acter strengths, we lose our connection to ourselves and little by little can develop self-directed frustration, anger, and mistrust that extends to others. The antidote is to practice strengths authenticity. Developing awareness and appreciation of our strengths, as well as those of others, is essential.

Conversely, trying to force oneself and others to fit into roles that are not authentic, over the long-term can have a deflating, withering ef-fect. In fact, there are studies indicating that heart patients have com-promised their hearts by faking smiles and positive attitudes, similar to the ventricle constriction that can be observed when people experience intensely negative emotions,[259] and new research shows that insincere positivity can be as corrosive as anger.[260]

This is where self-awareness comes in. It serves us better to reframe a negative state into a positive one, genuinely. Denying or stuffing negative emotions doesn't make them go away for good. "Fake it till you make it" is a well-known adage; however, keeping in mind that words matter, I'd like to propose a different, more authentic adage here: "try it to transform it." This acknowledges that we are a creative force in our own lives when we live authentically in the present moment.

So how do we summon sincere positivity in the midst of difficulties? We can make a mental list of the things that we are genuinely grateful for. At first, we may find it difficult to identify the good when we feel surrounded by the bad, but if we persist in looking for even the smallest blessing in our life, that awareness will grow. A friend told me about having such an experience in her hospital room before a serious surgery. As a single mom of two young children, and sole provider for her family, she was at first filled with fear as she waited in her hospital room. She decided to make a mental list (a prayer of thanksgiving) of all that she was thankful for, and she was surprised that half an hour later she was still adding to the list! She was overwhelmed with authentic positive emotion as one uplifting awareness expanded to another, and then another. Relaxed and smiling by the end of her massive gratitude list, she feels this beneficially impacted not only her surgery, but her recovery as well. And studies show that genuine smiles and positive emotions produce health-inducing physical reactions.[261] So the next time someone suggests that you fake a smile, instead take a moment to identify things (your blessings, even if few) that will honestly turn the corners of your mouth upward! Thus, the inner life that we cultivate affects our outer life. I have discovered that when people connect to their authentic strengths, they find that added measure of energy needed to transform challenging situations, genuinely.

Emotionally Intelligent Relationships

A wonderful thing about emotional intelligence (our awareness and management of our own emotions, and our ability to understand the feelings of others), is that it grows through the optimal use of our character strengths and, although it can develop naturally with age, it can also grow when one practices authenticity.[262] It's been shown that strengths related to positive relationships with oneself and others contribute to our resilience.[263] *Psychology Today* affirms our ability to increase our emotional intelligence, making the connection between emotional intelligence and the health of our relationships. *"An emotionally intelligent individual is both highly conscious of his or her own emotional states, even negativity—frustration, sadness, or something more subtle—and able to identify and manage them. These people are also especially tuned in to the emotions others experience. It's easy to see how a sensitivity to emotional signals from within and from the social environment could make one a better friend, parent, leader, or romantic partner. Fortunately, these skills can be honed."[264]*

It's not about learning a script. It is about developing a new perception of reality centered on genuinely being one's best self, understanding and valuing others. The key, as we learned earlier, is to approach defining moments in our relationships as a coach rather than as a critic.

Authentic Vulnerability

To live authentically, and in an emotionally intelligent way, requires some vulnerability. In her book, *Daring Greatly: How the Courage to be Vulnerable Transforms the Way We Live, Love, Parent and Lead*, Dr. Brené Brown offers a truth about vulnerability that I believe is foundational to emotional intelligence, *"Vulnerability sounds like truth and feels like courage. Truth and courage aren't always comfortable, but they're never weakness."[265]* In other words, self-awareness and social-awareness require the courage to be vulnerable—to relate authentically with others.

Our close relationships deepen when we allow ourselves to be vulnerable. Emotional intelligence is a reflection of this kind of honest vulnerability. By being vulnerable we lower our shields and open our hearts to others, engendering mutual, genuine understanding. This involves learning to see and appreciate the authenticity in others, as well as taking the risk to be seen for one's authenticity as well.

Trust

"We tend to grossly underestimate how much we can trust other people. Don't let the harmful effects of a few bad exchanges cause you to miss out on all the benefits that come from high-trust relationships... Trust makes our relationships resilient, allowing us to navigate change smoothly."266

—*Center for Ethical Leadership*

Interestingly, when you look at the research on what builds trust, character strengths come to the forefront of the discussion. The Center for Ethical Leadership at the University of Notre Dame, reports that *"the decision to trust is more emotional than rational; building trust requires emotional intelligence...generosity is the best way to build trust during a first impression. It makes your values and motivations clear."267* They go on to illustrate how being the first one to extend generosity (related to the character strength of kindness) is not acting on "blind faith," but rather it influences the other's behaviors in three important ways, summarized as follows:

1. **Trust invites trust.** By showing that you trust a person, you're inviting them to trust you.
2. **Others know where you stand**. By making it clear that you are not just motivated by your own interest. One study revealed that because it guards against the effects of inevitable disappointments in our

relationships, generosity is a more effective way to sustain long-term collaboration than a tit-for-tat strategy.[268]

3. **First impressions set the tone for future interactions.** Since trust is so difficult to build, you cannot afford to miss the opportunity a first impression offers. If you begin an interaction with doubt, trust will be very difficult to rebuild.[269]

The current global climate of trust, however, is far from ideal. The Edelman Trust Barometer, which documents global trust opinion shifts, reveals a crisis of low trust around the world, with the United States experiencing the largest decline of any country. A significant loss of trust toward government, business, media and NGO's—37 percentage points lower in recent years—or what they call a "trust crash" in the US since 2016. The good news is that people are stepping up to make a difference. Reportedly, there is a commonly felt need to build trust throughout the globe. According to Edelman Trust Barometer, *"The world is united on one front—all share an urgent desire for change. Only one in five feels that the system is working for them... In conjunction with pessimism and worry, there is a growing move toward engagement and action."*[270]

It is more important than ever to be co-creators of prosperity and abundance rather than to look over our shoulders to see who can outrun whom. Our character strengths develop self-awareness and social-awareness—our emotional intelligence. Appreciating strengths in ourselves and others is the opposite of comparanoia because it is focusing on what we and others do well. It is an act of generosity to look for the best in any human being. Such generosity celebrates everyone's unique strengths, leading to higher trust in relationships, and resulting in higher productivity and success overall.[271]

Positivity Journal STRONG Questions

As you explore the higher ground of interdependence, consider the following questions and how strengthening your relationships can boost your resilience:

- What strengths can you use to enhance your ability to listen to and better understand others?

- What is an important relationship that you would like to build? How will you use your strengths to nurture in this relationship?

- Identify the character strengths that increase self-awareness for you. How can you bring them forward more consistently?

- Which character strengths increase self-management (your ability to manage your emotions and actions) for you? How can you bring them forward more consistently?

- Which of your top character strengths could be used to understand others, and improve your relationships?

  - How do your strengths contribute in meaningful ways to others?

- What strengths have you noticed and appreciated in others? How can you make a habit of this?

- What strengths have others noticed in you? How did it feel when you were acknowledged and appreciated for your strengths?

- Why is it a generous act to spot strengths in oneself and in others?

Now, think of a time where you had a positive relationship, group or community experience—when everyone involved was engaged and accomplished a goal that was meaningful.

- What success did you experience?

- What were the interpersonal dynamics:

  - Was there clarity of purpose?

  - Were strengths appreciated and leveraged?

  - Were strengths matched to the different roles?

CHAPTER 9

A NEW STATE OF BEING: OPEN-HEARTED RESILIENCE

*"No matter how we may search outside ourselves...if the message we find
is authentic, it will send us right back to ourselves."*[272]
—*Jean Yves Leloup*

*"Every time we change our state of being and begin our day by opening
our hearts to the elevated states that connect us to a love for life...
and a level of kindness toward others, we must carry, maintain and
demonstrate that energy and state of being throughout the day—
whether we are sitting, standing, walking or lying down."*[273]
—*Dr. Joe Dispenza*

What is open-hearted resilience and why should we strive for this? I submit to you that an open heart is also a resilient heart—and making the important journey from the head to the heart, connecting the two—is essential to authentic resilience. Resilience is not an individualistic skill or outcome. As we've learned previously, resilience flows from not only a focus on our own strengths, but also our genuine appreciation of the best in others. It calls for us to let down our shields and to open ourselves to be in healthy relationships with others. In the words of Dr. Brené

Brown, *"Until we can receive with an open heart, we're never really giving with an open heart. When we attach judgment to receiving help, we knowingly or unknowingly attach judgment to giving help."*[274] Living in this way beckons forth our strength of hope, or as some would call it, our "faith" in a better tomorrow.

It's inspiring to see that many people, in the midst of the stress and chaotic noise of modern life, are choosing faith over fear, healthy relationships over barriers. More and more people are seeing the wisdom in building bridges rather than separating themselves with walls. What if you too turned your energy into building your own extraordinary life? Where would your new awareness of your character strengths lead you?

When we commit to expressing our character strengths optimally and consistently, we engage those strengths in a more authentic and natural expression. As Ralph Waldo Emerson has said, "That which we persist in doing becomes easier to do, not that the nature of the thing has changed but that our power to do has increased."[275]

This is why I have written this new book you hold in your hands—it has been written in a way that is applicable to everyday people living everyday lives—not just to professional coaches. My goal was to connect with you as I would with a friend, through our common human experiences. This book was written to empower you to become your own coach—based on tried and proven research. It is my hope that you have learned practical and helpful self-coaching principles that will serve you well, and that will help you build your resilience for the challenges you face now and in the future. And that you will share your newfound insights with those you love—improving your relationships as well.

Flow: A New State of Being

"It seems clear that flow serves as a buffer for adversity... [and] its major contribution to the quality of life consists in endowing momentary experience with value."[276]

—*J. Nakamura & M. Csikszentmihalyi,
Oxford Handbook of Positive Psychology*

Exploring the richness of our strengths, empowering all that we do with authentic strengths motivation, and engaging our strengths in our daily lives can produce a remarkable state of flow. What is flow? It is a movement characteristic of liquids. Water flows. When things flow, they are doing what they were made to do—think of a school of fish swimming. When flow is powerful and purposeful, you have optimal energy and full engagement. The resulting fulfillment you experience spills over into other areas of your life. You have learned to thrive.

What does a flow state look like? Recall any athlete you've watched achieve a peak experience, and you will see what it means to achieve flow. It is almost as exhilarating for the spectators as it is for the individual. It doesn't happen by accident. It requires practice, persistence, awareness, and optimal use of our character strengths. In order for springs to feed the streams that flow into the rivers that flow into the sea, conditions need to be cultivated. And the water needs an outlet or it will become stagnant and dead. A purposeful groove is cultivated in the earth over time, and the channel must be open in order to empty into the realm of great possibilities.

Why is understanding flow important and how do we get into this amazing state of flow more often? As Dr. Csikszentmihalyi has explained:

"Flow—the kind of knowledge or wisdom one needs for emancipating consciousness—is not cumulative. At least as much as intelligence, it requires the commitment of emotions and will. It is not enough to know how to do it; one must do it, consistently, in the same way as athletes and musicians who must keep practicing what they know in theory."[277]

You have learned some principles in this book that will cultivate conditions to express your character strengths—so that you can enjoy more flow in all aspects of your life. But make no mistake, you must do the heavy lifting, which means you must carefully consider and identify how, when, with whom, and to what degree you choose to employ and develop your strengths. This responsibility builds your commitment and will, as Csikszentmihalyi describes above. When you make this a consistent positive practice, it eventually becomes second nature; then, your strengths take on an intelligence of their own that enables them to flow.

Upstream vs Downstream

When you are in flow, you have more energy and awareness. The landscape (inner and outer) looks sharper; everything is more focused. You find yourself completely immersed in what you are doing—you are savoring every moment, not wanting it to end. Think of a time you have experienced a "flow state." Perhaps it was while you were working on a project where you felt purposeful and made a significant contribution, or engaging in your favorite sport, or spending meaningful, quality time with loved ones.

We all know what it feels like when something "clicks" and we suddenly are able to see, understand, or act on something that previously had baffled us. Our senses are engaged. We feel elated. Ideas spark and explode like fireworks. For example, listening to my inner coach instead of my inner critic, I chose to go into the field of coaching. A few years later, I found myself even more passionate about "being a contribution" to others and have felt completely energized while writing this book.

Being in flow with our strengths also creates a sense of happiness and well-being.[278] Author and positive psychologist Ed Diener commented to me once about what made him happy:

> *"Happiness is not just a place, but also a process. I once thought that when I had my 'ducks in a row,' the right wife, kids, house, and job, that I would be happy from then on. And, of course those things all helped a lot. But I learned that happiness is an ongoing process of fresh challenges, and that even when everything is in place, it takes the right attitudes and activities to continue to be happy."[279]*

Our attitude, or perception, can be the difference in experiencing the ease of flowing downstream, rather the struggle of going upstream.

Flow and Contribution

When we ask, "What are the needs I see around me?" what begins to emerge is the contribution we can make, the service we can render. When this service is grounded in and powered by the most authentic part of ourselves, our character strengths, we are in the position to make a valuable contribution. The best solutions or contributions in society, in business, and in personal life have emerged when people apply their strengths to serving a need. And it's an added bonus that people who give service or contribute to others in a meaningful way live on average 10 years longer![280] It seems easy on the surface, but oftentimes we get so busy in day-to-day life that we don't even know what we are passionate about any more. We have disconnected from those strengths that enliven us.

How do we bring passion and flow back into day-to-day life? Ask yourself what is happening around you that you care about deeply—in your relationships, family, community, workplace? Answering questions like this is a step toward reconnecting with your authentic strengths and enabling flow.

Positive Practices Enable Flow

When in a flow state, writers write unforgettable stories, musicians create memorable music, artists paint masterpieces, and scientists study everything around them. They all rely on regular practice to achieve optimum experiences. The same can be true of anyone whose life is grounded in regularly expressing and appreciating character strengths. I call these "positive practices." Every time we participate in a positive practice, we are expressing our commitment to empower and engage our strengths and to appreciate strengths in others. Families who sit down to dinner together regularly are saying without words that they believe in the need for families to have shared time together. Organizations that provide regular outlets for expression and appreciation of strengths are communicating that they invest in their people and want to develop their potential.

Far from precluding spontaneity, positive practices provide a level of comfort, continuity, and security that frees us to improvise and to take risks. Positive practices provide a stable framework for utilizing our strengths and enabling creative breakthroughs to occur. They can also open up time for renewal of our strengths, when relationships can be deepened, and reflection and growth become possible.

In other words, we can "train" for greatness. Much as it is possible to strengthen a muscle by subjecting it to stress and recovery, we can develop our ability to utilize and leverage our strengths. By building positive practices that become automatic—and subsequently relatively effortless—we ensure a strong showing in any pursuit to which we turn our efforts.

Riding the Waves

"Promise me you will not spend so much time treading water and trying to keep your head above the waves that you forget how much you have always loved to swim."[281]

—*Tyler Knott Gregson*

It's a great feeling to be in flow. However, that fluid, enjoyable ride can sometimes turn into a towering and imposing wave of challenge. Riding the wave frightens a lot of people. Seeing something coming toward you that has the power to take you down is equivalent to facing a crisis point—whether it's a wall of water, losing your job, relationship issues, or undergoing chemotherapy. But what if you could welcome that wave and learn to ride it to new heights? Beyond the fear lies the ecstasy of tackling the Big Kahuna (the *ultimate* wave).

Big waves and other challenges must be sized up and respected for their power. You want to be prepared for the challenge in body, mind, heart, and spirit. And sometimes you have to paddle away until conditions allow a ride. If you have explored, empowered, and engaged your character strengths, you have learned to focus on what's strong instead of what's wrong. With each new challenge, you can learn and grow and progress.

An example of this is a woman who had an unexpected opportunity to go to St. Martin for a weekend with her twenty-one-year-old son. Her son was a single father with joint custody, and the mother was helping him raise his daughter in their family home.

Mother and son went out on a group watercraft tour one morning, both on the same jet ski. The aqua Caribbean Sea was transparent and calm. As they rounded a cliff the water got choppy, then rough. Waves started slapping the mother in the face. Riding on the back of the jet ski with her arms wrapped tightly around her son's waist, she saw the waves get higher and higher. They'd coast up to the crest and then fall, slamming into the water and climbing the next wave almost before she could catch her breath. As her son wrestled the jet ski from crest to crest, he kept turning his head and yelling at her.

Due to the rough waters, they had traveled far from shore and gotten separated from the group, but finally the shoreline came into view around a bend. The waves subsided, and the mother, drained but grateful for her son's expert steering, finally heard what her son had been yelling each time he'd turned around: "Mom, isn't this beautiful!" Hearing his words made her realize something important.

During her son's childhood, the waves in her own path had been high—and it was her son who had been hanging on for dear life behind her as they rode from wave to wave. She had done her best to encourage him through those hard times to engage his own strengths in order to see the beauty of the ride.

Looking back, she realized that although the jet ski experience had been the ride of her life, she had been in good hands and trusted his judgment. Her son was up to the task. He had the ability to ride those rough waves just the way he had displayed his ability to raise his daughter in less-than-perfect circumstances. He had become an extraordinary father, a good student, and a responsible worker. Just as she was proud of the way he had handled the jet ski so capably in treacherous waters, she was also proud of the way he was using his authentic strengths to ride the waves in his life to shore.

Closing

I hope this book has been a call to action for living your best life, learning to ride your own waves to shore. As you go forward, you can approach each new day from a new state of being—using the positive practices in this book for authentic, elevated, open-hearted life experiences—one day at a time. The real work begins at each new choice-point, when upset by external events, you lean into a fresh, empowering vision of your highest and best self. Your connection to the many people in your life is strengthened by appreciating the best in yourself *and* in others—really seeing strengths—which helps build and sustain everyone's resilience.

As you finish this book, you have likely come to see that authentic resilience is an "inward" journey. One that demands deep reflection, and at times can be daunting, requiring a change in thinking and in habits. You may be wondering: What if I fail, is that normal? If I fail, what do I do, how do I get back on track? How do I measure success? Is there a community I can join? Is there an online class I can take? How do I know when I've achieved authentic resilience? How do I sustain the momentum I've gained, and not slip back while under stressful situations?

Authentic resilience is a process, not a destination. It's not a straight line, it's not perfect—it's often messy, in fact. There are inevitable "gaps" we will all confront—it's all part of discovering the best inside you—day by day, moment by moment.

Authentic resilience is also giving ourselves permission to be human, to not only discover our character strengths, but also over time to better understand how to apply our strengths when we fail. Then getting back up, dusting ourselves off, recommitting to do our best going forward. It's learning how to relate to the inevitable setbacks and "failures" when we "overuse" or "underuse" our strengths. It's understanding that "optimal use" of our strengths is about finding balance, honoring ourselves and others.

I encourage you to continue your journey and find ways to try some of your underused character strengths to solve a problem as part of becoming more resilient and pivoting forward. Look for ways to leverage your top strengths, and try less-familiar strengths on for size, to ultimately live a fuller, more fulfilling, happier life. Authentic resilience in that sense is not the goal, it's the day to day experience of realigning your life with your higher self—embracing your character strengths!

Final Note

As you prepare to reenter your life, I want to bring your focus back to your resilience journey with a challenge. This is perhaps the most important exercise you will have done throughout this book. Studies show this one exercise can significantly increase your sense of happiness and well-being, while decreasing negative emotional states such as anxiety, stress, and depression—boosting resilience. The measurable mood boost people get from this exercise can last up to 6 months![282]

Recall once again your top strengths. The challenge is to use one or two of your top strengths in *new ways* for one week.

- List your top strengths
- Pick one or two
- Look for ways to use the strength(s) daily for a week

The challenge is that simple! Email us at info@authenticstrengths. com and share your results from this challenge. We would love to celebrate your successes with you and to hear your stories! We also have blogs and articles on our website at AuthenticStrengths.com to help you stay positive and maintain your momentum. And you can check out my posts on Facebook, Instagram, LinkedIn, and YouTube by searching "Fatima Doman" for continual boosts on your journey.

Closing Mindfulness Practice

Awaken Resilience: 8 minutes *(Also available on YouTube at Fatima Doman Channel.)*
In this mediation you will calm your inner critic
and give voice to your inner coach.
Awakening your resilience is a matter of connecting
with your authenticity.
Amplifying this voice is a powerful guide,
bringing out your best self.
Your inner coach will inspire you to focus on your strengths
and to live your best life.

Now, find a comfortable seated position with your back straight.
Close your eyes and dedicate this mindfulness practice
for your greatest good.
Breathing in deeply, center yourself in this present moment.
Breathing out fully, relax and let all your worries go.

Breathing in, settle into your authentic self—your wholeness.
Breathing out, release all that does not serve you.
Continue breathing mindfully as you allow the following
Inner coach statements to settle into your awareness.

I see myself using my character strengths and I am energized.
My strengths reflect the real me and feel empowering.
I use my strengths in creating solutions to the challenges I face.
My strengths open me to growth, positive change, and fulfillment.

AUTHENTIC **RESILIENCE**

As I quiet my mind, I observe the solutions that emerge.
I visualize creative ways to accomplish my goals.
I am engaged and motivated to realize my aspirations.
I *feel* the positive emotions of the solutions that I envision.

I recognize the best in others, as well as in myself.
I enjoy healthy interdependence and connection with others.
I celebrate my successes and I am genuinely happy
for the successes of others.
My inner coach is awakened and inspires others to do the same.

ACKNOWLEDGEMENTS

It is with heartfelt thanks that I acknowledge the many people who have helped make this book possible. I am deeply grateful to my family for their unconditional love and encouragement. Words cannot express how much I adore them, and my heart is full with the joy they bring into my life daily.

To my parents, Tiberio and Isabel Silveira, for the courage, perseverance and hope they exercised when faced with uncommon challenges. They left behind their country of birth to provide greater opportunities and a better life for our family. With love and deep gratitude for their selfless gifts.

To my siblings whom I cherish—Phyllis Camboia, Joe Silveira, Isabel Pierce and Laurette Eslinger—you have always encouraged and supported me. We have comforted each other through life's difficulties and celebrated the joys. I am grateful for the beautiful, loving bond we share.

To Dr. Neal H. Mayerson and Donna Mayerson whose service to the cause of strengths education is helping to build a better world. I greatly appreciate your dedication to the mission of the VIA Institute on Character. And to Dr. Ryan Niemiec, Breta Cooper and Kelly Alluise at the VIA Institute on Character who work diligently to spread the empowering message of character strengths to the world.

To Dr. Martin E.P. Seligman, whose groundbreaking work in the field of positive psychology and hopeful message to the world inspired me to write this book.

To the Columbia University Coaching Certification Program and my friend and colleague, Dr. Terry Maltbia, who continues to inspire me toward coaching excellence. Your brilliant thought leadership, guidance, and contributions to the field of executive coaching have been invaluable.

To my friends and colleagues, David Covey and Stephan Mardyks, whose significant work at SMCOVEY helping content providers to share their empowering messages is increasing engagement and improving the way people show up in organizations around the world.

To Tiffany Yoast, my incredibly gifted friend and colleague who helped me as a sounding board while I discussed new tools and theories with her. Her beautiful work on the book design is greatly appreciated.

To Heather Moon who verified research citations and was a reader of the manuscript. To Echo Garrett, my friend and colleague, who helped with some of the stories from my previous book that are also included here.

To Matthew Morse and Jawad Mazhir who contributed to the design. Water images © Tatiana Shepeleva stock.adobe.com.

I am grateful to the many people who supported me through their reading of the manuscript and by providing their helpful feedback/edits, namely Dr. Felicia English, Dr. Michael Hunter, Carl Husa, Angie Pincin, Ann Larsen, Kendal Lukrich, Allyson Lyle, Chris McLaws, Rachel McLaws Nemelka, Liz Patterson, Laurinda Raquel, Phyllis Camboia, Isabel Silveira, Michelle Silva, Rebecca Espinola, Kristen Walton, Diane Williams, Karina Whetstine, Chris Whetstine, Shauna Wiest, Cheryl Anderson, Megan Heward, Echo Garrett, and Stacy Swain.

ENDNOTES

1   Williams, Ray. "Are We Hardwired to Be Negative or Positive?" International Coach Federation, June 30, 2014. https://coachfederation.org/blog/are-we-hardwired-to-be-negative-or-positive.

2   "When the Best Brings the Worst and the Worst Brings the Best." Outbrain 2014. https://www.outbrain.com/blog/headlines-when-the-best-brings-the-worst-and-the-worst-brings-thebest/

3   Williams, Ray. "Are We Hardwired to Be Negative or Positive?" International Coach Federation, June 30, 2014. https://coachfederation.org/blog/are-we-hardwired-to-be-negative-or-positive.

4   Hanson, Rick. "Confronting the Negativity Bias." Rick Hanson. Accessed September 1, 2019. http://www.rickhanson.net/how-your-brain-makes-you-easily-intimidated/

5   Csikszentmihalyi, Mihaly. *Flow: The Psychology of Optimal Experience*. 1 edition. New York: Harper Perennial Modern Classics, 2008.

6   "The 33 Most Inspirational Quotes from Our Live Webcasts." Oprah. Accessed March 27, 2020. http://www.oprah.com/oprahs-lifeclass/the-most-inspirational-quotes-from-our-live-webcasts_1/all.

7   Meah, Asad. "50 Inspirational Quotes on Awakening." Awaken the Greatness Within. Accessed March 27, 2020. https://www.awakenthegreatnesswithin.com/50-inspirational-quotes-on-awakening/.

8   "Resilience." Lexico powered by Oxford. Accessed August 31, 2019. https://www.lexico.com/en/definition/resilience.

9   Martínez-Martí, María Luisa, and Willibald Ruch. "Character Strengths Predict Resilience over and above Positive Affect, Self-Efficacy, Optimism, Social Support, Self-Esteem, and Life Satisfaction." *The Journal of Positive Psychology* 12 (April 25, 2016): 1—10.

10   Pennock, Seph Fontane. "Resilience in Positive Psychology: Bouncing Back & Staying Strong." PositivePsychology.com, March 3, 2017. https://positivepsychology.com/resilience-in-positive-psychology/; Ackerman, Courtney. "What Is Resilience and Why Is It Important to Bounce Back?" Positive Psychology. January 3, 2019. https://positivepsychology.com/what-is-resilience/.

11   Sirois, Maria. "Resilience is Possible at Any Time." Maria Sirois. Accessed September 8, 2019. http://mariasirois.com/news/entry/resilience_is_possible_at_any_time

12   Rowling, J.K. "Text of J.K. Rowling's Speech." The Harvard Gazette. June 5, 2008. Accessed September 8, 2019. https://news.harvard.edu/gazette/story/2008/06/text-of-j-k-rowling-speech/

13   Conley, Ember. "An Opioid Crisis Hits Home." AASA. August 2017. Accessed March 25, 2020. https://my.aasa.org/AASA/Resources/SAMag/2017/Aug17/Conley.aspx ; "Resilience, The Biology of Stress and the Science of Hope" KPJR Films. Accessed March 25, 2020. http://kpjr-films.co/resilience; "Chasing the Dragon: The Life of an Opiate Addict." FBI. Accessed March 25, 2020. https://www.fbi.gov/video-repository/newss-chasing-the-dragon-the-life-of-an-opiate-addict/view.

14   Peterson, C. and M.E.P. Seligman. *Character Strengths and Virtues: A handbook and Classification.* Washington, DC: American Psychological Association, 2004.

15   Peterson, C. and M.E.P. Seligman. *Character Strengths and Virtues: A handbook and Classification.* Washington, DC: American Psychological Association, 2004.

16   Peterson, C. and M.E.P. Seligman. *Character Strengths and Virtues: A handbook and Classification.* Washington, DC: American Psychological Association, 2004.

17   Rozin, Paul and Royzman, Edward B. "Negativity Bias, Negativity Dominance, and Contagion." SAGE Journals , (November 2001), https://journals.sagepub.com/doi/10.1207/S15327957PSPR0504_2

18   World Health Organization. ". Mental Health in the Workplace." May 2019. Accessed August 30, 2019. https://www.who.int/mental_health/in_the_workplace/en/ World Health Organization. "Depression." March 22, 2018. Accessed August 30, 2019. https://www.who.int/news-room/fact-sheets/detail/depression

19   Kauffman, Carol. "Positive Psychology: The Science at the Heart of Coaching." *Evidence Based Coaching Handbook: Putting Best Practices to Work for Your Clients*, edited by D. R. Stober & A. M. Grant 219-253. Hoboken, NJ: John Wiley, 2006.

20   Juma, Norbert. "Oprah Winfrey Quotes to Inspire Passion, Leadership, and Love." Everyday Power. April 16, 2018. Accessed March 25, 2020. https://everydaypower.com/oprah-winfrey-quotes-about-life/.

21   "67 Stephen Covey Quotes." Wow4U. Accessed March 27, 2020. https://www.wow4u.com/stephen-covey-quotes/.

22   "What the Research Says about Character Strengths." VIA Character. Accessed March 25, 2020. https://www.viacharacter.org/research/findings.

23   Niemiec, Ryan M. "Six Functions of Character Strengths for Thriving at Times of Adversity and Opportunity: a Theoretical Perspective." *Applied Research in Quality of Life* (January 2019). https://doi.org/10.1007/s11482-018-9692-2.

24   Hausler, M., C. Strecker, A. Huber, M. Brenner, T. Höge, and S. Höfer. "Distinguishing Relational Aspects of Character Strengths with Subjective and Psychological Well-Being." *Frontiers in Psychology*, 8 (2017a). https://doi.org/10.3389/fpsyg.2017.01159; Hausler, M., C. Strecker, A. Huber, M. Brenner, T. Höge, and S. Höfer. "Associations Between the Application of Signature Character Strengths, Health and Well-Being of Health Professionals." *Frontiers in Psychology*, 8 (2017b). https://doi.org/10.3389/fpsyg.2017.01307.

25   Peterson, C., W. Ruch, U. Beerman, N. Park, and M.E.P. Seligman. "Strengths of Character, Orientations to Happiness, and Life Satisfaction." Journal of Positive Psychology, 2 (2007): 149—156.

26   Seligman, Martin. *Authentic Happiness: Using the New Positive Psychology to Realize Your Potential for Lasting Fulfillment.* New York: Atria Books, 2003; *Flourish: A Visionary New Understanding of Happiness and Well-Being.* New York: Atria Books, 2012.

27   VIA Institute on Character. "Character Strengths and Virtues: A Handbook and Classification" Via Character. Accessed on Jun 8, 2015. http://www. viacharacter.org/www/About-Institute/Character-Strengths-and-Virtues.

28   Braden, Gregg. *The Science of Self-Empowerment: Awakening the New Human Story.* Reprint edition. Carlsbad: Hay House Inc., 2019.

29   "Muhammad Yunus on Microfinance." Enterprising Ideas NOW | PBS. Accessed September 1, 2019. http://www.shoppbs.pbs.org/now/enterprisingideas/Muhammad-Yunus.html.

30   "Spirituality" VIA Institute on Character. Accessed September 13, 2019. https://www.viacharacter.org/character-strengths/spirituality

31   "Spirituality" VIA Institute on Character. Accessed September 13, 2019. https://www.viacharacter.org/character-strengths/spirituality

32   "Spirituality" VIA Institute on Character. Accessed September 13, 2019. https://www.viacharacter.org/character-strengths/spirituality

33   "Nelson Mandela." Quotes. Accessed March 27, 2020. https://www.quotes.net/quote/3128.

34   Seligman, Martin. *Learned Optimism: How to Change Your Mind and Your Life.* New York: Vintage, 2006.

35   "Your Issues Are in Your Tissues." *MindBodyWise* (blog), August 9, 2016. https://mindbodywise.com/blog/your-issues-are-in-your-tissues/.

36   McDonough, Megan. "Defining Embodied Positive Psychology." Wholebeing Institute. Accessed March 25, 2020. https://wholebeinginstitute.com/defining-embodied-positive-psychology/.

37   The Number One Habit to Develop in Order to Feel More Positive." Amen Clinics. August 16, 2016. Accessed March 25, 2020. https://www.amenclinics.com/blog/number-one-habit-develop-order-feel-positive/.

38   Neff, Kristin. "The Motivational Power of Self Compassion." Self Compassion. 2016. https://self-compassion.org/the-motivational-power-of-self-compassion/

Allmendinger, Jutta, Hackman, J. Richard, and Lehman, Erin V. "Life and Work in Symphony Orchestras." The Musical Quarterly 80, no. 2 (July 1, 1996): 194—219. https://doi.org/10.1093/mq/80.2.194.

39   Neff, Kristin. "The Motivational Power of Self-compassion." Self-compassion. 2016. https://self-compassion.org/the-motivational-power-of-self-compassion/

40   Mayo Clinic Staff. "Positive Thinking: Stop Negative Self-Talk to Reduce Stress." Mayo Clinic. Accessed March 25, 2020. https://www.mayoclinic.org/healthy-lifestyle/stress-management/in-depth/positive-thinking/art-20043950.

41   Beck, Aaron T. "Thinking and Depression: I. Idiosyncratic Content and Cognitive Distortions." *Archives of General Psychiatry* 9, no. 4 (October 1, 1963): 324—33. https://doi.org/10.1001/archpsyc.1963.01720160014002.

42   Mayo Clinic Staff. "Positive Thinking: Stop Negative Self-Talk to Reduce Stress." Mayo Clinic. Accessed March 25, 2020. https://www.mayoclinic.org/healthy-lifestyle/stress-management/in-depth/positive-thinking/art-20043950.

43   Childre, Doc Lew, and Howard Martin. *The HeartMath Solution: The Institute of Heart-Math's Revolutionary Program for Engaging the Power of the Heart's Intelligence.* New York: Harper-One, 2000.

44   Reynolds, Gretchen. "How Meditation Changes the Brain and Body." New York Times. February 18, 2016. https://well.blogs.nytimes.com/2016/02/18/contemplation-therapy/; Cahn, B. Rael, Matthew S. Goodman, Christine T. Peterson, Raj Maturi, and Paul J. Mills. "Yoga, Meditation and Mind-Body Health: Increased BDNF, Cortisol Awakening Response, and Altered Inflammatory Marker Expression after a 3-Month Yoga and Meditation Retreat." *Frontiers in Human Neuroscience* 11 (June 26, 2017). https://doi.org/10.3389/fnhum.2017.00315; "Benefits of Mindfulness." Harvard Health. Accessed March 25, 2020. https://www.helpguide.org/harvard/benefits-of-mindfulness.htm

45   Powell, Alvin. "When Science Meets Mindfulness." *The Harvard Gazette* (April 9, 2018). https://news.harvard.edu/gazette/story/2018/04/harvard-researchers-study-how-mindfulness-may-change-the-brain-in-depressed-patients

46   Moss, Hanna. *The Practice of Mindful Yoga: A Connected Path to Awareness (Mindfulness).* Lewes, UK: Leaping Hare Press, 2018.

47   Discussion with Megan McDonough, CEO and Co-Founder of the Whole Being Institute. November 6, 2019.

48 "Understanding the Stress Response." Harvard Health Publishing. Modified May 1, 2018. Accessed March 25, 2020. https://www.health.harvard.edu/staying-healthy/understanding-the-stress-response.

49 Williams, Pat. *American Scandal*. Shippensburg: Destiny Image Publishers, 2003

50 HeartMath. Accessed September 13, 2019. https://www.heartmath.com

51 "Research Articles," HeartMath. Accessed September 13, 2019. https://www.heartmath.com/health-professionals/research-articles/.Ratanasiripong, Paul, Kevin Sverduk, Judy Prince, Diane Hayashino. "Biofeedback and Counseling for Stress and Anxiety Among College Students." *Journal of College Student Development*, 53:5 (September/October 2012): 742-749

Ratanasiripong, Paul, Nop Ratanasiripong, and Duangrat Kathalae "Biofeedback Intervention for Stress and Anxiety among Nursing Students: A Randomized Controlled Trial" *International Scholarly Research Network, ISRN Nursing* (2012). doi:10.5402/2012/827972.

Lemaire, Jane B., Jean E. Wallace, Adriane M. Lewin, Jillde Grood, Jeffrey P. Schaefer. The Effect of a Biofeedback-Based Stress Management Tool on Physician Stress: a Randomized Controlled Clinical Trial." *Open Medicine* **5(4), (2011).**

Linden, C. C. Linden, MA, FACHE, Cory Jackson, MA, Sheryl Rutledge, MS, DHES, RCEP, Chad Nath, Laura Nelson Todd. "The Heart of Grinnell: A Community-Wide Rural Health Wellness Initiative: a pilot Observational Study and A Prospective Study Design." *LofAlternative Therapies*, Vol. 16, no. 4 (2010): 46-49.

McCraty, Rollin PhD, Mike Atkinson and Dana Tomsino BA. "Impact of a Workplace Stress Reduction Program on Blood Pressure and Emotional Health in Hypertensive Employees." *The Journal of Alternative and Complementary Medicine*. Vol. 9, no. 3, (2003): 335-369.

Pipe, Teresa Britt, Vicki L. Buchda, Susan Launder, Barb Hudak, Lynne Hulvey, Katherine E. Karns, and Debra Pendergast. "Building Personal and Professional Resources of Resilience and Agility in the Healthcare Workplace" *Stress Health*. Mayo Clinic Hospital. DOI: 10.1002/smi.1396

McCraty, Rollin PhD, Mike Atkinson. "Resilience Training Program Reduces Physiological and Psychological Stress in Police Officers" *Global Advances in Health and Medicine*, Vol.1, no. 5 (November 2012): 44- 67.

Ginsberg, Jay P. PhD, Melanie E. Berry, MS, Donald A. Powell, PhD "Cardiac Coherence and Post Traumatic Stress Disorder in Combat Veterans" *Alternative Therapies*, Vol. 16, no. 4 (2010): 52-60.

Dunster, Christine RN, MA "Treatment of Anxiety and Stress with Biofeedback." *Global Advances in Health and Medicine*, Vol. 1, no. 4 (September 2012): 76-83.

52 HeartMath Institute. "Two Way Communication." HearthMath. Accessed September 1, 2019. Heartmath.org

53   Fredrickson, Barbara L., "The Broaden and Build Theory of Positive Emotions" *American Psychologist*, Vol 56(3), (March 2001): 218-226.

54   Fredrickson, Barbara L., and R. W. Levenson. "Positive Emotions Speed Recovery from the Cardiovascular Sequelae of Negative Emotions." *Cognitive Emotions* 12, no. 2 (1998): 191-220.

55   HeartMath Institute. "Heart Intelligence" (August 7, 2012). Heartmath.org

56   Frankl, Viktor. *Man's Search for Meaning*. Boston: Beacon Press, 2006.

57   Grant, A. M. "The Impact of Coaching on Goal Attainment, Meta-Cognition, and Mental Health." *Social Behavior and Personality, 31* (2003): 253-263.

58   Green, L. S., L.G. Oades, and A.M. Grant. "Cognitive-Behavioral, Solution-Focused Life Coaching: Enhancing Goal Striving, Well-Being, and Hope." *The Journal of Positive Psychology, 1* vol 3 (2006): 142-149.

59   Curry, Colleen. "Maya Angelou's Wisdom Distilled in 10 of Her Best Quotes." ABC News. May 28, 2014. Accessed March 27, 2020. https://abcnews.go.com/Entertainment/maya-angelous-wisdom-distilled-10-best-quotes/story?id=23895284.

60   Andrews, Evan. "9 Things You May Not Know About Michelangelo." HISTORY. August 31, 2018. Accessed August 31, 2019. https://www.history.com/news/9-things-you-may-not-know-about-michelangelo.

61   Carnegie, Dale. *How to Win Friends and Influence People*. New York: The World's Work, 1981.

62   Cunningham, Sachi, and Chandler Evans. "CRUTCH." YouTube video, 4:03. Posted by

"Viyabobo." https://www.youtube.com/watch?v=_zjfpdRlbbA.

63   Cunningham, Sachi, and Chandler Evans. "CRUTCH." YouTube video, 4:03. Posted by "Viyabobo." https://www.youtube.com/watch?v=_zjfpdRlbbA.

64   Maraboli, Steve. *Life, the Truth, and Being Free*. New York: A Better Today Publishing, 2009.

65   Carter, Christine "Happiness." *Gratitude Revealed*. Moving Art. 2018. https://www.christinecarter.com/2015/11/happiness-gratitude-revealed/

66   Skiffington, Suzanne, and Perry Zeus. *The Coaching at Work Toolkit*. 1 edition. New York, N.Y. London: McGraw-Hill Book Company Australia, 2002; Tichy, Noel M. *The Cycle of Leadership: How Great Leaders Teach Their Companies to Win*. Reprint edition. New York: HarperCollins, 2009.

67   Tolle, Eckhart. *The Power of Now: A Guide to Spiritual Enlightenment*. Novato: New World Library, 2004.

68   Tedeschi, R.G. and L. G. Calhoun. *Trauma and Transformation: Growing in the Aftermath of Suffering*. Thousand Oaks CA: Sage, 1995.

69   Nijdam, M.J., C.A.I. van der Meer, M. van Zuiden, P. Dashtgard, D. Medema, Y. Qing, P. Zhutovsky, A. Bakker, M. Olff. "Turning Wounds into Wisdom: Posttraumatic Growth over the Course of Two Types of Trauma-Focused Psychotherapy in Patients with PTSD." *J Affect Disord*, 227 (2017): 424-431.

70   World Health Organization. "Depression." March 22, 2018. Accessed August 30, 2019. https://www.who.int/news-room/fact-sheets/detail/depression

71   World Health Organization. "Mental Health in the Workplace." May 2019. Accessed August 30, 2019. https://www.who.int/mental_health/in_the_workplace/en/

72   "The Top Mental Health Challenges Facing Students." Best Colleges. Accessed August 30, 2019. https://www.bestcolleges.com/resources/top-5-mental-health-problems-facing-college-students/

73   World Health Organization. "Suicide" August 24, 2018. Accessed August 31, 2019. https://www.who.int/news-room/fact-sheets/detail/suicide

74   World Health Organization. "Suicide" August 24, 2018. Accessed August 31, 2019. https://www.who.int/news-room/fact-sheets/detail/suicide

75   Breel, Kevin. "Confessions of a Depressed Comic." TED Talks. May 2013. Accessed August 29, 2019. https://www.ted.com/talks/kevin_breel_confessions_of_a_depressed_comic

76   Martínez-Martí, María Luisa, and Willibald Ruch. "Character Strengths Predict Resilience

over and above Positive Affect, Self-Efficacy, Optimism, Social Support, Self-Esteem, and Life Satisfaction." *The Journal of Positive Psychology* 12 (April 25, 2016): 1—10.

77   Niemiec, R. "Six Functions of Character Strengths for Thriving at Times of Adversity and Opportunity: A Theoretical Perspective." *Applied Research in Quality of Life, (2019).* http://doi.org/10.1007/s11482-018-9692-2 CS_thriving_6_functions_-theory_article(Niemiec_2019).pdf

78   Barton, Y. A., S.H. Barkin, and L. Miller. "Deconstructing depression: A latent profile analysis of potential depressive subtypes in emerging adults." *Spirituality in Clinical Practice* 4(1), (2017): 1-21. http://dx.doi.org/10.1037/scp0000126

79   National Suicide Prevention Lifeline. Accessed March 25, 2020.https://suicidepreventionlifeline.org

80   Hyman, Mark. *The UltraMind Solution. Fix Your Broken Brain by Healing Your Body First.* New York: Scribner, 2008.

81   Tindle, Hilary A., Yue-Fang Chang, Lewis H. Kuller, JoAnn E. Manson, Jennifer G. Robinson, Milagros C. Rosal, Greg J. Siegle, and Karen A. Matthews. "Optimism, Cynical Hostility, and Incident Coronary Heart Disease and Mortality in the Women's Health Initiative." *Circulation* 120, no. 8 (August 25, 2009): 656—62.

82   Holt-Lunstad, Julianne, Timothy B Smith, and J Bradley Layton. "Social Relationships and Mortality Risk: A meta-analytic Review." *PLoS Medicine* 7, no. 7 (2010). DOI: 10.1371/journal. pmed.1000316.

83   Williams, R. *Anger Kills: Seventeen Strategies for Controlling the Hostility That Can Harm Your Health.* New York: Harper Torch 1998; Rosenbert, E.L., P. Ekman, et al. "Linkages between facial expressions of anger and transient myocardial ischemia in men with coronary artery disease," *Emotion* 1 (2001):107:15.

84   Gielan, Michelle. "The Financial Upside of Being an Optimist." Harvard Business Review. March 12, 2019. https://hbr.org/2019/03/the-financial-upside-of-being-an-optimist

85   Davidson, Richard. "Be Happy Like a Monk." Presentation at Wisconsin Academy, Columbus WI, February 13, 2007.

86   Huppert F. A., Baylis N., Keverne B., and Fredrickson Barbara L. "The Broaden—and— Build Theory of Positive Emotions." *Philosophical Transactions of the Royal Society of London. Series B: Biological Sciences* 359, no. 1449 (September 29, 2004): 1367—77.

87   Winerman, Lea. "Suppressing the 'White Bears.'" American Psychological Association. October 2011. Accessed March 27, 2020. https://www.apa.org/monitor/2011/10/unwanted-thoughts

88   Wegner, Daniel M., David J. Scheider, Samuel R. Carter, and Teri L. White. "Paradoxical Effects of Thought Suppression." *Journal of Personality and Social Psychology* 53, no. 1, (1987): 5-13.

89   Wenzlaff, Richard M., and Daniel M. Wegner. "Thought Suppression." *Annu. Rev. Psychology* 51 (2000): 59-91.

90   Booth, DeJanay. "Study: 20 Minutes in Nature Reduces Stress Hormone Levels." Detroit Free Press. April 4, 2019. https://www.freep.com/story/news/local/michigan/2019/04/04/stress-blood-pressure-cholesterol-nature/3362288002/

91   Exercise-Induced Neuroplasticity - Creating New Neural Pathways." Ausmed. August 13, 2017. https://www.ausmed.com/cpd/articles/exercise-induced-neuroplasticity

92   Coelho, Paulo. "Doubt and Fear." Paulo Coelo Blog. August 25, 2011. Accessed March 27, 2020. https://paulocoelhoblog.com/2011/08/25/doubt-and-fear-editar/

93   Juma, Norbert. "25 Malala Yousafzai Quotes that Have Changed the World." Everyday Power. March 18, 2019. Accessed March 23, 2020. https://everydaypower.com/malala-yousafzai-quotes/.

94   Emoto, Masaru. *Secret Life of Water.* New York: Atria Books, 2011.

95   Susan Fendler. Park City Spa Yoga. Accessed September 9, 2019. parkcityspayoga.com

96   Stahl, Lesley. "Architect Goes Blind, Says He's Actually Gotten Better at His Job." CBS News. January 13, 2019. https://www.cbsnews.com/news/architect-chris-downey-goes-blind-says-hes-actually-gotten-better-at-his-job-60-minutes/

97   Zone, Eric. "Without Failure, Jordon Would Be a False Idol." Chicago Tribune May 19, 1997. http://articles.chicagotribune.com/1997-05-19/ news/9705190096_1_nike-mere-rumor-driver-s-license .

98   "Richard Branson." Biography. June 5, 2019. https://www.biography.com/business-figure/richard-branson

99   "Albert Einstein Biography, Education, Discoveries, & Facts | Britannica.Com." Accessed September 1, 2019. https://www.britannica.com/biography/Albert-Einstein.

100   "Mark Twain Quotes." Goodreads. Accessed September 1 2019. https://www.goodreads.com/quotes/548857-comparison-is-the-death-of-joy

101   boutje777. "Keeping up with the Joneses." *Newspaper Comic Strips* (blog), February 20, 2016. https://newspapercomicstripsblog.wordpress.com/2016/02/20/keeping-up-with-the-joneses/.

102   Price, Catherine. "Trapped — The Secret Ways Social Media is Built to be Addictive (and What You Can do to Fight Back.)" Science Focus. October 29, 2018. https://www.sciencefocus.com/future-technology/trapped-the-secret-ways-social-media-is-built-to-be-addictive-and-what-you-can-do-to-fight-back/.

103   Haynes, Trevor. "Dopamine, Smartphones & You: A Battle for Your Time" May 1, 2018. Harvard University. http://sitn.hms.harvard.edu/flash/2018/dopamine-smartphones-battle-time/

104   Blankson, Amy. *The Future of Happiness: 5 Modern Strategies for Balancing Productivity and Well-Being in the Digital Era*. Dallas: BenBella Books, 2017.

105   Greenspon, Thomas *Moving Past Perfect*. Minneapolis: Free Spirit Publishing, 2012.

106   Dahl, Melissa. "The Alarming New Research on Perfectionism." *The Cut*. September 30, 2014. https://www.thecut.com/2014/09/alarming-new-research-on-perfectionism.html

107   Greenspon, Thomas. *Moving Past Perfect*. Minneapolis: Free Spirit Publishing, 2012.

108   Jiang, Jia. "What I Learned from 100 Days of Rejection." Ted Talks. May 2015. https://www.ted.com/talks/jia_jiang_what_i_learned_from_100_days_of_rejection?language=en

109   Carter, Christine "Happiness." *Gratitude Revealed*. Moving Art. 2018. https://www.christinecarter.com/2015/11/happiness-gratitude-revealed/

110   Schwartzburg, Louie. *Gratitude Revealed*. Moving Art. 2018. https://movingart.com/gratitude-revealed/

111   Brown, Brene. *The Gifts of Imperfection: Let Go of Who You Think You're Supposed to Be and Embrace Who You Are*. Center City: Hazelden Publishing, 2010.

112   Clark, M. C. "Off the Beaten Path: Some Creative Approaches to Adult Learning." *New Directions for Adult and Continuing Education* 89 (Spring 2001): 83-91.

113   Dominice, Pierre. *Learning from Our Lives: Using Educational Biographies with Adults*. San Francisco: Jossey-Bass, 2000.

114   Huppert F. A., Baylis N., Keverne B., and Fredrickson Barbara L. "The Broaden—and—Build Theory of Positive Emotions." *Philosophical Transactions of the Royal Society of London. Series B: Biological Sciences* 359, no. 1449 (September 29, 2004): 1367—77.

115   Martínez-Martí, María Luisa, and Willibald Ruch. "Character Strengths Predict Resilience Over and Above Positive Affect, Self-Efficacy, Optimism, Social Support, Self-Esteem, and Life Satisfaction." *The Journal of Positive Psychology* 12 (April 25, 2016): 1—10; Martínez-Martí, María Luisa, and Willibald Ruch. "Character Strengths and Well-Being across the Life Span: Data from a Representative Sample of German-Speaking Adults Living in Switzerland." *Front. Psychol.*, 2014; Fredrickson, Barbara L., and R. W. Levenson. "Positive Emotions Speed Recovery from the Cardiovascular Sequelae of Negative Emotions." *Cognitive Emotions* 12, no. 2 (1998): 191-220.

116   Martínez-Martí, María Luisa, and Willibald Ruch. "Character Strengths Predict Resilience Over and Above Positive Affect, Self-Efficacy, Optimism, Social Support, Self-Esteem, and Life Satisfaction." *The Journal of Positive Psychology* 12 (April 25, 2016): 1—10.

117   Peterson, Christopher, Nansook Park, and Martin E. P. Seligman. "Greater Strengths of Character and Recovery from Illness." *The Journal of Positive Psychology* 1, no. 1 (January 1, 2006): 17—26. https://doi.org/10.1080/17439760500372739.

118   Peterson, Christopher, Nansook Park, Nnamdi Pole, Wendy D'Andrea, Martin E. P. Seligman. "Strengths of Character and Posttraumatic Growth." *Journal of Traumatic Stress* 21, no. 2 (2008): 214-217

119   Martínez-Martí, María Luisa, and Willibald Ruch. "Character Strengths Predict Resilience over and above Positive Affect, Self-Efficacy, Optimism, Social Support, Self-Esteem, and Life Satisfaction." *The Journal of Positive Psychology* 12 (April 25, 2016): 1—10

120   Peterson, Christopher, Nansook Park, Nnamdi Pole, Wendy D'Andrea, Martin E. P. Seligman. "Strengths of Character and Posttraumatic Growth." *Journal of Traumatic Stress* 21, no. 2 (2008): 214-217

121   Martínez-Martí, María Luisa, and Willibald Ruch. "Character Strengths Predict Resilience over and above Positive Affect, Self-Efficacy, Optimism, Social Support, Self-Esteem, and Life Satisfaction." *The Journal of Positive Psychology* 12 (April 25, 2016): 1—10.

122   Martínez-Martí, María Luisa, and Willibald Ruch. "Character Strengths Predict Resilience over and above Positive Affect, Self-Efficacy, Optimism, Social Support, Self-Esteem, and Life Satisfaction." *The Journal of Positive Psychology* 12 (April 25, 2016): 1—10.

123   Fredrickson, Barbara L., and R. W. Levenson. "Positive Emotions Speed Recovery from the Cardiovascular Sequelae of Negative Emotions." *Cognitive Emotions* 12, no. 2 (1998): 191-220.

124 Fredrickson, Barbara L., "The Broaden and Build Theory of Positive Emotions" American Psychologist, Vol 56(3), Mar 2001, 218-226

125 Covey, Stephen M.R. *The Speed of Trust: The One Thing that Changes Everything*. New York: Free Press, 2008.

126 Brown, Brene. "Own our History. Change the Story." Brenebrown.com. June 18, 2015. Accessed March 23, 2020. https://brenebrown.com/blog/2015/06/18/own-our-history-change-the-story/

127 "Mindfulness." Wikipedia. Accessed March 25, 2020. https://en.wikipedia.org/wiki/Mindfulness.

128 Niemiec, R. M. "Mindful living: Character Strengths Interventions as Pathways for the Five Mindfulness Trainings." *International Journal of Wellbeing*, 2(1), (2012): 22—33. https://doi.org/10.5502/ijw.v2i1.2.

129 Fredrickson, Barbara L., Ph.D. *Love 2.0: How Our Supreme Emotion Affects Everything We Feel, Think, Do, and Become,* New York: Hudson Street Press, 2013.

130 McDonough, Megan. "Defining Embodied Positive Psychology." Wholebeing Institute. Accessed March 25, 2020. https://wholebeinginstitute.com/defining-embodied-positive-psychology/.

131 Tolle, Eckhart. *The Power of Now: A Guide to Spiritual Enlightenment.* Novato: New World Library, 2004.

132 Greenspon, Thomas S. "Is There an Antidote to Perfectionism?" *Psychology in the Schools*, 51:9, 986-998.

133 "Understanding the Stress Response." Harvard Health Publishing. Modified May 1, 2018. Accessed March 25, 2020. https://www.health.harvard.edu/staying-healthy/understanding-the-stress-response.

134 Neff, K. D., & Germer, C. K. (2013). "A Pilot Study and Randomized Controlled Trial of the Mindful Self-Compassion Program." *Journal of Clinical Psychology*, 69, (2019): 28-44.

135 Neff, K. D., & Germer, C. K. (2013). "A Pilot Study and Randomized Controlled Trial of the Mindful Self-Compassion Program." *Journal of Clinical Psychology*, 69, (2019): 28-44.

136 Benson, Herbert. *Relaxation Revolution: The Science and Genetics of Mind Body Healing.* Scribner: New York, 2011.

137 "Mindfulness" in *The Cambridge Advanced Learner's Dictionary & Thesaurus.* Cambridge University Press, 2020. https://dictionary.cambridge.org/us/dictionary/english/mindfulness.

138 Niemiec, Ryan M. *Mindfulness and Character Strengths: A Practical Guide to Flourishing. Kirkland: Hogrefre Publishing*, 2013.

139 Faulds, Danna. Go In and In: Poems from the Heart of Yoga. Morris Publishing, 2002.

140 Young, Shinzen. "Break Through Pain: Practical Steps for Transforming Physical Pain into Spiritual Growth." Shinzen.org. Accessed Jun 8, 2015. http://www.shinzen. org/Articles/artPain. htm.

141 "Sallatha Sutta: The Arrow" (SN 36.6). Translated from the Pali by Thanissaro Bhikkhu. Access to Insight (Legacy Edition) 30 November 2013.

142 Delia, Lalah. *Vibrate Higher Daily: Live Your Power.* San Francisco: HarperOne, 2019.

143 Fredrickson, Barbara L., R. A. Mancuso, C. Branigan, and M. M. Tugade. "The Undoing Effect of Positive Emotions." *Motiv Emot.* 24 no. 4 (2000):237-258.

144 Fredrickson, Barbara L., and R. W. Levenson. "Positive Emotions Speed Recovery from the Cardiovascular Sequelae of Negative Emotions." *Cognitive Emotions* 12, no. 2 (1998): 191-220.

145 Fredrickson, Barbara L., "The Broaden and Build Theory of Positive Emotions" American Psychologist, Vol 56(3), Mar 2001, 218-226

146 Fredrickson, Barbara L., "The Broaden and Build Theory of Positive Emotions" American Psychologist, Vol 56(3), Mar 2001, 218-226.

147 Armenta, Fritz, Lyubomirsky. "Functions of Positive Emotions: Gratitude as a Motivator of Self-Empowerment and Positive Change." Emotion Review (2017). http://sonjalyubomirsky.com/ files/2012/09/Armenta-Fritz-Lyubomirsky-2017.pdf

148 Halliwell, Ed. "When the Mind Goes Dark." Mindful. 21 May 2018, www.mindful.org/ mind-goes-dark/

149 "Karaniya Metta Sutta: The Buddha's Words on Loving-Kindness." Translated from the Pali by The Amaravati Sangha. Access to Insight. 2004. Accessed March 25, 2020. https://www.access-toinsight.org/tipitaka/kn/snp/snp.1.08.amar.html

150 Dyer, Wayne W. " The Power of I Am." Drwaynedyer.com. Accessed March 24, 2020. https:// www.drwaynedyer.com/blog/the-power-of-i-am/

151 Tolle, Eckhart. *The Power of Now: A Guide to Spiritual Enlightenment.* Novato: New World Library, 2004.

152 Hanson, Rick. "Find What's Sacred." Psychology Today. October 1, 2013. Accessed September 1, 2019. https://www.psychologytoday.com/us/blog/your-wise-brain/201310/find-whats-sacred

153 Ghandi, Mahatma. *Soul Force: Ghandi's Writings on Peace.* Chennai: Tara Publishing, 2004

154 Hanson, Rick. "Find What's Sacred." Psychology Today. October 1, 2013. Accessed September 1, 2019. https://www.psychologytoday.com/us/blog/your-wise-brain/201310/find-whats-sacred

155 Boroditsky, Lera. "How Does Our Language Shape the Way We Think?" Edge. June 11, 2019. Accessed March 25, 2020. https://www.edge.org/conversation/lera_boroditsky-how-does-our-language-shape-the-way-we-think

156 Seligman, Martin. Third World Presentation Congress on Positive Psychology. 2013 International Positive Psychology Association.

157 Razetti, Gustavo. "Appreciative Inquiry: A Positive Approach to Change." Liberationist. Accessed September 1, 2019; "Words Create Worlds." The Center for Appreciate Inquiry. Accessed September 1, 2019. https://www.centerforappreciativeinquiry.net/words-create-worlds

158 Emoto, Masaru. Interviewed by Fatima Doman. 2013.

159 Emoto, Masaru. *Messages from Water and the Universe.* Carlsbad: Hay House, 2010; *The True Power of Water: Healing and Discovering Ourselves.* Hillsboro: Beyond Words Publishing, 2005; Introduction

160 "The Water in You: Water and the Human Body." USGS. Accessed September 1, 2019. https://www.usgs.gov/special-topic/water-science-school/science/water-you-water-and-human-body?qt-science_center_objects=0#qt-science_center_objects

161 Hay, Louise. "The Man Who Talks to Water." Heal Your Life. July 22, 2010. Accessed March 25, 2020. https://www.healyourlife.com/the-man-who-talks-to-water.

162 Ross, Christina L Ph.D. "Energy Medicine: Current Status and Future Perspectives," *Journal of Global Advances in Health and Medicine,* 8 (2019)

163 Goswami, Amit. *The Self-Aware Universe: How Consciousness Creates the Material World.* New York: Tarcherperigree, *1995;* "Mind Over Matter," Wired April 1, 1995, https://www.wired.com/1995/04/pear; Lincoln, Don. "The Good Vibrations of Quantum Field Theories." PBS. August 5, 2013. Accessed September 1, 2019. https://www.pbs.org/wgbh/nova/article/the-good-vibrations-of-quantum-field-theories/

164 Dispenza, Joe. You Are the Placebo: Making Your Mind Matter. Carlsbad: Hay House, 2015; Dispenza, Joe. Becoming Supernatural: How Common People are Doing the Uncommon. Carlsbad: Hay House, 2019; "Physicists Count Sound Particles with Quantum Microphone." PHYS. July 27, 2019. Accessed September 2019. https://phys.org/news/2019-07-physicists-particles-quantum-microphone.html

165 Bedrij, Orest. *Exodus III: Great Joy and Glory to the Most High as You.* Xlibris Corporation, 2011.

166 Garfinkel, Perry. "Four Noble Buddha Quotes." HuffPost. March 28, 2008. Accessed September 1, 2019. https://www.huffpost.com/entry/four-noble-buddha-quotes_b_86728

167 *The Bhagavad-Gita.* Chicago: The University of Chicago Press, 1929.

168 Soundings of the Planet. "Joan Borysenko, Ph.D. - Clip from 'Sonic Healing' Meet the Masters Video Course." Youtube video, 4:25. "SoundingsofthePlanet," October 30, 2014. https://www.youtube.com/watch?v=RT9YBkxTHos

169 "What is the Meaning of Om?" *Gaia. February 28, 2017.* https://www.gaia.com/article/what-meaning-om

170 "Six Nikola Tesla Quotes that Might Change the Way You See the World." Learning Mind. Accessed September 1, 2019. https://www.learning-mind.com/nikola-tesla-quotes/ .

171 Gilbert, Paul and Liotti Giovanni. "Mentalizing, Motivation, and Social Mentalities: Theoretical Considerations and Implications for Psychotherapy." *Psychology and Psychotherapy: Theory, Research, and Practice* 84 (2011): 9-25.

172 Team Tony. ""Life is Happening For Me:" World-Class Triathlete and Coach Siri Lindley on How Pain Can Serve You." Tony Robbins. Accessed September 1, 2019. https://www.tonyrobbins.com/mind-meaning/life-is-happening-for-me/

173 Phelps, Michael. "NBC's 2016 Rio Preview Show." Interviewed by Bob Costas. August 3, 2016.

174 Pace, Noelle Pikus. Focused. Salt Lake City: Desert Book Company, 2014

175 Clarey, Christopher. "Olympians Use Imagery as Mental Training." New York Times. February 22, 2014. Accessed September 9, 2019. https://www.nytimes.com/2014/02/23/sports/olympics/olympians-use-imagery-as-mental-training.html; Cohn, Patrick. "Sports Visualization: The Secret Weapon of Athletes." Peak Sports. Accessed September 9, 2019. https://www.peaksports.com/sports-psychology-blog/sports-visualization-athletes/

176 Stambulova, Natalia B., Craig A. Wrisberg, and Tatiana V. Ryba. "A Tale of Two Traditions in Applied Sport Psychology: The Heyday of Soviet Sport and Wake-Up Calls for North America." Journal of Applied Sport Psychology 18, no. 3 (September 1, 2006): 173–84. https://doi.org/10.1080/10413200600830182.

177 Nicklaus, Jack. Golf My Way. New York: Simon & Schuster, 2005.

178 Adams, AJ. "Seeing is Believing: The Power of Visualization" Psychology Today. December 3, 2009. Accessed September 9, 2019. https://www.psychologytoday.com/us/blog/flourish/200912/seeing-is-believing-the-power-visualization

179 Taylor, Shelley E., and Lien B. Pham. "The Effect of Mental Simulation on Goal-Directed Performance." Imagination, Cognition and Personality 18, no. 4 (1999): 253-268.

180 Fredrickson, Barbara L., "The Broaden and Build Theory of Positive Emotions" American Psychologist, Vol 56(3), Mar 2001, 218-226

181 Armenta, Fritz, Lyubomirsky. "Functions of Positive Emotions: Gratitude as a Motivator of Self-Empowerment and Positive Change." Emotion Review 9(3), (2017): 183-190. http://sonjalyubomirsky.com/files/2012/09/Armenta-Fritz-Lyubomirsky-2017.pdf

182 "15 Quotes to Inspire Your Employee Wellness Program." Zipongo. Accessed March 25, 2020. https://meetzipongo.com/blog/15-quotes-inspire-employee-wellness-program/

183 "15 Quotes to Inspire Your Employee Wellness Program." Zipongo. Accessed March 25, 2020. https://meetzipongo.com/blog/15-quotes-inspire-employee-wellness-program/

184 Proyer, R. T., F. Gander, S. Wellenzohn, and W. Ruch "What Good Are Character Strengths Beyond Subjective Well-Being? The Contribution of the Good Character on Self-Reported Health Oriented Behavior, Physical Fitness, and the Subjective Health Status." The Journal of Positive Psychology 8 (2013): 222-232.

185 Leontopoulou, Sophie and Sofia Triliva. "Explorations of Subjective Well-being and Character Strengths Among a Greek University Student Sample." International Journal of Well-being 2, no. 3 (2012): 251-270.

186 Proctor, C., J. Maltby, and P. A. Linley. "Strengths Use as a Predictor of Well-Being and Health-Related Quality of Life." Journal of Happiness Studies 10 (2009): 583-630.

187 Achor, Shawn, and Michelle Gielan. "Resilience Is About How You Recharge, Not How You Endure." Harvard Business Review, June 24, 2016. https://hbr.org/2016/06/resilience-is-about-how-you-recharge-not-how-you-endure.

188 Achor, Shawn, and Michelle Gielan. "Resilience Is About How You Recharge, Not How You Endure." Harvard Business Review, June 24, 2016. https://hbr.org/2016/06/resilience-is-about-how-you-recharge-not-how-you-endure.

189 Huffington, Arianna. The Sleep Revolution: Transforming Your Life, One Night at a Time. 1 edition. New York: Harmony, 2016.

190 Prather, Aric A., Denise Janicki-Deverts, Martica H. Hall, and Sheldon Cohen. "Behaviorally Assessed Sleep and Susceptibility to the Common Cold." Sleep 38(9), (September 2015): 1353–1359, https://doi.org/10.5665/sleep.4968

191 Huffington, Arianna. The Sleep Revolution: Transforming Your Life, One Night at a Time. 1 edition. New York: Harmony, 2016.

192 Achor, Shawn, and Michelle Gielan. "Resilience Is About How You Recharge, Not How You Endure." Harvard Business Review, June 24, 2016. https://hbr.org/2016/06/resilience-is-about-how-you-recharge-not-how-you-endure.

193 Peterson, C. & Seligman, M.E.P. Character Strengths and Virtues: A handbook and classification. Washington, DC: American Psychological Association Press and Oxford University Press, 2004.

194 David Whyte, The Heart Aroused: Poetry and the Preservation of the Soul of Corporate America. New York: Crown Business, 1996.

195 "The Wisdom of Booker T. Washington. Leadership Now. February 14, 2011. Accessed March 25, 2020. https://www.leadershipnow.com/leadingblog/2011/02/the_wisdom_of_booker_t_washing.html

196 Borysenko, Joan Z. Fire in the Soul: A New Psychology of Spiritual Optimism. New York: Grand Central Publishing, 1993.

197 Brown, Brene. "Brene Brown: 3 Ways to Set Boundaries." Oprah.com. Accessed March 25, 2020. http://www.oprah.com/spirit/how-to-set-boundaries-brene-browns-advice.

198 Anderson, Amy Rees. "'Resentment Is Like Taking Poison And Waiting For The Other Person To Die'" Forbes. April 7, 2015. Accessed September 8, 2019. https://www.forbes.com/sites/amyanderson/2015/04/07/resentment-is-like-taking-poison-and-waiting-for-the-other-person-to-die/#38e9f536446c

199 Kor, Eva. "Eva Kor." The Forgiveness Project. Accessed September 6, 2019. https://www.theforgivenessproject.com/eva-kor

200 Saffarinia, Majid and Mohammadi, Narges and Afshar, Hamid (2016) "The Role of Interpersonal Forgiveness in Resilience and Severity of Pain in Chronic Pain Patients." Journal of Fundamentals of Mental Health 18 (4) (2016): pp. 212-219. http://eprints.mums.ac.ir/1926/l; Harris, A.H, F.M. Luskin, S.V. Benisovich, S. Standard, J. Bruning, S. Evans, and C. Thoresen. "Effects of a Group Forgiveness Intervention on Forgiveness, Perceived Stress and Trait Anger: A Randomized Trial." Journal of Clinical Psychology. 62(6), (2006): 715-733; "Studies Suggest Forgiveness Has Health Benefits." National Public Radio. January 2, 2008. Accessed September 8, 2019. https://www.npr.org/templates/story/story.php?storyId=17785209

201 Lees, Adena Bank. "Forgiveness: A Path To Healing and Emotional Freedom." Psychology Today. November 13, 2018. Accessed September 5, 2019. https://www.psychologytoday.com/us/blog/surviving-thriving/201811/forgiveness-the-path-healing-and-emotional-freedom; Jr, Everett L. Worthington, and Michael Scherer. "Forgiveness Is an Emotion-Focused Coping Strategy That Can Reduce Health Risks and Promote Health Resilience: Theory, Review, and Hypotheses." Psychology & Health 19, no. 3 (June 1, 2004): 385–405. https://doi.org/10.1080/0887044042000196674.

202 Mayo Clinic Staff. "Forgiveness: Letting Go of Grudges and Bitterness." Mayo Clinic. September 5, 2019. https://www.mayoclinic.org/healthy-lifestyle/adult-health/in-depth/forgiveness/art-20047692

203 Mayo Clinic Staff. "Forgiveness: Letting Go of Grudges and Bitterness." Mayo Clinic. September 5, 2019. https://www.mayoclinic.org/healthy-lifestyle/adult-health/in-depth/forgiveness/art-20047692

204 Aten, Jamie D. "Resilience and Forgiveness: An interview with Dr. Everett Worthington on this important connection." Psychology Today. January 8, 2019. Accessed September 5, 2019. https://www.psychologytoday.com/us/blog/heal-and-carry/201901/resilience-and-forgiveness

205 Aten, Jamie D. "Resilience and Forgiveness: An interview with Dr. Everett Worthington on this important connection." Psychology Today. January 8, 2019. Accessed September 5, 2019. https://www.psychologytoday.com/us/blog/heal-and-carry/201901/resilience-and-forgiveness

206 "REACH Forgiveness." Everett Worthington. Accessed September 5, 2019. http://www.evworthington-forgiveness.com/reach-forgiveness/

207 Aten, Jamie D. "Resilience and Forgiveness: An interview with Dr. Everett Worthington on this important connection." Psychology Today. January 8, 2019. Accessed September 5, 2019. https://www.psychologytoday.com/us/blog/heal-and-carry/201901/resilience-and-forgiveness

208 Shapiro, Joseph. "Amish Forgive School Shooter, Struggle with Grief." National Public Radio. October 2, 2007. Accessed September 8, 2019. https://www.npr.org/templates/story/story.php?storyId=14900930; Walters, Joanna. "'The Happening': 10 Years After the Amish Shooting." The Guardian. October 2, 2016. Accessed September 8, 2019. https://www.theguardian.com/us-news/2016/oct/02/amish-shooting-10-year-anniversary-pennsylvania-the-happening

209 Kor, Eva. "Eva Kor." The Forgiveness Project. Accessed September 6, 2019. https://www.theforgivenessproject.com/eva-kor

210 Luskin, Frederic. Forgive for Good. Reprint edition. New York, NY: HarperOne, 2003.

211 Luskin, Frederic. "About." Learning to Forgive. Accessed September 6, 2019. https://learningtoforgive.com/about/

212 Luskin, Frederic. "9 Steps." Learning to Forgive. Accessed September 6, 2019. https://learningtoforgive.com/9-steps/

213 Luskin, Frederic. "9 Steps." Learning to Forgive. Accessed September 6, 2019. https://learningtoforgive.com/9-steps/

214 Tolle, Eckhart. The Power of Now: A Guide to Spiritual Enlightenment. Vancouver, B.C., Canada : Novato, Calif: Namaste Publishing, 2004.

215 "Buddy Hackett Quotes" Goodreads. Accessed March 25, 2020. https://www.goodreads.com/quotes/75453-don-t-carry-a-grudge-while-you-re-carrying-a-grudge-the

216 Tolle, Eckhart. The Power of Now: A Guide to Spiritual Enlightenment. Vancouver, B.C., Canada : Novato, Calif: Namaste Publishing, 2004.

217 "Elizabeth Earnshaw." A Better Life Therapy. Accessed March 25, 2020. https://abetterlifetherapy.com/about

218 Covey, Stephen R. The 7 Habits of Highly Effective People: Powerful Lessons in Personal Change. Anniversary edition. New York: Simon & Schuster, 2013.

219 Pury, Cynthia, and Shane Lopez. The Psychology of Courage: Modern Research on an Ancient Virtue. Washington, DC, US: American Psychological Association, 2010. https://doi.org/10.1037/12168-000.

220 Brown, Brené. Rising Strong: How the Ability to Reset Transforms the Way We Live, Love, Parent, and Lead. New York: Random House Trade Paperbacks, 2015.

221 Brown, Brené. "Brené Brown: 3 Ways to Set Boundaries." Oprah. Accessed September 6, 2019. http://www.oprah.com/spirit/how-to-set-boundaries-brene-browns-advice

222 Buck, Chad. Establishing Effective Personal Boundaries, Vanderbilt University Faculty and Staff Health and Wellness (2015, 2016). Accessed September 6, 2019.

223 Holmes, Lindsay. "10 Great Things that Happen When You Set Boundaries." Huffington Post. April 4, 2016. Accessed September 6, 2019. https://www.huffpost.com/entry/setting-boundaries-benefits_n_57043126e4b0b90ac27088bb

224 Holmes, Lindsay. "10 Great Things that Happen When You Set Boundaries." Huffington Post. April 4, 2016. Accessed September 6, 2019. https://www.huffpost.com/entry/setting-boundaries-benefits_n_57043126e4b0b90ac27088bb

225 Brown, Brené. Rising Strong: How the Ability to Reset Transforms the Way We Live, Love, Parent, and Lead. New York: Random House Trade Paperbacks, 2015.

226 Holmes, Lindsay. "6 Times It's Totally Okay to Say 'No'." Huffington Post. January 28, 2016. Accessed March 25, 2020. https://www.huffpost.com/entry/when-to-say-no_n_56a7c904e-4b01a3ed1240e0d

227 Holmes, Lindsay. "10 Great Things that Happen When You Set Boundaries." Huffington Post. April 4, 2016. Accessed September 6, 2019. https://www.huffpost.com/entry/setting-boundaries-benefits_n_57043126e4b0b90ac27088bb

228 Holmes, Lindsay. "10 Great Things that Happen When You Set Boundaries." Huffington Post. April 4, 2016. Accessed September 6, 2019. https://www.huffpost.com/entry/setting-boundaries-benefits_n_57043126e4b0b90ac27088bb

229 Wong, Brittany. "Second Marriages Are More Likely to End in Divorce. Here's Why." Huffington Post. March 2, 2017. Accessed March 25, 2020. https://www.huffpost.com/entry/second-marriages-are-more-likely-to-end-in-divorce-heres-why_n_58b88e38e4b0b99894162a07

230 1 Happy Life. Accessed March 25, 2020. 1HappyLife.com

231 "Stepfamily Statistics." Stepmom Magazine. Accessed March 25, 2020. https://www.stepmommag.com/stepfamily-statistics/

232 "The Delusion." Letters of Note. November 10, 2011. Accessed March 25, 2020. http://www.lettersofnote.com/2011/11/delusion.html

233 Ranasinghe, Eshanthi. "A Mental Health Pandemic: Is the World Getting More Addicted, Anxious, and Lonely?" Medium, March 27, 2019. https://medium.com/positive-returns/a-mental-health-pandemic-is-the-world-getting-more-addicted-anxious-and-lonely-4e45bf533ae5.

234 Barbara L. Fredrickson, Ph.D. (2013). *Love 2.0: How Our Supreme Emotion Affects Everything We Feel, Think, Do, and Become,* New York: Hudson Street Press, 2013. Page 161

235 "Giving Thanks Can Make You Happier - Harvard Health." Harvard Medical School. Accessed September 13, 2019. https://www.health.harvard.edu/healthbeat/giving-thanks-can-make-you-happier.

236 Johnson, Kareem J., and Barbara L. Fredrickson (2005). "We All Look the Same to Me: Positive Emotions Eliminate the Own-Race Bias in Face Recognition." *Psychological Science* 16:11(2005): 875-81; Waugh, Christian E, and Barbara L Fredrickson. "Nice to Know You: Positive Emotions, Self-Other Overlap, and Complex Understanding in the Formation of a New Relationship." *The Journal of Positive Psychology* vol. 1,2 (2006): 93-106. doi:10.1080/17439760500510569

237 Fredrickson, Barbara L., Ph.D. *Love 2.0: How Our Supreme Emotion Affects Everything We Feel, Think, Do, and Become,* New York: Hudson Street Press, 2013.

238 Johnson, Kareem J., and Barbara L. Fredrickson. "We All Look the Same to Me: Positive Emotions Eliminate the Own-Race Bias in Face Recognition." *Psychological Science* 16:11(2005): 875-81; Waugh, Christian E, and Barbara L. Fredrickson. "Nice to Know You: Positive Emotions, Self-Other Overlap, and Complex Understanding in the Formation of a New Relationship." *The Journal of Positive Psychology* vol. 1,2 (2006): 93-106. doi:10.1080/17439760500510569

239 Covey, Stephen R. *The 7 Habits of Highly Effective People: Powerful Lessons in Personal Change.* Anniversary edition. New York: Simon & Schuster, 2013.

240 Peterson, C. and Martin Seligman. *Character Strengths and Virtues: A handbook and classification.* Washington, DC: American Psychological Association Press and Oxford University Press, 2004.

241 Peterson, C. and Martin Seligman. *Character Strengths and Virtues: A handbook and classification.* Washington, DC: American Psychological Association Press and Oxford University Press, 2004.

242 Zenger, Jack and Joseph Folkman. "The Ideal Praise-to-Criticism Ratio." Harvard Business Review. March 15, 2013. Accessed September 6, 2019. https://hbr.org/2013/03/the-ideal-praise-to-criticism; Losada, Marcial, and Emily Heaphy. "The Role of Positivity and Connectivity in the Performance of Business Teams: A Nonlinear Dynamics Model." *American Behavioral Scientist,* July 27, 2016. https://doi.org/10.1177/0002764203260208.

243 White, Chris. "The Deeper Meaning of Respect." Essential Parenting. Accessed September 8, 2019. http://www.essentialparenting.com/2014/10/11/the-deeper-meaning-of-respect/

244 Childre, Doc. HeartMath. Accessed March 25, 2020. https://www.heartmath.com/

245   McCraty, Rollin. *Science of the Heart, Volume 2 Exploring the Role of the Heart in Human Performance An Overview of Research Conducted by the HeartMath Institute*, 2016. https://doi.org/10.13140/RG.2.1.3873.5128.   https://www.researchgate.net/figure/The-hearts-magnetic-field-which-is-the-strongest-rhythmic-field-produced-by-the-human_fig11_293944391

246   HeartMath. Accessed September 6, 2019. https://www.heartmath.com/

247   Abulela, Amy. "Wherever You are, be There Totally: An Excerpt from The Power of Now by Eckhart Tolle." New World Library. December 12, 2014. Accessed September 8, 2019. https://www.newworldlibrary.com/Blog/tabid/767/articleType/ArticleView/articleId/294/WHEREV-ER-YOU-ARE-BE-THERE-TOTALLY-An-Excerpt-from-THE-POWER-OF-NOW-by-Eckhart-Tolle.aspx#.XXNAy5NKit9

248   Isen, A.M. Positive Affect, Cognitive Processes, and Social Behavior." *Advances in Experimental Psychology* 20 (1987): 203-53.

249   Fredrickson, Barbara L. *Positivity: Top-Notch Research Reveals The Upward Spiral that Will Change Your Life*. Edinburgh: Harmony, 2009.

250   "Tal Ben Shahar." Azquotes. Accessed June 8 2015. http://www.azquotes.com/quote/672859

251   Taylor, Shelley E., and Lien B. Pham. "The Effect of Mental Simulation on Goal-Directed Performance." *Imagination, Cognition and Personality* 18, no. 4 (1999): 253-268.

252   Drew, Emily. "Dr. David Cooperrider Works With Nepal's President and Constitutional Assembly." Weatherhead School of Management. December 1, 2009. Accessed September 8, 2019. https://weatherhead.case.edu/news/detail?idNews=1437

253   Cooperrider, David. "The Three Circles of Strengths Revolution: Moving from the Micro to the Macro Magnification of Strengths via Appreciative Inquiry." Presentation from VIA Institute on Character. n. d.

254   Park, Nansoon, and Christopher Peterson. "Character Strengths: Research and Practice." *Journal of College and Character* 10, no. 4 (2009a): n.p.

255   "We are all Connected!" HeartMath. Accessed September 8, 2019. https://www.heartmath.com/blog/articles/new-science-its-not-just-the-world-wide-web-that-connects-us/

256   "Compete." Online Etymology Dictionary. Accessed September 6, 2019. https://www.etymonline.com/word/compete

257   Covey, Stephen R. *The 7 Habits of Highly Effective People: Powerful Lessons in Personal Change*. Anniversary edition. New York: Simon & Schuster, 2013.

258   Phillips, Jonathan. "Kevin Garrett." Capture Life Through the Lens. November 30, 2012. Accessed September 8, 2019. https://capturelifethroughthelens.com/2012/11/30/kevin-garrett/

259 Rosenberg, E.L., P. Ekman, et al."Linkages between Facial Expressions of Anger and Transient Myocardial Ischemia in Men with Coronary Artery Disease," *Emotion* 1:107:15 (2001).

260 Donaldson, S.I., M. Csikszentmihalyi, and J. Nakamura. *Applied Positive Psychology: Improving Everyday Life, Health, Schools, Work, and Society.* Applied Psychology. Psychology Press, 2011.

261 Johnson, Kareem J, Christian E Waugh, and Barbara L Fredrickson. "Smile to See the Forest: Facially Expressed Positive Emotions Broaden Cognition." *Cognition & Emotion* 24, no. 2 (February 19, 2010): 299—321. https://doi.org/10.1080/02699930903384667.

262 Bradberry, Travis. *Emotional Intelligence 2.0.* TalentSmart, 2009.

263 Martínez-Martí, María Luisa, and Willibald Ruch. "Character Strengths Predict Resilience over and above Positive Affect, Self-Efficacy, Optimism, Social Support, Self-Esteem, and Life Satisfaction." *The Journal of Positive Psychology* 12 (April 25, 2016): 1—10.

264 "Emotional Intelligence." Psychology Today. Accessed September 1, 2019. https://www.psychologytoday.com/basics/emotional-intelligence.

265 Brown, Brené. *Daring Greatly: How the Courage to Be Vulnerable Transforms the Way We Live, Love, Parent, and Lead.* New York: Avery, 2015.

266 "How Generosity Builds Trust." Notre Dame Deloitte Center for Ethical Leadership. Accessed September 6, 2019. https://ethicalleadership.nd.edu/news/leading-through-the-trust-crisis-part-1-begin-with-generosity/

267 "How Generosity Builds Trust." Notre Dame Deloitte Center for Ethical Leadership. Accessed September 6, 2019. https://ethicalleadership.nd.edu/news/leading-through-the-trust-crisis-part-1-begin-with-generosity/

268 Klapwijk, A., & Van Lange, P. A. M. (2009). Promoting cooperation and trust in "noisy" situations: The power of generosity. *Journal of Personality and Social Psychology, 96*(1), 83-103. http://dx.doi.org/10.1037/a0012823

269 Dunning, D., and D. Fetchenhauer. "Understanding the Psychology of Trust." *Frontiers of Social Psychology. Social Motivation* (pp. 147-169). New York, NY, US: Psychology Press, 2011; Fetchenhauer, D., and D. Dunning. "Do People Trust Too Much or Too Little? *Journal of Economic Psychology* 30(3), (2009): 263-276. http://dx.doi.org/10.1016/j.joep.2008.04.006; Klapwijk, A., and P.A. Van Lange. "Promoting Cooperation and Trust in 'Noisy' Situations: The Power of Generosity." *Journal of Personality and Social Psychology (2009).*

270 "2017 Edelman Trust Barometer." Edelman. January 21, 2017. Accessed September 6, 2019. https://www.edelman.com/research/2017-edelman-trust-barometer; "2018 Edelman Trust Barometer." Edelman. January 21, 2018. Accessed September 6, 2019. https://www.edelman.com/research/2018-edelman-trust-barometer; "2019 Edelman Trust Barometer." Edelman. January 21, 2019. Accessed September 6, 2019. https://www.edelman.com/research/2019-edelman-trust-barometer

271   Covey, Stephen M.R. *The Speed of Trust: The One Thing that Changes Everything.* New York: Free Press 2008.

272   Leloup, Jean-Yves. *The Gospel of Mary Magdalene.* Rochester: Inner Traditions, 2002.

273   Dispenza, Joe. *Becoming Supernatural: How Common People are Doing the Uncommon.* Carlsbad: Hay House, 2019.

274   "Brene Brown Quotes." Goodreads. Accessed March 25, 2020.https://www.goodreads.com/quotes/544061-until-we-can-receive-with-an-open-heart-we-re-never

275   "Ralph Waldo Emerson Quotes." Goodreads. Accessed September 8, 2019. https://www.goodreads.com/quotes/19755-that-which-we-persist-in-doing-becomes-easier-to-do

276   Nakamura, Jeanne & Csikszentmihalyi, Mihaly. "Flow Theory and Research." *The Oxford Handbook of Positive Psychology.* Oxford: Oxford University Press, 2011.

277   Csikszentmihalyi, Mihaly. *Flow: The Psychology of Optimal Experience.* 1 edition. New York: Harper Perennial Modern Classics, 2008.

278   Peterson, Christopher, and Martin Seligman. *Character Strengths and Virtues: A Handbook and Classification.* Washington DC: American Psychological Association, 2004.

279   Ed Diener. Interview. July 9, 2009.

280   Jenkinson, Caroline E., Andy P. Dickens, Kerry Jones, Jo Thompson-Coon, Rod S. Taylor, Morwenna Rogers, Clare L. Bambra, Iain Lang, and Suzanne H. Richards. "Is Volunteering a Public Health Intervention? A Systematic Review and Meta-Analysis of the Health and Survival of Volunteers." *BMC Public Health* 13, no. 773 (2013): doi:10.1186/1471-2458-13-773.

281   Gregson, Tyler Knott. *Chasers of the Light: Poems from the Typewriter Series.* New York: TarcherPerigee, 2014.

282   Gander, Fabian & Proyer, René & Ruch, Willibald & Wyss, Tobias. "Strength-Based Positive Interventions: Further Evidence for Their Potential in Enhancing Well-Being and Alleviating Depression." *Journal of Happiness Studies.* 14 (2012). Doi:10.1007/s10902-012-9380-0.

ABOUT AUTHENTIC STRENGTHS ADVANTAGE®

Our mission is helping people engage their character strengths to increase their resilience, well-being and fulfillment in all aspects of life. We provide transformative, evidence-based, microlearning, training, coaching and certification—empowering people to maximize their energy, engagement and contributions—at work, at school, in communities, and in life. Visit us at AuthenticStrengths.com to take the free VIA strengths survey, and discover your own unique strengths profile.

ABOUT THE VIA INSTITUTE ON CHARACTER

In 1998, Dr. Neal H. Mayerson and then President of the American Psychological Association, Dr. Martin E.P. Seligman, conceived a robust effort to explore what is best about human beings and how we can use those best characteristics in our lives. They launched an effort of unprecedented magnitude to lay the groundwork for the new science of positive psychology. Dr. Mayerson created a nonprofit (now the VIA Institute on Character) to do this work and provided the funding to support Dr. Seligman in orchestrating a diverse collection of scholars and practitioners who took three years to complete the development of the VIA Classification of Character Strengths and Virtues, and the VIA Surveys for adults and youth. The enormous response of people worldwide taking the survey has made it clear that VIA's work is resonating broadly and deeply.

The mission of the VIA Institute on Character is to advance the science and the practice of character strengths. The nonprofit offers the scientifically validated VIA Survey, free of charge, across the globe. Millions of people from more than 200 countries have taken the survey, now translated into many languages.

ABOUT THE AUTHOR

FATIMA DOMAN, AUTHOR, SPEAKER AND EXECUTIVE COACH, has motivated audiences across six continents to leverage their authentic strengths for transformation. An influential voice in resilience, well-being, leadership, and positive change, she is passionate about empowering people for sustainable high performance–at work, at school, in communities and in life. For decades, Fatima has worked successfully with Fortune 100 and Fortune 500 clients representing a variety of industries, and with educators, non-profits, and government agencies around the globe. Her books, *Authentic Strengths* and *True You* have been featured by the Huffington Post, Psychology Today, ThriveGlobal, on TV, radio, podcasts, and YouTube. Her online programs, microlearning, workshops, coach training, and certifications have been translated and licensed throughout the world.

As CEO of Authentic Strengths Advantage, Fatima shares innovative, evidence-based tools rooted in the groundbreaking science of Positive Psychology–engaging people to bring out the best in themselves and in those they influence. Fatima has served as Co-Founder and Co-Director of FranklinCovey's Global Executive Coaching Practice, as Faculty for the FranklinCovey/Columbia University Executive Coach Certification Program, and as manager of certification for the internationally acclaimed 7 Habits of Highly Effective People. Her post-graduate work includes an MA from California State University, an Advanced Executive Coaching Certification from the Columbia University Coaching Program, and she holds numerous academic, leadership and well-being certifications. Fatima's holistic approach to coaching and well-being includes certification from the HeartMath Institute and certification from the California College of Ayurveda as an Ayurvedic Yoga Therapist. Fatima's greatest fulfillment comes from enjoying time with family and friends.

Learn more: AuthenticStrengths.com

www.ingramcontent.com/pod-product-compliance
Lightning Source LLC
Chambersburg PA
CBHW060256100426
42742CB00011B/1767